William Green

SUNY Series in Labor History
Robert Asher and Charles Stephenson, Editors

WILLIAM
GREEN

Biography of a Labor Leader

Craig Phelan

State University of New York Press

Published By
State University of New York Press, Albany

© 1989 State University of New York

For information, address State University of New York
Press, State University Plaza, Albany, NY 12246

Library of Congress Cataloging-in-Publication Data

Phelan, Craig, 1958–
  William Green: biography of a labor leader / Craig Phelan.
      p.   cm.—(SUNY series in American labor history).
  Bibliography: p. 209
  Includes index.
  ISBN 0–88706–870–7.   ISBN 0–88706–871–5(pbk.)
  1. Green, William, 1872–1952.   2. Trade-unions—United States—
Officials and employees—Biography.   3. AFL-CIO—Biography.
4. American Federation of Labor—Biography.   I. Title.   II. Series.
HD8073.G7P54   1988
331.88′32′0924—dc19
[B]   88–12356
                                                               CIP

10   9   8   7   6   5   4   3   2   1

Contents

Preface

IN THE TEXTILE mills which dominated the economic life of southern Appalachia, the year 1929 witnessed a dress rehearsal of the militant labor uprising which would occur across the United State in the 1930s. Sixty-hour work weeks, subsistence wages, and oppressive working conditions had long been the predicament of Southern textile operatives. When mill owners further intensified the pace of work, the operatives resisted with a vengeance. Beginning in 1929, a series of spontaneous strikes wracked the mill towns of Tennessee and North and South Carolina. Battle lines hardened throughout Appalachia as contestants on both sides prepared for an aggressive struggle.[1]

For the first time since William Green had assumed the American Federation of Labor presidency in 1924, the Federation had an opportunity to organize large numbers of hitherto nonunion workers. Unlike the auto workers whom the AFL was also attempting to organize in 1929, the textile operatives could not be accused of indifference to unionism. Nor were craft unionists apathetic to their plight. Delegates to the 1929 AFL convention exhibited, in the words of one observer, "a pitch of enthusiasm not seen in labor gatherings since the spring tide of the Knights of Labor."[2] Indeed, they agreed to launch a massive campaign, involving all international affiliates, to organize Southern workers.[3]

On January 6, 1930, the AFL opened its drive with a conference at Charlotte, North Carolina. Although delegates from the South urged militancy, Green, in a two-hour speech, explained that while he sincerely desired to unionize Southern workers, he would not countenance force or violence. In fact, he devoted much of his speech to contrasting the methods of the Communists (who were also organizing mill workers) with the peaceful, constructive, and Christian mission of the AFL. The AFL would achieve better results, Green suggested, if it set out not to antagonize, but to convince employers and the public of the social and economic benefits of trade unionism. "There is no sword in our scabbard," he declared. "There is no weapon in our hand. We come not with the mailed fist but with the open hand to the employers of the South appealing to them to give us the opportunity, to try us out and see whether we can help this industrial situation in the South."[4]

Green formulated a tripartite strategy for the drive: organizers would try to interest workers in the AFL; an industrial engineer, Geoffrey Brown, would attempt to persuade employers of the merits of trade unionism; and Green himself would sell the idea of unionism to the Southern public. Green made two extensive speaking tours through the South in the early months of 1930. He mustered all the charm and eloquence at his command as he appealed to college gatherings, chambers of commerce, Rotary and Kiwanis clubs, three state legislatures, and four governors.[5] Green assured the South that the AFL was not composed of godless radicals and troublemakers. Rather, members fully believed that, in resolving differences between employers and employees, "the law of righteousness, religion and morality must control if settlements arrived at are to be just and fair to all." Above all, he declared that the AFL was not a violent, destructive force. Its ultimate purpose was to create "a healthy environment, a favorable psychological condition in the homes and communities where workers dwell so that the seeds of Gospel Truth may not fall upon stony ground. . . ."[6]

Although the Southern public responded favorably to Green and his message, the AFL organizers and Geoffrey Brown met only resistance. Green had instructed organizers to counsel against spontaneous strikes in the hope that employers would recognize the AFL's peaceful mission.[7] But such advice alienated the operatives who sought tangible support in their struggles. Only three employers, all of them located in Columbus, Georgia, agreed to allow the AFL to organize their workers. The combined workforce at the three firms—a syrup factory, a food packing plant, and a hosiery mill—was at most eighty-two workers.[8] Not a single textile employer expressed interest in working with the Federation.

The climax of the Southern campaign occurred at Danville, Virginia, home of the Dan River and Riverside cotton mills, the largest in the South. Confronted with a ten percent wage cut imposed in early 1930, employees asked the United Textile Workers to help them form a union. UTW Vice-President Francis Gorman took personal charge of the organizing activities, while Geoffrey Brown and Green tried to sell the AFL to the mill's management. In response, Dan River began to fire all operatives suspected of union affiliation. By September, two thousand workers had been dis-

missed. Thus the AFL had little choice but to override Green's protests and
support the workers in a strike that lasted four months. The management
of the mills resorted to injunctions, evictions, and the state militia. In the
end, the strike failed, and with it died the hope of a peaceful campaign to
introduce unionism to the South.[9]

Several factors account for the defeat of the Southern organizing campaign: cotton manufacturers proved determined and resourceful foes of
unionism; Southern political leaders inevitably brought state power to the
aid of corporations; AFL affiliates proved unwilling and sometimes unable
to provide the necessary financial support for a large-scale campaign; and
the South had a large pool of unskilled workers willing to break strikes, a
pool made larger by the onset of the Great Depression.[10] Added to these
factors was Green's adamant refusal to sanction militant rank-and-file
action to secure union recognition and collective bargaining rights. All
that Southern workers received from the Federation were warnings against
ill-advised strikes. Oppressed mill workers found no relief in Green's religious commitment to industrial peace and cooperation between labor
and capital.

Strange as Green's preachment of a Christian cooperative ideal may
seem in the face of Southern realities, it was nonetheless explicable. Green
was among the last heirs of a strain of labor thought that can be traced
back to the nineteenth century. Religious idealism had been a major component of the Knights of Labor ideology in the 1870s and 1880s, and
Green's own union, the United Mine Workers, was particularly suffused
with social gospel thought in its early years. Moreover, in the Progressive
Era, as Green rose to power in both the AFL and the UMW, the Federation
sought to establish close ties with churches through such activities as
"Labor Sunday," and association with groups such as the Federal Council
of Churches of Christ in America. A surprising number of labor officials
joined Father Peter Dietz in the Militia of Christ for Social Service, and
from 1912 to 1916, the AFL launched an organizing drive, the Labor
Forward movement, that borrowed the methods of evangelism and the
ideals of the social gospel. Thus as Green matured, he was only one of
many trade union officials who embraced a religiously inspired dream of
labor-management cooperation.

By the 1920s and 1930s, however, as industrial relations became
increasingly complex and depersonalized and as society became more secular, the ideal of Christian cooperation waned. Yet Green was so strongly
wedded to those values that he proved incapable of abandoning them even
after years of failure. His became an increasingly estranged and isolated
voice for Christian fellowship in industrial relations. Under his guidance,
the evangelical-labor tradition, while still upholding the virtue and human-

ity of labor, became, as we shall see, a hindrance to working-class organization, a handmaiden to craft unionists, and a contributor to the division
of the labor movement.

I

Christian Ideals and Union Politics:
The Rise to the AFL Presidency

IN 1868 A TWENTY-eight-year-old English miner, his new bride—the twenty-year-old daughter of a Welsh miner, and his twenty-three-year-old brother said farewell to their friends and families. The parting was probably the most painful experience of their lives. Hugh Green, Jane Oram Green, and Joseph Green were saying goodbye forever to all that they knew. Never again would Hugh see his parents, the little mining village of Frampton-Cottrell where he had spent his entire life, his workmates and union brothers, or his fellow worshippers in the local Baptist church.

Hugh Green's decision to leave England was more a matter of economic necessity than personal choice. The mining industry in Great Britain had fallen on hard times. Throughout England, Ireland, Scotland, and Wales, there were simply too many miners and not enough work. Frampton-Cottrell, situated just a few miles outside Bristol near the Welsh border, fared no better than other mining communities. Although coal mining had been a way of life there for hundreds of years, the mines in which Hugh Green worked for more than a decade were all but played out.[1]

As their ship left port, the Greens could reflect upon all they had left behind. They could also share their dreams about the new life awaiting them. They were bound for America as part of the great influx of Scottish and English miners into the coal fields of the New World between 1860 and 1870. To some extent these miners were inspired by the acclaimed leader of the British miners, Alexander McDonald, who urged his men to emigrate to the United States where land was so cheap and plentiful that they eventually might escape the pits and become farmers.[2] If this was the dream of Hugh Green, he never realized it; for upon his death the 1925 he owned a small plot of land, but not enough to make a living as a farmer.[3]

1

Hugh and Joseph arrived in America with few possessions. They did, however, carry a great deal of cultural baggage. While neither man was literate, they possessed skills of which they were proud. They were members of an elite class of workmen, set apart from general laborers in and around the mines by virtue of their ability to use a pick. And, as coal mining in the United States matured from a surface to an underground operation, the need for able pick miners grew. In large measure, pick mining was a handicraft introduced in America by the British. Along with skills, Hugh and Joseph brought with them a heritage of trade unionism. Both men were strong supporters of the miners' union in Great Britain, and they fully understood, unlike many American miners, the need and the means to pool labor's strength. Finally, the Green brothers carried with them unshakable religious convictions. Their fervent Baptist faith became ingrained even more deeply as they struggled to adapt to their new country.

Immediately upon reaching the United States, the three immigrants made their way to eastern Ohio and the mining village of Coshocton. As is so often the case with working people, especially those who were illiterate, no written record exists to explain why the Greens chose Coshocton as their new home. Perhaps a cousin lived there, or a miner they once knew in England. We will never know the exact reason, but the choice of Coshocton proved a fortunate one.

In 1870 Coshocton was relatively prosperous. Originally laid out in 1802 upon the site of an old Indian village, the town was nestled in the fertile, gently rolling hills at the confluence of the Muskingum and Tuscarawas Rivers. Almost two thousand people lived within the town limits, although nearly all the miners lived about a mile outside of town in what became known as Hardscrabble Hill.[4] "Hardscrabble," a word meaning the gaining of a meager living by hard labor, was an appropriate name for a mining community.

As early as 1775, mapmaker Louis Evans had noted the existence of coal near the Tuscarawas River. What he discovered later became known as the Hocking Valley coal bed, a major seam of high quality coal beneath 12,000 square miles of eastern and southern Ohio. As Ohio industry expanded in the mid to late nineteenth century, demand for this coal spiraled. In the year 1840 only about 140,000 tons of Ohio coal were extracted, but in 1870 nearly 3 million tons were brought to the surface. Shipping the coal was augmented by the completion of Ohio's extensive canal system, linking Lake Erie on the north and the Ohio River on the South. Hocking Valley coal could thus be marketed throughout Ohio, the Great Lakes region, and beyond.[5]

Numerous mines opened in the locality of Coshocton in the 1860s and 1870s. Almost all of these mines were small enterprises that opened and closed within a matter of years, usually failing in the face of competition or the playing out of the mines. Two larger, more permanent operators at this time were the Morgan Run and the Cassingham mining companies. These companies operated a series of mines and employed most of the men living on Hardscrabble Hill.[6]

Upon their arrival, the greens found a situation in many ways typical of English miners emigrating to America. Hardscrabble Hill was a primitive enclave of miners, shacks and company houses isolated from the rest of the community. And while most of that community was of native birth, most of the miners were foreigners. Of the 198 households in Franklin township (where the Hill was located), twenty-five belonged to miners. Ten of the miners were from England, two from Wales, and one from Ireland. Of those miners who were born in the United States, three were from Pennsylvania and nine from Ohio. In addition, five of the nine Ohio-born miners had at least one parent of foreign birth.[7]

Times were undoubtedly hard for the Greens as they adjusted to their new home. Conditions on the Hill in 1870 were harsh. The Greens were long familiar with the coal dust and cinders that filled the air in mining communities, dust that coated everything and everyone, inside and outside houses. And they were probably familiar with the reality of the company town, where public sanitation was practically nonexistent and housing consisted of rickety frame dwellings with no insulation or paint. The Morgan Run Company owned most of the Hill, and thus could charge high rents for these shacks and force workers to buy necessities, such as food and mining supplies, at the company store for exorbitant prices. With the mines offering the only chance of employment and with few social diversions, it was no wonder that Hugh Green hoped for a better life for his children. Nevertheless, those miners who settled on the Hill were perhaps more fortunate than most, for while few were able to escape the pits and become farmers, they were able to build a stable community. This helped cushion the adjustment to life in a foreign land and also saved the Greens from the fate of so many immigrant miners, who were forced to move from town to town in search of steady work.

As Jane struggled to make the miner's shack a home, Hugh and Joseph trekked to the pits to start work. The work they found could not have impressed them. American mines were primitive and unsafe by British standards. Moreover, operators engaged in cutthroat competition and extracted far more coal than the market could bear, leading to erratic employment and meager wages for mine workers. Even near prosperous Coshocton, miners could expect to remain idle at least fifteen weeks every spring and summer. Their pay, often in company scrip, was often insufficient to cover bills at the company store, leaving them perpetually in debt. According to an 1879 survey, seventy-five percent of Ohio miners reported family expenses exceeding incomes.[8]

Under these circumstances Hugh and Jane Green gave birth to their first child, William, born March 3, 1870. When William was two years old, Hugh and Jane moved into a new house built and owned by the Morgan Run Company. Joseph did not move with them. He found a new mining job in neighboring Tuscarawas county, and by 1880 he was married with two children of his own.[9] Again, the absence of written records leaves us with little concrete knowledge of William Green' early years. Later in life he recalled a happy childhood. Although he remembered the Hill as a "drab mining village," he carried fond memories of his "proud" father and "loving" mother. He recalled that his father was tall, thin, quiet, sported long white hair and a beard and that, with respect to his circumstances, he provided well for his family. Never once did the family want for food.[10]

As there were few diversions for little boys, life on the Hill was quiet enough. Bill collected acorns for use as marbles in games with other children. But for youth in mining towns, fear and horror played a much greater role in the formative years than peace and joy. An understanding of desperate poverty and the gruesome reality of mine accidents left permanent scars on Green's childhood memories. "Even as a child," Green wrote, "I realized the horrors of mine accidents and saw the sorrow and deprivation which loss of bread winners brought to families and sensed the ever-present fear of impending tragedy that dwells in miners' homes."[11]

William was an energetic and precocious child, excelling at school and developing an appetite for reading. He attended a one-room schoolhouse on the Hill and, in a rare achievement for the son of a miner, completed the eighth grade before his labor was required to supplement the family income. He recalled especially enjoying history and biographies, a preference that lasted throughout his life.[12]

Other than school, the only outlet for young Green's energies was the Baptist church. The Greens were devout believers who shunned smoking, drinking, and gambling. Twice each day, at 6 a.m. and 6 p.m., the family would hold religious services in their home. Since neither his father nor mother could read, it was up to William, the eldest of five children, to read from Scripture.[13] Soon William mastered the teachings of the *Bible* and began to take a more active role in the church. The First Baptist Church of Coshocton was located, symbolically enough, not on Hardscrabble Hill but in the town itself. Attending service, Sunday school, church socials, and debates provided Green with his only contact with mainstream Coshocton society, his only break from the fraternity of mining families that justly deserved the distinction as "a people apart unto themselves."[14] At the Baptist church Green was not looked down upon as a dirty "Hardscrabble boy." And his desire to win acceptance by the "respectable" people who lived in neat white houses with picket fences perhaps gave

Green, already intensely religious, an extra incentive to learn his lessons and excel in church debates.

At an early age, Green heard the Lord's calling to the ministry. Both he and his father were aware that such a calling was not something to be taken lightly. It was divinely inspired and required certain "signs and evidences" of worthiness. According to the 1859 Baptist *Directory*, the "greatest" sign was "the inward teaching of the Spirit, by which, after long, deliberate, and painful consideration, and perhaps painful conflict, the convictions become deep and permanent in the mind, that to teach the Gospel is the work which God has assigned to him."[15] Green himself believed he possessed the qualifications for such a career and his father actively encouraged William's *Bible* studies. Imbued with the power of the Holy Spirit, then, Green sought a life devoted to the contemplation of Scripture and spreading the word of the Lord. And while circumstances prevented him from becoming a minister, Green would always consider himself God's agent in human affairs.

Green' religious aspirations were dashed by economic reality. The paltry earnings of a coal miner denied him the requisite training for the ministry. Although he continued to entertain hopes of attending *Bible* college, he abandoned this dream is 1892 when he married Jenny Mobley, the daughter of a local miner.[16] Later, as a local union official, Green would conduct Sunday school classes, and as AFL president, he pursued opportunities to address churches and religious organizations.[17]

The working life of a coal miner's son began early, and Green was no exception. At the age of fourteen, he completed his formal education and went to work as a waterboy for railroad laborers laying track for the Wheeling Railroad line. Two years later, Hugh Green took his son along with him on the two-and-a-half mile journey in the dark of morning to Morgan Run mine No. 3. Nothing his father said could have prepared him for the experience of working in a late nineteenth-century bituminous mine. Working conditions facing coal miners were unmatched in terms of privation and danger. Only flickering lamps distributed the total darkness as miners descended sometimes miles underground. Each miner either worked alone or with an assistant in his own small chamber that was never big enough to stand up in. Lying on his side, usually in about a foot of slimy black water, the miner struck at the coal face with his pick. It was excruciating work, but necessary to form holes into which the powder was inserted. With skill and a little luck, the miner blasted the coal onto the floor, then hand-loaded the large and heavy pieces into cars hauled to the surface by mules. Such arduous labor was compounded by the very real threat of death or injury. While few large-scale mining disasters hit Ohio in the 1880s or 1890s, hundreds of miners perished alone or in small numbers as a result of cave-ins, asphyxiation, or the unintentional ignition of methane gas. Thousands more suffered slower deaths due to crippling injuries, the slow poisoning by noxious gases, or gradual strangulation by inhaled particles—"black lung" disease.[18]

Green recalled that going to work in the pits at the age of sixteen was part of the "normal course of life" for boys on the Hill. Although he had grown up aware of the danger and hardship his father faced, Green joined him "without any feeling of self-pity on my part. On the contrary, I was glad to take on a man's work that I might have some income to add to the family's purse." Green learned quickly. Within a few years, he had become a skilled pick miner in his own right, and his skill was reflected in the fact that by the 1890s he was one of two miners drawing the biggest pay at Morgan Run.[19]

Despite his skill with the pick and powder, Green received little enjoyment from his work. His twenty years in the mines were remembered as particularly bleak ones: "The mine-worker spends all working hours of his life stripped of the light of day. He breathes stale mine air, saturated with coal dust and often tainted with gas. Through narrow seams of coal, the miner often works in strained, cramped positions for long periods. The shafts are often saturated with moisture and sometimes the miner works ankle-deep in water, within narrow, dripping walls." These conditions made Green and his fellow miners "abnormally susceptible to tuberculosis, rheumatism and other diseases." And illness "became almost inevitable" when he and his neighbors had to return from their jobs "to spend their unemployed hours crammed in small, ill-lighted, unventilated huts."[20]

This seemingly unbearable situation was relieved to some extent by the love and nurturing of his family, which ultimately included five daughters and one son, his religious beliefs, and Green's devotion to the community on Hardscrabble Hill. Life in a nineteenth century mining village—in which the entire economy rested on the pits—created a communal solidarity born out of a common plight. A strike or shutdown could spell disaster, not just for the miners, but for the shopkeepers and professionals who were dependent upon the miners' business. Especially among the miners, recalled Green, there was always "a sort of friendly, fraternal feeling. . . . The very nature of the work brings the men engaged in it into a close, friendly and sympathetic relationship."[21] Another miner rose in the ranks of the United Mine Workers, John Brophy, remembered that feelings of solidarity bound the whole community. "Especially when the work became slack the whole community drew together," he wrote, adding that "we were all the same breed of cats; we shared the burdens of the mine."[22]

Green was twenty-three years old before he left Coshocton for the first time to attend a union meeting in nearby Columbus, and by then his character was well marked by this sense of community.[23] Coshocton remained Green's home for his entire life, and even as AFL president, he would try to return there twice each month to be with family and friends.[24] Throughout his life, he remained an active participant in community affairs, a member of not only the local union, but also such fraternal societies as the Elks, Odd Fellows, and Masons.[25]

Feelings of solidarity with fellow miners led to active participation in union affairs. Just as it had been "normal" for Green to follow his father into the mines, so, too, was it normal for him to follow his father into the local chapter of the Progressive Miners' Union in 1888. An eighth-grade education served him well, for he was one of the few men in his local of about sixty-five miners who was able to record the minutes of a meeting, compose a formal letter, or frame a resolution for subdistrict or district conventions. In 1891, one year after the Progressive Miners' Union merged with Knights of Labor District 35 to form the United Mine Workers, Green was elected secretary of his local.[26]

Green threw himself wholeheartedly into his union work and served his local in every capacity: as secretary, business agent, vice-president, on committees, and ultimately as president. The union movement became for him the "calling" he had once sought in the Baptist ministry. As he later described the experience, the union offered "work that appealed to me. Organizing the men in the mines to better their lives and give new opportunities to their children was God's work. The union became for me an opportunity as well as a duty."[27] Trade unionism presented Green with the chance to serve his fellow miners while at the same time receive recognition, gain status, fulfill his need to be useful, and put his religious beliefs into practice.

Green's tendency to regard union work as a form of religious commitment was not unusual for members of the newly-formed UMW. Early issues of the *United Mine Workers Journal* revealed that the union was steeped in Christian idealism. Religious tracts, sermons, and prayers could be found in most issues. Early UMW national conventions always began with a prayer, and even resolutions might be drowned in religious rhetoric. Members regarded the union as more than an economic institution; it was a righteous cause that promised its adherents dignity and religious meaning. Miners often described their struggles through the use of biblical parables, portrayed Jesus and Moses as leaders of the working class, and considered the *Bible* "a gospel of unionism and a handbook of social justice."[28] Thus Green was not alone in attaching religious significance to his involvement in the miners' union.

The tumultuous first decade of the UMW, punctuated with instability and numerous lost strikes, tested Green's new faith. Depression and the ruthlessness of operators nearly killed the union in its infancy. The union survived, however, and even began to prosper by the end of the decade. Numerous factors account for the UMW's ability to survive its early years, but three of the most important were a high degree of unity within the ranks of miners, a lenient use of the strike weapon at the local and national levels, and a growing realization among major operators that the UMW could aid their efforts to reduce competition in the coal fields by standardizing production costs. This last factor proved to be the most important in the development of Green's trade union philosophy. The late 1890s offered him tangible proof that sensible employers, acting in their own interests, had no reason to oppose unionism. And it fostered his belief that capital and labor, once organized, could cooperate for mutual gain.

If developments in the late 1890s led Green to stress accommodation with industry, events in the early part of the decade convinced him that economic warfare with employers was suicidal. In 1891, the young secretary of UMW local 379 and the other miners of Hardscrabble Hill learned the hard facts of securing union recognition in the coal fields. On March 15, the five major coal companies Coshocton county, including Morgan Run, notified the miners that they refused to recognize their union. Green and his union brothers has no recourse except the strike. By the following month the miners' *Journal* reported that "already the Morgan Run company is shipping in Italians, Huns, Poles and Negroes." The importation of strikebreakers was a favorite tactic of operators. By pitting immigrant against immigrant, foreign against native born, black against white, operators hoped to enlist the prejudice of miners in their attempt to destroy union organization. Morgan Run followed up with two other familiar strikebreaking tactics: injunctions and evictions. Under force of law, miners on the Hill were thrown out of their homes to provide living quarters for the strikebreakers. In the face of this employer onslaught, Green and his local remained firm, finally forcing a settlement on May 1 that provided for the departure of the strikebreakers and union recognition.[29] Local 379 was now established, but the price had been high—the temporary destruction of the community.

Coal diggers on the Hill had reason to rejoice, but the new local and the national union were still very weak. A leading cause of that weakness was the depression of the early 1890s, during which coal prices plummeted, wages were slashed, and thousands of miners either lost their jobs altogether or were retained on a part-time basis. Miners and their supporters cried for assistance from state governments, but their appeals went unanswered.[30] Amid these disheartening conditions, local 379 selected William Green to attend his first state UMW convention, which opened February 1894 in Columbus. At twenty-three years old, Green was less than one year married and had never before set foot outside his hometown. This would be the first time in his life that Green would not be present at the evening *Bible* readings, the first time he would miss home cooking. As Jenny was pregnant with their first child, he must have been especially anxious.

But Green had important union business to consider. Operators under contract with the UMW had demanded a reduction in pay of over twenty-eight percent from the existing scale when the contract expired on April 30. Whether to strike or accept the reduction became the major dispute at the convention. Having no desire to experience again the hardships of the 1891 strike, Green voted to accept the wage cut. Even at this early stage of his career, Green displayed his boundless optimism in appeasement and rational discourse with employers. He told the convention that miners should try to talk operators into a "corresponding reduction in house rents, tool sharpening, mine supplies and house coal." In the end, Ohio miners voted to accept the reduction.[31]

Despite the vote in Ohio, the national union made preparations for a strike. National leaders took their cue from English miners who, only a few years earlier, called a strike to eliminate the existing glut of coal and then tried to reestablish the prevailing wage. On April 11, the national convention voted to go on strike as of Saturday afternoon, April 21. By April 27, miners in Ohio were out to a man, including the reluctant Green. The early weeks of the strike increased the strength and unity of the fledgling national union. When the strike began, the UMW could claim only 13,000 dues-paying members; eight weeks later 180,000 miners had responded to the strike call. But by mid-summer the strike was failing. The continued depression, the increased coal production in the unorganized fields of Maryland, Virginia, and West Virginia, employer injunctions, and the calling of state militias against the strikers all undermined the chance of success. The failure of the strike dealt a harsh blow to the national and, in many areas, the UMW disappeared entirely. In Ohio, Green and his union brothers voted to return to work at reduced rates.[32]

One major effect of the failed 1894 strike was the temporary destruction of the Central Competitive Field, an arrangement in which the union and major operators established wages nationally instead of locally. This forced miners, already beaten and disorganized, to negotiate wage scales separately in each locality. Local 379 did not fare well. When contract talks began in 1895, Green found himself, for the first time, participating directly in wage negotiations with his employers. He confronted operators who were adamant that wages, already down twenty-eight percent from 1893 levels, be further reduced. Unable to appease them, Green had little choice but to follow his local to the picket line on February 11, the third strike in five years. Again the miners of Coshocton stood firm to a man, and again, operators emerged from the debacle victorious. The wage scale dropped from seventy-five to sixty-five cents a ton for pick mining.[33]

The successive failures of the UMW in its early years put its future in doubt. The union seemed incapable of preventing reductions in wage rates. In 1896, the union could claim less than 10,000 members and $600 in its treasury.[34] Sixty-five cents a ton for pick mining, the lowest rate since 1890, was barely enough to keep food on the table. And the Green family now had another mouth to feed. Yet never once did Green abandon his faith in the union. Indeed, he considered the miners' organization the only way out of the present predicament. In a letter to miners of eastern Ohio, Green tried to raise the ebbing morale of his union brothers. His letter represents his unflappable devotion to organization and education, and his boundless optimism in the future, traits he exhibited throughout his career. Unless we "educate ourselves in the principles which it is intended to teach," Green lectured, the union "is nothing but a form, a shadow, or a name with nothing real about it." For education to take place, "it is necessary to attend all meetings of our locals; discuss the principles of our organization; our condition as a craft; our duty to our fellow miners, our families and ourselves." Green then asked local secretaries to call meetings, read his letter to members, and appoint committees to visit union men who were lax in their commitment to the union.

While Green's letter stressed that the UMW was the only vehicle by which miners could improve their lot, it also contained hints that Green was displeased with the union's strategy of waging economic warfare on an almost annual basis. And the conclusion pointed to a growing conviction that the welfare of the miners rested not only upon their own efforts, but also upon the moral conduct of employers. "What with very little work and low wages, it has been very trying to us as a craft, but I feel there is a brighter future in store for us. The Lord lights our path and I am certain that the majority of operators are guided by His principles."[35]

Positive collective action, not Christian-minded employers, saved the union from collapse. At the national convention of January 1897, delegates voted for yet another strike in an effort to prevent further wage reductions. Although Green was not a delegate to the convention, he, along with 28,000 other Ohio miners, answered the strike call on July 4.[36]

A report from the president of the Ohio district hailed the solidarity of purpose among miners in Coshocton county during the strike. All miners were out and all had pledged to remain out until victory was secured. The president also observed an unusual degree of serenity among Coshocton miners engaged in a full-scale struggle for economic justice. "A person would hardly know a great strike is on," he noted. "Most of the boys have formed themselves into fishing clubs . . . and are having a good time." The depth of community support for the strikers also surprised observers. Another UMW official was pleased to find that "all professional and business men here (in Coshocton) are strongly in favor of the miners."[37] From experiences such as these, Green developed a commitment to win public support for labor and a belief in the reasonableness of businessmen.

The strike of 1897 was a tremendous victory and reversed the fortunes of the UMW. Although the wage increase was small, the UMW had at last stopped wage cuts and proved its viability to miners and operators. President Ratchford was able to inform the 1898 national convention that, as a result of the strike, the union now had 33,000 members and $11,000 in its treasury. The strike was also a godsend to Coshocton miners. One organizer noted in 1898 that the county "was never better organized than at the present time," and one year later Coshocton was deemed "the banner union mining county in Ohio."[38] Miners had achieved success largely through their own militant efforts. But it must be wondered why the 1897 strike succeeded while earlier ones had failed. The answer lies in the passive acceptance of unionism on the part of progressive operators.

For years, major operators had been concerned about the ruinous competition and overproduction that beset the soft coal industry. Because a relatively small capital outlay was required to begin operations and because soft coal had defied the rationalization common to other major industries at this time. Forward-looking operators recognized the need for the establishment of uniform costs of production and limitation of output. Many even understood that a national union, by standardizing wage rates, could help stabilize the industry. Thus more than a few operators privately welcomed the UMW's victory in 1897. During settlement talks, progressive employers successfully appealed for the re-establishment of the Central Competitive Field and a system or resolving labor-management disputes.[39]

Leading economists such as John R. Commons and W. J. Ashley praised the new system of labor-management cooperation in the soft coal industry.[40] So, too, did William Green. He believed the accords ushered in a new dawn for the men of coal. Miners would receive increased job security and more stable wages, while operators could reduce wasteful competition and strikes. As a frequent participant in later wage scale committees and joint conferences on labor disputes, Green came to the conclusion that when labor and capital were both well organized, they could work together for mutual benefit. He reasoned that the interests of capital and labor, far from being irreconcilable, were in fact mutually dependent. The relationship was "an interdependence so fixed and irrevocable as to make complete success attainable only through understanding and cooperation."[41] The accommodationist views of the future AFL president were not ethical abstractions divorced from economic reality, but rather lessons he drew from the policies and practices of the infant UMW.

Nor was Green alone in his view that the 1897 settlement established a new basis for union dealings with operators. In December 1900, delegates gathered in Zanesville for the annual convention of Subdistrict 5 of District 6, which included the eastern Ohio counties of Coshocton, Guernsey, and Muskingum. President James Stewart was proud to announce that the year 1900 witnessed the creation of seven new locals and the signing of a new wage agreement. The new agreement meant not only "a year's peace and comparative prosperity for both miners and operators," Stewart declared, it meant "a continuation of the friendly relations between employer and employee, and further established the principles of joint action, which had proven mutually advantageous to all parties concerned, and which has done more towards lifting the coal industry out of the disorder and chaos caused by unscrupulous competition, into which it had fallen, than any other agency." It was at this convention, when delegates were extolling the virtues of cooperation with operators, when union resources and membership were higher than ever before, that the miners of eastern Ohio elected William Green to replace Stewart as their president.[42] Green rode a wave of prosperity into office.

At the age of thirty, Green had at last received a small measure of recognition for his union work. He was now the area's chief organizer, speechmaker, and contract negotiator. While he was not officially a salaried employee, he did receive money for his expenses and for days he missed work because of union business. In his first year this amounted to $226.72.[43] But a subdistrict president was still a mine worker, and on most days Green still had to descend below the earth's surface, imperiling his life for the sake of extracting coal. Green's union duties were not oppressive. In 1891, for example, he settled a few contract disputes, gave a number of speeches to locals, and raised funds for an ongoing strike in his district.[44]

In December 1901, Green presided over his first subdistrict convention, held in Cambridge. After calling the fifty-six delegates from twenty-four locals to order, Green reported on the current state of affairs. The address is remarkable in that Green described his subdistrict's success in terms he would use the rest of his life: the union as a moral force; the need for public support of the union cause; the securing of management's respect; and disdain for strikes. "We were never more powerful or ever exerted a greater influence for good than at present. We have enlisted the support of public opinion, without which we could not succeed; commanded the respect of our employers . . . thereby insuring comparative peace and prosperity to both employer and employe." Above all, Green stressed that the lesson of the UMW's first decade was that industrial warfare was futile, that negotiations proved far more successful than militancy. "The success of the joint method of transacting business between operators and miners is so plainly apparent that those who were inclined to condemn it . . . are certainly forced to admit its beneficial results. While we cannot ever surrender the right to strike, we certainly prefer the conference hall to the strike field, and I trust the morality, wisdom and intelligence of both parties to the yearly agreements may prevail."[45]

With operators apparently willing to cooperate with the union, Green's major area of concern was forcing the rank-and-file to abide by all the rules of the joint agreements. These contracts covered not only wage scales, but every aspect of mine work, such as loading coal, weighing procedures, and grievance policies. If miners expected operators to carry out their part of the bargain, Green, as chief labor negotiator, had to force miners to live up to their side. Green therefore assumed the role of policeman. Other union officials, within and without the UMW, also appreciated their role as contract enforcer at this time. As one historian put it, the union leaders' "insistence that contracts be upheld stemmed from their belief that organized labor could exist only as a working-class institution which functioned in ways acceptable to middle-class society. Failure to live up to agreements would alienate public support."[46] At subdistrict conventions, Green often bemoaned the lack of discipline on the part of miners that was essential to union-management cooperation. "There is lacking the proper discipline so necessary to the success of any well-organized body," he told delegates in 1901. "Better discipline can be brought about by a strict adherence to the constitution and a careful study of the joint agreements," he informed them in 1902. At the heart of the matter, at least to Green, was the need to instill in his fellow miners an abiding respect for the rules of their organization and a temperance of action. "The principles upon which it (the UMW) rests are everlasting as the hills and can never be destroyed; but in order to perpetuate its power for good we must be cautious in our deliberations and conservative in our action."[47] Conservatism, cautiousness, respectability, responsibility in behavior—these were the lessons Green learned about unionism in the chaotic and strike-filled years of the infant UMW. They were lessons he would preach to union men and women the rest of his life. That others in the UMW believed in these virtues can be gleaned from the fact that Green ran unopposed in elections for subdistrict president from 1900 to 1905 and became the most popular UMW leader in Ohio.

In the fall of 1905, William Haskins, president of District 6, which included all of Ohio and the West Virginia panhandle, announced that he would not seek reelection the following year. He had served in that post for seven years and planned to retire. Upon the urging of national president, John Mitchell, however, Haskins consented to run again. But by early January 1906, Haskins was again telling the press that he did not want the office, and when delegates arrived at the state convention in Columbus later that month, they learned that Haskins had withdrawn from the race.

The other candidate therefore ran unopposed. The other candidate was William Green.[48] At the age of thirty-five, Green was making steady, if not spectacular, progress up the UMW hierarchy.

According to the local Coshocton newspaper, when news of Green's victory reached home on the night of Tuesday, January 9, the entire town celebrated. The paper described Green as a very popular and likeable man, with literally "hundreds of friends" in town. Stout and healthy, with no sign yet of the paunch he would carry in later years, he lived with his wife, five daughters and one son on East Chestnut Street on the outskirts of town, and could be seen on his way to visit his father who still lived near the one-room schoolhouse on Hardscrabble Hill. Upon his election, Green's first act was to call his wife long-distance to give her the happy news. To Jenny and William, the election meant more than prestige and power, it meant that William would no longer have to mine coal. Now most of his work would be done in an office, the 77 Ruggery Building in Columbus, or travelling from mine to mine, town to town, in his district. Green would spend most of his weekday in Columbus and his weekends with his family back home.[49] Although the change from a coal mine to an office in a sprawling city of over 180,000 was a dramatic one, the move seemed to have little impact on Green's approach to union questions.

Green's election did force his attention, perhaps for the first time, to national affairs. Although he had been a delegate to every national convention since 1899, Green would now be asked to participate more fully in decisions affecting miners across the country. And by 1906, the affairs of the national UMW were once again in a turbulent state. On the political front, the caution and conservatism advocated by Green and other leading UMW spokesmen were being challenged from the left. Just a few years earlier, the Socialist Party of America had been formed and was now making marked progress. The eloquent Eugene Debs, leader of the young party, was an outspoken opponent of the national presidency of John Mitchell. When Mitchell accepted a slight wage-scale decrease for bituminous miners in 1904, Socialists inside and outside the union began calling for his dismissal. By 1905, there rose an even more strident voice decrying the UMW and labor-management cooperation. The voice belonged to William D. "Big Bill" Haywood and his Industrial Workers of the World. The IWW, or Wobblies as they became known, stood directly opposed to the UMW-type of unionism that seemed more intent upon making friends with capital than advancing the cause of labor. Wobblies advocated the general strike as a tactic to overturn the existing economic order. Both the Wobblies and the Socialists attracted followings among the rank-and-file, forming able and aggressive opposition blocs.[50]

Economic problems facing the UMW in 1906 were perhaps even more pressing than political ones. The relative peace and prosperity enjoyed by miners in Green's subdistrict between 1900 and 1905 had been the result of concentration of ownership in the bituminous fields. Larger and wealthier coal operations decreased competition and stimulated industrial peace. But the sheer vastness of coal deposits in American worked against the rise of an oligarchy of mine owners. Small mines continued to spring up next to large ones, employ nonunion labor, and begin underselling the corporations. This led to a renewal of the old competitive cycle of overproduction, wage cuts, and lay offs. The UMW had accepted a wage decrease in 1904, but when operators demanded another cut in early 1906, the union balked. Green was a member of the wage scale committee that met with operators of the Central Competitive Field during the national convention of 1906. When his committee returned to the delegates without a new scale agreement, the convention voted on a national strike.[51]

Green disembarked the train from Indianapolis to Coshocton on the night of Saturday, February 3 exhausted. The date set for the strike, April 1, was also the date he was to assume the responsibilities of his new office. As he told a reporter at the train station, he was still hoping for a settlement, for if a strike comes, "it will be the greatest ever seen in history, and bitter to the end."[52]

As a last effort to avert a strike, the UMW called a special convention in March. Green attended. No new wage scale had been hammered out but, in a surprise move, President Mitchell put fort a resolution stating that the best way to make sure the strike was of short duration was to allow districts to sign wage agreements, rather than hold out for a national contract. Green, obviously aghast, rose to address the delegates. "The resolution now under consideration means that we (the UMW) are taking the initiative in dissolving the interstate movement." Stating that the Central Competitive Field formula was a necessary component of the working partnership between labor and capital in coal and that its destruction would lead once again to wage slashing and the erratic employment of earlier years, Green voiced his abject disapproval. Green was careful lest his objection to the Mitchell resolution place him in the camp of the militants who longed for a showdown between operators and the union. Instead, Green counseled moderation and even hinted that he did not approve of the strike call. "The proper thing for us to do is to stand together and wait until the time when reason and moderation will possess the minds of the operators of this country." Despite Green's protests, Mitchell's resolution passed.[53]

As Green moved into his office at the Ruggery Building on April 1, half a million miners walked off their jobs. After two months of difficult negotiations and often violent confrontations at the mines, Green was finally able to reach an agreement with Ohio operators. His skill as a negotiator was revealed when he not only resisted demands for a reduction in wages, but won back the decrease Mitchell had accepted in 1904 and reestablished the wage scale of 1903.[54]

By no means did Green's success and the relatively short duration of the strike convince him that Mitchell had been correct when he dissolved the Central Competitive Field. Green found himself in the strange position during the next two years of siding, at least on the issue of national contracts, with Mitchell's opponents, including the Socialists. Obviously, Green had much more in common with Mitchell's brand of union leadership than he did with the objectives of the leftists, but his insistence on national agreements placed him in a temporary alliance with the opposition forces. For this reason, the 1908 national convention proved very peculiar for Green.

Reeling from the attacks that came his way from progressive operators and militants within his union, John Mitchell fell sick in late 1907 and handed in his resignation. He claimed to be unable to carry out his last duty, that of presiding over the 1908 convention. This honor fell to William Green. Exactly why the UMW executive board chose Green cannot be established from the written record. An editorial in the miners' *Journal*, appearing just before the convention, called Green one of the "younger leaders looming upon the horizon of the organization," and it was well known that Green was a student of parliamentary rules of order. But his selection was probably a result of the fact that he was president of the largest district in the union. Green's first spot in the national limelight began sedately enough, as he formed committees, read reports, and handled resolutions. His personal interests remained in the background until time came for a discussion of the wage scale, whereupon he made a plea for the restoration of the Central Competitive Field. "It was to me a matter of sincere regret when two years ago the joint movement was dissolved," Green said. This seemingly innocuous speech touched off a hail of condemnations on the departing Mitchell, a storm led by T. L. Lewis of Ohio and the Socialists. Lewis at this point literally took over the convention, attacking operators, radicals, and even the temporary chairman whenever Green dared to protest the course of events. Until this time, Lewis had served under Green as vice-president of District 6, but he now rode the crest of the wave of sentiment to restore the Central Competitive Field and was voted in as the new national president.[55]

Lewis kept his promise and successfully restored the Central Competitive Field, but not without making enemies along the way. Although he was no more militant than other UMW leaders when it came to negotiations, Lewis was a fighter by nature and his tendency to attack everyone around him, including his supporters, alienated him from the other top men in the union, such as Frank Farrington and John Walker of Illinois,

Alex Howat of Kansas, and John P. White of Iowa. His attitude and policies also led him into open opposition with William Green.

In less than a year, Lewis's enemies were organizing an attack. In the spring of 1909, former President Mitchell gathered together in Chicago the most powerful men in the union: Green, Farrington, Walker, White, and Edwin Perry, the UMW's secretary-treasurer. At this meeting the leaders pledged to unite their forces and select a candidate powerful enough to unseat Lewis at the 1909 convention. All present agreed that John P. White was the obvious choice. However, White was unwilling to run for president so long as Edwin Perry, also from Iowa, retained his post as secretary-treasurer. White argued that two candidates for the top three slots in the union hailing from the same state would weaken his chances. When Perry refused to give up his job, the plotters had to make another selection. According to Mitchell, Green "seemed to be the logical choice." He represented the largest district, was popular himself, and his pleasant personality would contrast well with the bellicose Lewis. With all in agreement, Green was chosen to run for the presidency of the UMW in 1909.[56]

Mitchell became Green's unofficial campaign director. Although he had been rejected by the miners in 1908 and Green himself had opposed him, Mitchell still had a strong backing among the rank-and-file and he and Green shared similar union ideals. Both preferred the conference table to the strike field, both held high hopes for the cooperation of labor and capital, and both regarded the UMW as an agent of uplift in all aspects of society. Indeed, Mitchell informed Green that it was "because of my anxiety to see preserved the integrity and helpfulness of our union that I feel it my duty to further your cause."[57]

As a seasoned professional of union politics, Mitchell counseled Green on every aspect of his campaign. He told Green what to say when announcing his candidacy, gave advice on the selection of a running mate (Green chose the relatively unknown Frank Hayes of Illinois), suggested that Green write each district president, and devised the key campaign issue: "Green has heretofore been a consistent supporter of Lewis while at the same time retaining the confidence and esteem of those who disagreed with him. Consequently he is the best man to restore the harmonious relationship that should exist between the various branches of the organization."[58]

For his part, William Green was a willing tool of Mitchell and the opposition bloc. First, Green undoubtedly was flattered that the "big boys" in the union should accept him into their confidence and respected abilities. After all, only a little more than three years earlier Green had been only a subdistrict president, and now he was privy to the inner workings of the union's top echelon. Second, Green was convinced, as were the rest of the opposition leaders, that he had a more than fair chance of winning the election. By nature cautious, Green would not have ventured into such an undertaking if he believed the odds were against him. Third, ambition played a role. The UMW was his chosen career, and Green craved recognition from his peers and advancement in his profession as much as the next man. Finally, there were serious issues in the campaign to defeat Lewis. In a campaign circular dated November 25, Green spelled out why Lewis should be unseated. "Unity of purpose and harmony of action" were the chief elements of union strength, Green declared, and Lewis had undermined these by his quarrelsome personality. Lewis had also subverted "the autonomy of district organizations in handling their own internal affairs" by ordering miners in Pennsylvania to stay on the job even though state officials had called a strike. Further, Lewis had done little to organize nonunion mines in Kentucky, Tennessee, and West Virginia, creating a situation that "threatens the security and the work of those now in our union." Above all, Lewis had failed the UMW by erecting a personal machine to maintain his power. He selected organizers personally responsible to him rather than to officers in areas to which they were assigned, and he transformed the miners' *Journal* from a forum of discussion to a personal mouthpiece for his policies.[59]

The campaign itself was a rude awakening for the earnest and moralistic Green. Mitchell and the other insurgents quickly realized the strength of Lewis's personal machine. The incumbent used the pages of the *Journal* to print articles favorable to his own candidacy and refused to publish letters in support of Green. He also used his corps of organizers to campaign for him in areas already organized. He fabricated membership increases in union rolls, and he hand-picked officials to administer the election. By October 13, most of the opposition leaders were resigned to the fact that Green had little or no chance of victory.[60]

Green himself was not convinced the campaign was a lost cause, however, and he looked forward confidently to the December 14 election. The campaign trail took Green to all the organized districts, and his speeches focused on the viability of labor-management cooperation and the issue of morality in industrial relations. "Force has given way to reason," he told Illinois miners. "Morality, reason and intelligence prevail where physical force and passion once ruled."[61]

On the eve of the election, Green sent a long telegram to Mitchell, telling him that he was still confident of success. Moreover, he expressed his satisfaction with the campaign, congratulating himself and his supporters for having conducted "a clean and honorable campaign." In true Green fashion, he prided himself on not having stooped to "immoral" tactics as Lewis had done. "Everything honorable has been done that could be done, and I am hoping that we will win so that our organization will then take on new life and vigor."[62] It would be many decades before another UMW presidential hopeful could make a similar claim in good conscience.

The election results revealed that Lewis had administered a sound drubbing of Green and the other insurgents. Bitterly frustrated, Green still managed to write Lewis a letter of congratulations. He then wrote a scathing letter to the *Journal*, criticizing the editors, and vowing to introduce a resolution that would "effectively prohibit the use of the *Journal* during any future campaigns as it has been during this one." As a final slap to the vanquished Green, the editors retorted that they had been eminently fair during the campaign and that Green was "inconsistent" because the *Journal* had in fact presented his side by printing his congratulations to Lewis.[63]

Despite his defeat, Green had the savvy to retain his alliance with Mitchell and the insurgents. At another Chicago meeting in 1910, the group reformulated their strategy. This time they received Perry's assurance that he would not seek another term as secretary-treasurer. The path was thus cleared for the selection of John P. White as the presidential candidate. And by virtue of his popularity in the largest district, Green was chosen to run for secretary-treasurer. Lewis's campaign tactics were as corrupt as the previous year, but this time his personal machine was no match for the opposition. Cries of fraud and illegalities abounded during and after the campaign, but when the smoke cleared, White became president. However, Green had again suffered defeat. At the last minute, Perry reneged on his promise not to run and used the resources of his office to earn a narrow victory over the hapless Green. Although Green rejoiced in White's triumph, he knew very well that the election was a personal disaster.[64]

Having lost two elections in two years, Green had reason to question his future. Just two years earlier, he had been one of the most popular figures in the union. But he had abandoned his District 6 presidency in the hope of attaining higher office, and now, at the age of forty, he no longer held a job in the labor movement. He explained his predicament to John Mitchell and asked his advice. That Green sought Mitchell's opinion at this point was itself curious, for Mitchell was in the midst of deciding his own future in the UMW. Mitchell served as the miners' representative on the Executive Council of the American Federation of Labor and, at the same time, was being paid $10,000 per year to investigate labor matters for the National Civic Federation, an organization of progressive employers. His dubious role as both union official and NCF representative was unpalatable to many in the labor movement. At the 1911 UMW convention, delegates told Mitchell that he could either relinquish his job in the

NCF or his membership in the union. Reluctantly, Mitchell withdrew from the employer organization. Green consoled Mitchell in his dilemma, telling the former president that he saw nothing wrong in colluding with liberal employers who sponsored harmony between labor and capital.[65]

Green was loathe to find employment outside the union that meant so much more than employment to him, but he had a family and his own ambition to feed. He received several offers from coal operators who recognized his talents during wage scale negotiations, but Green considered a position directly in the employ of an operator "distasteful."[66] In an abrupt move, Green decided to seek a seat in the Ohio State Senate as a Democrat in the largely Democratic 18th and 19th districts. He captured the nomination and, in part due to the heavy turnout of the many miners in these districts, he won the election handily. E. E. Vorhies, Green's opponent, commented on the "fairness and honesty of your campaign against me" in his congratulatory letter.[67]

The seventy-ninth General Assembly to which Green now belonged marked Ohio's heyday of progressivism. A coalition of Democratic and Republican progressives held majorities in both houses, but conservatives were united in their goal to prevent passage of any reform platform. Conservatives wielded enough power to prevent progressives from naming the Senate president *pro tempore*. But they were not strong enough to put through their own choice. The two factions were forced to select a compromise—the political unknown, William Green.[68] Green's selection proved a disaster for conservatives. He immediately established a close working relationship with the progressives, pushing for many of their reforms and introducing a number of his own.

The Coshocton coal digger quickly mastered the art of formal politics. His election as Senate president placed him in the position of mediator between contending political lobbies, the most powerful of which at this time were the Ohio Manufacturers' Association and the Ohio State Federation of Labor. As he had done in the UMW, Green pursued a course of mutual accommodation, hoping to improve capital-labor relations through the rationalization of industry. During his first term, Green authored and led the successful fight for passage of the 1911 Workmen's Compensation Act, which established a state insurance fund to be paid into by all employers with five or more workers who chose to participate. This act was rewritten with support from both employers and organized labor when the Ohio General Assembly unanimously approved the Green Compulsory Workmen's Compensation Act on February 16, 1913. By compelling employers to contribute, the new law rationalized production costs at the same time that it benefitted workers. It proved so successful that it served as model legislation for other states.[69]

Another example of how Green pressed for labor advances by accommodating industry was his Ohio Mine Run Law, enacted in February 1914. Miners were paid according to the weight of coal dug, but until this law passed, Ohio miners were not compensated for coal falling through the mine screen, the size of which varied from mine to mine. The Mine Run Lew rectified this situation, thereby increasing miners' wages and, at the same time, standardizing labor costs for operators.[70]

As a preacher of harmony between labor and capital, Green denounced radical unionism as vociferously as any employer. When armed police and vigilantes in Akron crushed a rubber workers' strike led by the Industrial Workers of the World, Green headed up an investigating committee that exonerated employers for their refusal to deal with the strikers because the Wobblies' doctrines were "immoral and destructive." The report of the Green investigating committee made no mention of police brutality, arrests of strikers, or the role of vigilantes. Green held that the radical union's espousal of sabotage justified the employers' refusal to settle with the strikers.[71]

During his second term, Green authored and campaigned successfully for bills establishing a maximum nine-hour work day for women, a one percent income tax measure, the direct election of senators, and the non-partisan election of judges. He labored fruitlessly for a minimum wage law and a state health insurance plan. By promoting legislation which advanced the interests of capital and labor through mutual accommodation, Green not only implemented that which he had learned as a UMW official, he also became quite popular in state politics. Rumors circulated in Columbus that Green would become the next lieutenant governor.[72] Yet just when his political career seemed most promising, Green returned to full-time work as a UMW official.

The affinity he felt for miners and the UMW was the chief reason Green did not pursue a career in politics. Even while a state senator, he considered himself to be first and foremost "the servant of the miners."[73] Never had he desired to leave the union, and he returned to his "calling" as soon as the opportunity arose. More than politics, trade unionism offered him spiritual meaning and the chance to participate in a righteous cause. Thus he was pleased when his opposition ally, President White, who considered Green "one of the finest young men on the Organization," appointed him as an international statistician in 1911.[74] He served so dutifully at this post in between Senate sessions that it was not long before he advanced in the UMW hierarchy.

According to Frank Farrington, another member of Mitchell's opposition movement in 1909 and 1910, White decided to oust UMW

Secretary-Treasurer Edwin Perry and appoint Green to that post for political reasons. White distrusted Perry because he had broken his promise not to seek reelection in 1910, and White was still concerned that Perry weakened his appeal in UMW elections because both men came from Iowa. Years later, Farrington insisted that White assigned him and two other executive board members to dredge up any incriminating evidence with which they could force Perry to resign. Farrington discovered that Perry had accepted a small Victrola as a gift from an operator, an indiscretion Farrington used to browbeat Perry into resigning. Under such sordid circumstances, White offered Green the post of secretary-treasurer on August 1, 1913.[75] At the time Green was perhaps unaware of the maneuver that led to his advancement, but the machinations of UMW officials revealed how difficult it was to maintain a high standard of morality in the world of trade unions.

Green was unusually active both as statistician and secretary-treasurer, a champion of White's administration, and an advocate of progressive union reform. As a leading official of the union, he was afforded the chance to express his views in the pages of the miners' *Journal* on a regular basis. Making the most of his first opportunity to write for public consumption, he penned articles on a wide range of topics. These articles offer important insights on Green's thoughts before he became AFL president. And the most striking aspect of these articles was his propensity to discuss labor issues in religious terms.

Throughout his life, Green was, above all else, a devoutly religious man. Inherited from his parents, nurtured in his childhood, and expressed in his desire to pursue the ministry, Green's Christian faith was unshakable. Despite the circumstances that prevented him from becoming a preacher, Green remained steadfast in his commitment to spread the word of the Lord. Each Sunday for the twenty years he spent as a coal miner in Coshocton, he not only attended church services but served as the sole Baptist Sunday school teacher in town. Every day of his life Green found time to read the *Bible*.[76] Religion was so much a part of his life that it was impossible for him to separate his union principles from his religious beliefs. Every question facing labor was, for Green, ultimatedly a spiritual question.

As were his union and political views, Green's religious convictions tended to be mildly progressive rather than conservative or radical. He sided neither with those preachers and laymen who used the *Bible* to justify the acquisition of great wealth nor those, such as W. D. P. Bliss, who used religion as a means to alter the existing social and economic structure along socialist lines. Green's views can be described best as belonging to the "progressive social Christian" tradition or, as it came to be known, the social gospel.

Protestantism underwent profound changes in late nineteenth century America. The rise of industrial capitalism and a permanent working class forced churches to address the sufferings of working people and the problems attending the rise of cities. The social gospel was a loose term applied to ideas that came to dominate Protestant thought from about 1900 to 1940. Never a movement in the strict sense, the social gospel was a body of ill-defined common beliefs about the proper role of religion in industrial society, beliefs that cut across denominational lines and even penetrated the Catholic Church. Basically, the social gospel referred to advocacy of moderation, accommodation, and social harmony between all classes in society. The most vocal champions of the social gospel in regard to labor issues were Washington Gladden, a Congregationalist, and Walter Rauschenbush, a Baptist.[77] Green was undoubtedly aware of Gladden, who served as minister in Columbus from 1882–1918, although no correspondence between them exists.

The principle message of Gladden and Rauschenbush was that "the power of Christian love" was the only force powerful enough "to smooth and sweeten all relations of capitalists and labor."[78] Gladden defended "responsible" unionism and labor's right to strike, yet he considered strikes "often unwise, unprofitable and injurious to the community." Rather than economic force, Gladden believed that "reason and moral influence" should be the unions' "primary weapons." According to his biographer, "Gladden's ideal was an industrial society based on cooperation (between labor and capital), permeated by the spirit of the Golden Rule, and geared to human welfare rather than profits."[79]

While it is not known whether Green ever met Gladden, the two men were of like mind when it came to the proper role of unions. They often quoted the same biblical passages to support identical points, and they backed many of the same causes. Both admired the National Civic Federation for its contributions to an open dialogue between employers and unions, and both stood behind the Federal Council of Churches, and ecumenical body that held lectures and debated on labor throughout the 1910s, 1920s, and 1930s.[80] Green frequently offered his time and expertise to such gatherings.

When Green was thus called upon to begin writing on a wide range of union subjects, he did so as a deeply religious man immersed in the principles of the social gospel. He constantly remined both employers and the rank-and-file that the *Bible* should serve as their guide in industrial relations. As he wrote in the 1911 Christmas issue of the *Journal*, "The teachings of the Master if obeyed and practiced would establish the Brotherhood of Man." The selfishness and greed of those employers who refused to cooperate with unions were responsible for much of the misery in the world, and it was up to union members to show recalcitrant employers the light, to make the UMW a "vital force for righteousness and social progress." On another occasion, Green emphasized the need to establish the basis of capital-labor relations "upon the principles of morality, righteous and truth. Each requires the other; capital cannot do without labor, nor labor without capital. Mutual agreement results in pleasantness and good order; perpetual conflict necessarily produces confusion and outrage."[81]

By no means was Green the sole advocate of religiously inspired unionism in the Progressive Era. He was only one of many labor officials who shared a vision of society perfected through trade unionism and Christianity. The ideas of the social gospel appealed as well to rank-and-file union members, as evidenced by the success of the Labor Forward movement, an AFL organizing drive in 150 cities advertising labor's commitment to Christianity and cooperation with management. Labor Forward organizers across the country reported massive turnouts from workers and favorable responses by employers and the public. Green no doubt shared the desire of one such organizer who wrote in 1912 that he hoped some day to see the rise of a "band of preacher-labor leaders" who would not be "bound by narrow creeds, but . . . will teach the intensely human gospel which Christ Himself preached."[82]

Along with becoming UMW secretary-treasurer, yet another unexpected honor befell Green in 1913. The death of an AFL vice-president created a vacancy on the Executive Council, and AFL president Samuel Gompers offered the post to White because the powerful miners' union was unrepresented. White scorned the position of seventh vice-president as beneath his dignity, pointing out that the last UMW official to serve on the Council, the now-retired John Mitchell, had been second vice-president. Gompers, still eager to have the UMW represented, then offered the post to Green, who proudly accepted.[83] In just a few years, Green had risen from unemployment to one of the top three positions in the UMW and, now, one of the most powerful slots in the entire labor movement.

In light of later events, it is ironic that before 1924 Green, as a Council member, was a persistent critic of AFL policy. His experiences as a progressive politician and as an official of a relatively forward-looking union led him to speak out against a number of established AFL practices, practices he would later have to enforce as AFL president. First, Green was the highest ranking spokesman for industrial unionism in the AFL. In 1912 and again during World War I, he introduced resolutions to AFL conventions calling for the restructuring of the labor movement along industrial lines. He railed against the "selfishness, ill-feeling and obstinacy" of the craft organizations as they butted heads in jurisdictional disputes.[84] When the industrial union resolution was defeated in 1912, Green wrote in the *Journal* that "great reforms come slowly. Men are slow to change their views even in the labor movement. However, this progressive change will come—in fact, it is inevitable, because it is fundamentally right and economically sound."[85] Little did he imagine that in the 1930s he would be the agent of those standing in the way of industrial unionism.

Second, Green rejected the AFL's knee-jerk opposition to political involvement. He struggled to secure Federation endorsement for a government-sponsored health insurance plan. And at the 1915 convention, he spoke strongly in favor of an eight-hour day law for all workers. He made an eloquent, if unsuccessful, attempt to convince Gompers, the Executive Council, and delegates that political action was a viable means of advancing worker interest. "Is there anyone here," he asked, "who believes that the man who enjoys the benefit of the eight-hour day through the strength of his economic organization, appreciates and enjoys it more than the man who secured the eight-hour day through legislation?"[86]

The rise of William Green in the labor movement was a matter of ambition, talent, and luck. But it also attested to the pervasiveness of the vision of cooperation in labor circles. His tremendous popularity among the UMW rank-and-file would have been impossible had not his ideals struck a responsive chord. The failure of the Labor Forward movement by 1920, however, revealed that a religious commitment of cooperation resonated less among unorganized workers in mass-production industries, many of whom were immigrants less influenced by the social gospel. And the dramatic emergence of John L. Lewis demonstrated that even in established unions, such as the UMW, hard-nosed, opportunistic union leadership was becoming increasingly common.

In the fall of 1917, John P. White resigned the presidency of the UMW to accept a position on the Federal Fuel Board and, in fulfillment of the union's constitution, Vice-President Frank Hayes automatically succeeded to the top post. Hayes and White together selected John L. Lewis of Illinois, at the time UMW statistician, for the vice-presidential slot. But when Hayes proved to be an alcoholic and an incapable administrator, Lewis literally took over. On January 1, 1920, Hayes' drinking problem forced him to resign and Lewis replaced him.[87]

Working for Lewis was a novel and not entirely pleasurable experience for the virtuous Green. Between 1922 and 1924, Lewis authorized the expenditure of more than $12,000 in union funds to secure information or influence. When he told Green not to record these expenditures in the union's books, the secretary-treasurer was appalled. Green protested, but ultimately bowed to his boss's will. In 1923 and again in 1924, when Green performed his duties in accordance with the UMW constitution and precedent, Lewis upbraided him. "I would be very glad to have you accommodate your bookkeeping arrangements . . . so as to square with the president's office.[88]

While the working relationship between the two men was hardly ideal, there is no evidence that Green ever defied Lewis or spoke out in opposition to him. On the contrary, Green praised his boss in public, as he

did in 1921 when he nominated Lewis for the AFL presidency. A successful bid by Lewis would have closed Green's only avenue for advancement
in the Federation, yet he supported him. In 1924, when the Executive
Council chose Green to replace Gompers, Green accepted the position
only after conferring with Lewis and receiving his approval.[89] Green's
actions as secretary-treasurer under Lewis showed neither timidity nor an
unwillingness to stand up for his convictions so much as loyalty to his
organization, a trait he would later exhibit as AFL president.

Gompers trounced Lewis in the 1921 election for the AFL presidency.
The result was hardly a surprise since Gompers dominated the affairs of
the Federation. He had served as president for all but one of the thirty-
eight years of the AFL's existence. Not only was he the founder, but many
considered him the Federation's life blood and guiding spirit. Thus his
death in 1924 was such a profound blow that there was some concern over
the AFL's ability to survive without him. John P. Frey, president of AFL's
Metal Trades Department, articulated the despair of Federation officials
upon Gompers" death when he wrote a friend that "the stars by which we
have guided our ship have suddenly been blotted out."[90] Even the selection
of a successor threatened to tear the AFL assunder.

Certainly Green seemed an unlikely choice for the vacant post. Other
men wielded far more power in the labor movement, particularly John L.
Lewis, president of the largest affiliate, and Matthew Woll of the Photo
Engravers' Union, considered Gompers' favorite and known as the "crown
prince." Neither candidate, however, could command a majority of votes
on the Executive Council. It was Lewis, in his determination to keep Woll
out of the presidency, who offered Green as the compromise candidate.
Lewis used his influence to persuade Council members to vote for his
lieutenant. This proved an easy task, for although Green had been a critic
of AFL policy, he had always upheld majority rule, was well-liked by
Council members, and was not prone to aggrandize power. In the end,
even Woll decided to vote for Green.[91]

Compromise had been the reason for Green's selection by John Mitchell in 1909 to run for the UMW presidency and by the Ohio Senate in
1911 to serve as its president, and now compromise was responsible for
his rise to labor's most exalted position. More than being in the right place
at the right time accounted for Green's appeal as a compromise candidate.
Above all, the lessons he had learned in the early UMW gave him the
attributes of a natural compromise choice. As could be seen in his reaction
to the destruction of the Central Competitive Field in 1906 and his advocacy of industrial unionism, Green was a passionate man. Yet his early
trade union career taught him to temper his passion, to appreciate caution
and conservatism in word and action, and to recognize the need to

accommodate all interests in any dispute. Green had developed a considerable gift for finding common ground between disputants and for avoiding the making of enemies. This skill accounted for his ability to thrive in the treacherous waters of union politics and to lead men without imposing his authority. This quality made Green attractive to Executive Council members in 1924. But when no common ground existed between contending parties and a more forceful style of leadership become necessary, Green appeared very weak, as we shall see in our discussion of the 1930s.

Amid the fanfare attending his election, Green gave the outward appearance of calm and reserve. Now, at the age of fifty-four, Green no longer looked much like a mine worker. It had been over eighteen years since he had last toiled in the darkened depths of a mine, over eighteen years since he had risked life and limb to earn a living. The once-hardened body had turned to fat, he wore tailored suits instead of overalls, and he had moved his family from Hardscrabble Hill to a comfortable two-story house in the heart of town. He was himself one of the "respectable" people he had met only in church as a youth. The feelings of solidarity he felt toward miners on the Hill were now only memories, to be rekindled every other weekend when he left his paperwork to visit his family and friends.

Despite the outward calm, when Green assumed the presidency on December 19, 1924, he was a man torn by contradictions. He was an intensely spiritual man, and yet he was now in charge of the oftentimes crassly materialist affairs of the largest trade union federation in North America. And although he was the product of an industrial union, he now became the executor of the will of craft union leaders who dominated the AFL Executive Council.

The key to understanding how Green resolved these contradictions lies in his unswerving commitment to majority rule. Regardless of his opposition to various AFL policies, Green always respected the decisions of the Executive Council or convention majority. Indeed, Green's willingness to allow the Council majority to determine policy may have been the deciding factor in his election, for Council members were well aware of Green's conviction that "if a policy is adopted by a majority, objectionable as it may be, it is our duty as loyal union men to subordinate our individual sentiments and submit to the majority will."[92] Thus Green's advocacy of religiously-inspired cooperation with management, industrial unionism, and political action posed no threat to the continued rule of the craft unionists. Although Green's dedication to the principle of majority rule was a result of many years of union experience, cynics regarded it as a copout, a sign of weakness. As journalist Benjamin Stolberg wrote in 1926, Green could "continue to lead the American Federation of Labor as long as the hard men on its Executive Council . . . think he is safe . . . They found him weak. They are for him."[93]

Upon entering office, Green immediately put to rest any possible doubts Council members may have had regarding his intentions. Council members expected a pledge from Green that he would not in any way attempt to control Federation policy, and Green did not disappoint them. The new president assured the high command that he would follow Gompers' precedent and leave the formation of strategy in the hands of the Council. In one of his first editorials in the AFL monthly journal, the *American Federationist*, Green promised to "adhere to those fundamental principles of trade unionism which President Gompers so ably promoted and defended and which form the greatest foundation of our movement." Foremost among those "fundamental principles" was the supposedly democratic way in which Gompers had managed the AFL:

> The American Federation of Labor stands as a monument to the rightness of the principle of voluntary action—of action by common agreement. The American Federation of Labor is bound together by common agreement upon the rightness of an ideal. There is no force that can for an instant hold a single union in affiliation, but there is a moral power in a common idealism and a common purpose that holds all together in an unbreakable unity.[94]

In practice, the policy of voluntarism placed strict limits on the powers of the AFL president. The AFL was a loose confederation of autonomous unions, and real power rested in the international unions. "To the International Union," Gompers had declared, "belong all power not specifically delegated to the Federation."[95] The presidents of the most powerful internationals composed the executive Council, and the role of AFL president was merely that of mediator. His function was to coax, advise, and reconcile differences between the internationals, but he did not possess the power to impose his will on them. Throughout the twenty-eight years of his presidency, Green never questioned this role. It was for him the essence of the AFL's democratic approach. He did not consider it his duty or privilege to initiate policy, only carry it out. And if by executing the will of the Executive Council or convention majority he inevitably placed his stamp on Federation policies, the policies always originated with the powerful union leaders. Nevertheless, Green wholeheartedly accepted many of the policies put forth by these men. The conservative strategy of the AFL in the 1920s, as we shall see, suited Green's temperament and his deepest convictions.

II

Marketing Unionism to Business:
The 1920s

T HE AFL PRESIDENCY was a prestigious office but not a powerful one. The president was the servant and not the master of the Federation. His principal duties were presiding over Executive Council sessions and annual AFL conventions, lobbying on Capitol Hill, settling squabbles between affiliates, and publicizing the AFL's program. In his first years in office, Green devoted most of his energies to publicizing work He directed the Federation's massive but ineffective marketing campaign in the 1920s to sell unionism to industry and the public. Audiences responded favorably to Green's moralistic addresses, but the campaign netted few tangible union gains. Green had much better success as the AFL's chief lobbyist in the 1920s, securing legislative relief from the labor injunction.

Becoming AFL president was a crowning distinction for Green, but the honor came at a time when the resources of the Federation were in decline and the opposition to it most powerful. The membership of many of the most powerful affiliates were dwindling; the glorification of the free enterprise system that marked the 1920s did not provide a climate favorable to union growth; and labor faced the hostility of both the judiciary, through the increased use of the labor injunction, and employers. In the early part of the decade a great number of employers implemented the American Plan, a frontal assault on unions using every conceivable belligerent tactic. By the end of the decade a more subtle approach to the "labor problem," paternalistic welfare capitalism, grew in popularity as employers consciously sought to supplant unions by directly providing employees' benefits.[1]

Under Green, the AFL reacted to these developments by changing strategy. The new strategy was simple—the AFL endeavored to sell itself to industry. In the hope that employers voluntarily would allow their workers to organize and bargain collectively, the AFL leadership abandoned whatever militancy it retained and advertised all the virtues of trade unionism.[2] For most, if not all, Executive Council members, the shift in strategy was a calculated response to union weakness and employer hostility, a temporary maneuver they would readily abandon when times grew more auspicious for union growth. But Green viewed the new approach as a secularized expression of the timeless ideal of Christian cooperation, a major step toward establishing an ethical basis for capital-labor relations. His role would be that of public relations director. He packaged and marketed the new AFL, and he took his product door-to-door to industrial associations, financial groups, patriotic organizations, college campuses, churches—in short, to anyone willing to listen.

The most publicized expression of the AFL's campaign for respectability and acceptance was union-management cooperation. In many ways similar to Green's religious vision of cooperation, union-management cooperation was a concrete plan to extend collective bargaining procedures. Once a union had been recognized, collective bargaining would determine wages, hours, and working conditions. Militancy would then give way to harmony, and unions would join with management to make production more efficient. Green set out on a quixotic quest to persuade employers of the benefits of such a scheme. He described his ideal of union-management cooperation in May 1927 to a labor gathering in Reading, Pennsylvania:

> I would like to see a condition established where the manufacturers, exercising their right to organization would grant to the workers the exercise of the same right and then I would like to see their respective committees sit down around a conference table, at stated periods, and discuss together the common problems of industry. At these conferences, the workers . . . could point out to the management how waste could be eliminated, how duplication could be avoided, how economies could be introduced . . . [3]

Green based his appeals for union-management cooperation on labor's commitment to efficiency, on labor's newly found readiness to avoid strikes and work stoppages, and, most importantly, on the employers' sense of justice and fair play. Indeed, the moral dimension of industrial relations was central to Green's approach. He remained forever the Baptist minister calling on sinner to repent. Employers who denied their workers the right to organize, let alone attempt union-management cooperation, were simply not good Christians. The root cause of all industrial controversies, the real reason behind employers' disregard of labor's rights, was the failure to follow the teachings of the *Bible*. Most of the suffering, bitterness, and hate in the world resulted from the un-Christian vices of selfishness and greed. "We are far from observing the Golden Rule in the relationship between employers and employees," Green told an audience at Carnegie Hall in September, 1926. "The rule of brute force and selfishness prevails in the policies of many large employing groups rather than the rules of morality, religion, and Christianity." A willingness to implement union-management cooperation, Green concluded, was the first step toward rectifying this situation.[4]

Green and the Executive Council clearly distinguished between union-management cooperation and company unions. The AFL had always denounced the company union, but by the time Green took over as president, it was apparent that denunciation alone would not do away with the menace. The AFL's high command could not ignore claims that employee representation plans spurred productivity. In 1925 Green proposed a "scientific" study of the operation of company unions. Although the 1926 AFL convention authorized such a study, the results of any possible investigation that might have been made were never released.[5] Green, nonetheless, was always confident that the benefits of union-management cooperation far outweighed those of company unions.[6]

An essential corrollary to union-management cooperation in the packaging of the AFL was the new wage policy. In order to stimulate rank-and-file interest in cooperation, the AFL leadership devised a wage policy that promised high wages and periodic wage increases based on labor's constructive contributions to efficient production.[7] Thus employers were told that cooperation from unions carried a price tag.

In his endeavor to convert industry and the public to the new wage policy, Green employed both economic and moral arguments. He often posed the question of how employers planned to market the ever-increasing volume of goods produced. Unions, he asserted, could not only aid industry by eliminating waste and improving efficiency, they were also central to the process of distribution. If unions were unable to maintain high wage rates, manufacturers would have no market for their products. Green offered industry what he thought was a fair exchange. Workers would cooperate with management to increase productivity if "employers will cooperate with labor in making it possible for labor to buy back the things it produces."[8]

Progressive businessmen, engineers, economists, and others warmly applauded the AFL's new wage policy. The *New York Times*, for instance, welcomed the new policy as a "wholesome change." By relating wages to productivity, the AFL had finally recognized that "the pockets of the 'capitalist' were not inexhaustable."[9] At first the AFL did not claim vital significance for the new policy, but once Green and other AFL leaders realized that the new policy was being well received by segments of the business community, the wage policy grew in importance. At the 1927 AFL convention, John P. Frey, a leader of the metal trades, praised the Federation for "being the first trade union movement to open the book of sound and true economics."[10] Speaking at the same convention, Green expressed his joy that the AFL had finally presented a policy that evoked a positive response from the business community, and declared that the new wage policy signalled "the beginning of a new era—a position far in advance of any we have ever taken before."[11]

In speeches across the country, Green focused on the one truly novel aspect of the AFL's new wage policy—that wages should increase in proportion to labor's increased productivity. By 1927 Green referred to compensation based on this ideal as "social wages." The social wage, Green argued, was the third phase of the AFL's struggle for higher pay. Organized workers, he claimed, had already won their battles for higher "money wages" and "real wages." But higher "money wages" did not improve the workers' economic situation if price increases outstripped any advance, and higher "real wages" did not improve their situation if productivity rose faster. If "real wages" did not keep pace with productivity, it meant that the additional product was being consumed by others than workers. The social position of wage earners in comparison to other groups actually worsens, because the workers' standard of living did not increase in proportion with those of other groups. Social wages, therefore, would not only give workers bigger paychecks, but would raise their social status as well.[12]

Not only did continued prosperity demand the social wage, but justice and morality necessitated it. "It would be unjust for employers to appropriate to themselves all the benefits resulting from increased productivity through the installation of new and improved methods of production," Green lectured. "Decency and justice require that the workers share fully and equitably in all the blessings and benefits which flow from the source of enlarged and everincreasing production."[13]

Closely related to the new wage policy was the call for a shorter work week. Although the reduction of working hours had been a goal of the AFL from its birth, only in 1926 did an AFL convention officially endorse the five-day week.[14] The Federation did not seek to attain the five-day week through legislation; it hoped that employers would accept the plan without compulsion. As was the new wage policy, the push for the five-day week was an attempt to capitalize on the staggering increase in productivity that occurred in the 1920s.

Green endeavored to convince the public and employers that working fewer hours would benefit industry by making workers better consumers.

"With leisure time people develop greater and more discriminating needs and therefore a greater desire to buy the goods that industry is producing."[15] Thus if employers accepted union-management cooperation and social wages, they would surely recognize the need to give workers more free time to consume.

The moral dimension always took precedence over economic arguments in Green's addresses, however. The monotony and high speed of work in automated factories meant that workers required more time to recover—physically, mentally, and spiritually. The five-day week would also provide workers the time to become active in civic affairs. It would give rise to a "better citizenship, with finer qualities and higher ideals."[16]

Union-management cooperation, social wages, and the five-day work week were the key tenets of the AFL's marketing campaign. If accepted by employers, they would have secured the same results the AFL had always sought: union recognition and collective bargaining, better working conditions, higher wages, and fewer working hours. But instead of flexing economic muscle to bring these conditions about, the AFL and its constituent unions developed arguments to convince, rather than force, employers to accept them. For most Executive Council members, the shift in strategy was a response to union weakness and employer hostility. But for Green, the new approach represented the great strides unions had made. No longer must unions fight tooth and claw for gains; now they could use their brain power to convince employers of the reasonableness of their position. The conservatism of the AFL in the 1920s promised to raise labor-management relations to a higher, ethical plane.

From Green's perspective, the AFL in the 1920s was not simply pursuing "more, more, now." Union-management cooperation promised a new era in industrial relations. It could improve workers' social as well as economic status. Under it, management might come to respect the opinions of workers. Employers would recognize that their employees were something more than production costs, that they could contribute to the successful operation of industry. And once relieved from the strain of excessive working hours, workers could become active community leaders advancing the common good. Green thus sought for workers a voice in decision-making on the job, a rising standard of living, and the respect and status due productive and responsible citizens.

Green perceived himself not as a mere trade unionist pursuing higher wages, but also as a missionary among the public and industry. He recognized, quite correctly, that if the AFL marketing campaign were to be successful, employers would have to experience something akin to a religious conversion. Green was calling for nothing less than a radical change in human behavior. Spiritual values must overcome material concerns, and the nature of industrial relations must be permanently altered. "Human welfare, spiritual values and social well-being," he wrote, "must be made paramount to industrial success. Industry must be made a contributing force to the advancement and promotion of all that is good and beautiful in life."[17]

Despite his conviction that the AFL had a moral mission, Green was not a utopian visionary. He held that human nature contained so many contradictions that perfection in human or industrial relations was unattainable. Yet he did believe that America had the resources—both natural and human—to create a cooperative and egalitarian society. Capitalist structure would be maintained, but the rights of each party to the production process would be guaranteed by mutual need and respect.

In futherance of his marketing campaign, Green tried to dispel long-held assumptions that organized labor was dangerous and un-American. Time after time Green would tell his audiences that he loved America and American institutions, and that the AFL had no desire to alter the nation's system of government. The AFL hoped to organize workers "in accordance with American traditions, and in thorough-going, American fashion. We have at no time employed any other than American means and American methods."[18] The AFL and its affiliates were red, white, and blue, Green declared, and they wanted only the chance to prove it.

One prominent aspect of the AFL's campaign to appear loyal and patriotic was the ties it established with the military in the 1920s. Relations with the military were initiated under Gompers, but they expanded under Green.[19] When Green accepted an invitation to address the Army War College in Washington, as Gompers had done from 1919 to 1924, he took the opportunity to declare that the AFL "is intensely patriotic and conscientiously devoted to American ideals, to American institutions and to the American form of government."[20] Green went to great lengths to make sure that his own patriotism was never brought into question. In 1925 he made a special point of urging workers to observe Flag Day. He led the Executive Council to West Point in 1929 where they received the cadets. And he also joined the U.S. Flag Association and the National Security League.[21]

The AFL was marketed not only as a defender of American political institutions, but as a champion of American capitalism. Green saw praise of capitalism as the best defense against charges of radicalism. "With all its imperfections the so-called capitalist administration of industry is the best of any thus far devised."[22] But AFL actions in the 1920s spoke louder than its words. In the labor banking and labor insurance movements of that decade, AFL business unionism was transformed into trade union capitalism.

The independent Brotherhood of Locomotive Engineers launched the first labor bank in 1920, and by 1926 there were thirty-five labor banks with assets totaling more that $126 million.[23] The reasoning behind labor banking was that the savings of workers' should be pooled in order to promote trade union activities. Green encouraged the growth of labor banks, but when the Locomotive Engineers' bank collapsed in 1927, he joined with the executive Council in issuing a "solemn warning" to AFL unions to "halt further expansion in labor banking until the labor movement makes a critical study of banks."[24] The decline of the Engineers' bank was followed by the decline of other labor banks, so that by 1929 there were only eighteen left.[25]

In response to employer-sponsored insurance programs, the AFL in 1925 created the Union Labor Life Insurance Company. Green presided over the founding conference represented by fifty internationals. By 1927 over sixty internationals, hundreds of locals, and over 300 individual union members owned stock in the company. Green himself purchased ten shares for $500 in 1927.[26]

The proper packaging of the AFL required not merely support of American political and economic institutions, but vociferous denunciation of those who dared to offer an alternative. All Executive Council members were accomplished Red-baiters, and upon Green's election, some feared that he was too progressive and that his condemnation of radicals was not strenuous enough. Green, after all, was from one of the more radical union, the UMW. He had supported the Plumb Plan at the 1920 AFL convention which would have led to partial government ownership of the railroads, and some traditional unionists were wary that his advocacy of old-age pensions smelled of creeping socialism.[27]

But Green soon dispelled all doubts as he set about sharpening his Red-baiting skills. In August 1925, Green warned black trade unionists not to attend the American Negro Congress to be held by the Workers' (Communist) Party in Chicago later that year.[28] Green really proved his Red-baiting mettle at the 1925 AFL convention, the first over which he presided. When Green recognized delegate A. A. Purcell, former president of the British Trades Union Congress and current president of the International Federation of Trade Union, he probably expected little more than a formal but hollow greeting from the international body. But Purcell was also a member of the Anglo-Russian Committee and a recent visitor to the Soviet Union. Purcell urged the convention to send its own delegation to the Soviet Union and, among other heresies, to support U.S. recognition of the Soviet Union, and to move toward establishing closer ties between Russian unions and the AFL. If there were still Council members uncertain as to the depths of Green's anti-Communist militancy, his response must have pleased them. Green told Purcell that the AFL would never send a delegation, would continue to oppose recognition of the Soviet regime, and would never establish ties with any organization that supported Communism.[29]

Within the United States, the actual Communist threat to "bore within" AFL unions, represented by the Trade Union Educational League, was weak throughout the 1920s. The only major TUEL success in the decade came in the fur industry. Led by Ben Gold, the Communists captured a number of New York City Fur Workers' locals. Their strength was such that they almost took control of the AFL union at the 1925 convention. Gold led a strike in 1926 in New York that was so successful that locals in Philadelphia, Boston, Newark, and Chicago came under Communist control. It looked as though Gold and the Communists would take over the Fur Workers' International at the 1927 convention.[30]

Green was alarmed. Loss of the Fur Workers would prove a damaging blow to the marketing campaign. In July 1926, Green appointed a committee to investigate the 1926 New York strike. To no one's surprise, the committee's report condemned the strike and accused Communists of attacking non-Communists, misappropriating union funds, and even bribing police in New York. On January 12, 1927, Green publicly vowed to purge New York unions of all Communist influence.[31] The following day the Executive Council instructed the executive board of the Fur Workers to expel Communist officers and revoke the charters of Communist locals. Yet the executive board, lacking funds and rank-and-file support, was never able to carry out the Executive Council's order. Communist domination of the Fur Workers remained firm. Green was never able to admit defeat in the fur industry. As late as February 1928, Green still claimed an AFL victory.[32]

The Communists also had some temporary success boring within the International Ladies' Garment Workers Union. The climax of the battle between the Communists and the conservative ILGWU executive board, led by President Morris Sigman, occurred in the 1926 Communist-led strike in the New York City cloak industry, which began in July and lasted for twenty-eight weeks. Green did not intervene as he had done in the fur industry, because the strike was not going well and defeat would guarantee the end of Communist influence. In November 1926, the strike collapsed and Sigman again resumed control of the union. Green then appointed a five-man committee to assist Sigman and the ILGWU rid the union of Communist influence.[33]

When the Communists shifted their strategy from one of boring from within AFL unions to boring from without by creating independent organizations in December 1928, Green was relieved. The disbanding of the TUEL and the creation of the Trade Union Unity League meant that

Communists would no longer subvert established AFL affiliates. Their approach was now one of competition with AFL unions, or dual unionism, and Green felt confident that the AFL could defend itself. In a March 1929 interview, Green commented that although there was a "red element" in the U.S., "its bark was more dangerous than its bite."[34] For the time being, Green felt the AFL was safe from Communist attack.

It was not just the Communist Party and the TUEL that Green and the AFL hoped to disassociate themselves: it was every smack of radicalism. If the AFL were to be properly packaged, it had to be divorced from every progressive labor effort within and without the AFL. For instance, Green received an invitation to speak at the semi-annual meeting of the American Academy of Political Science set for March 9, 1925. It would have been a golden opportunity to discuss his views on union-management cooperation. But when an invitation was extended to Sidney Hillman of the Amalgamated Clothing Workers, considered at this time to be an advocate of the Soviet Union, Green declined to attend.[35] If the AFL's marketing strategy were to have any chance of success, Green reasoned, all progressive criticism of AFL policies would have to be silenced. Thus Green had little patience with a potentially hostile and independent Workers' Education Bureau, and he led the assault on Brookwood Labor College.

The Workers' Education Bureau was formed in 1921 by labor educators and trade unionists, headed by James Maurer, president of the Pennsylvania Federation of Labor, John Brophy, president of UMW District 2, and J. B. S. Hardman, education director of the Amalgamated Clothing Workers. Their hope was to reform the leadership and policies of the AFL. They wanted to popularize the need for industrial unionism, a labor party, and greater militancy in the labor movement.[36] From the beginning, the AFL expressed an interest in the affairs of the WEB, and by 1922 had effected a "working plan of cooperation" with it. Slowly but surely, the AFL assumed control of the bureau. In 1927 Green took control of WEB publications, and received assurances that the WEB "would not concern itself in any way with trade union policies but would function strictly as an educational and research organization."[37] The WEB was thus slowly transformed into a defender of the conservative policies of the Federation.

While a few labor progressives remained in the WEB throughout the decade, most of them focused their attention on the activities of Brookwood Labor College. Maurer, Brophy, A. J. Muste of the independent Amalgamated Textile Workers, and Rose Schneiderman, president of the Women's Trade Union League, were among the founders of Brookwood, which opened its doors in October 1921 at Katonah, New York. The objectives of the college were similar to those of the original WEB, except that the founding convention of Brookwood explicitly called for the emancipation of the working class and the destruction of capitalism.[38]

The abolition of capitalism did not figure prominently in the curriculum, however, and most courses dealt directly with trade union principles. AFL unions were quick to offer their support and, within a few years, thirteen international unions provided financial support and four others had spoken highly of the school at their conventions.[39] One member of the Brookwood board of directors wrote Green in January 1927 asking for an official AFL endorsement of the college, but Green refused on the grounds that such an endorsement "would open the way for similar requests" and cause the AFL to become "involved in the problem of making decisions which properly belong to the Workers' Education Bureau."[40]

Most of the Brookwood faculty were progressive labor reformers and, since there were no faculty members sympathetic to old-line craft unionism, lectures and reading material did not often reflect the official AFL point of view. William Green was one of the first to sense the danger of the Brookwood heretics. He made several inquiries about the faculty and curriculum as early as 1926. the answers he received confirmed his suspicions. In an *American Federationist* editorial in April 1927, Green made a veiled threat against the college when he wrote that workers' education must be "a safeguard against revolutionary doctrines."[41] Green's suspicion became alarm at the May 1927 Executive Council meeting in Indianapolis when Martin Ryan, president of the Railway Carmen, handed him a letter from a Canadian Official of Ryan's union, a certain Mr. Rattigan. According to Green, the letter "contained much inside information regarding certain activities being carried on at Brookwood," and even though Green had "rather suspected the atmosphere at Brookwood was sort of surcharged with radical tendencies," he had not realized the situation was "quite as bad as reported by Mr. Rattigan."[42]

Green took no action against the college, however, until he received letters from students there concerning the celebration of May 1 as a labor holiday. With the letters as a pretext, Green authorized Matthew Woll, chairman of the executive committee of the WEB, to make an official investigation of the school. Woll's report was made in secret, and the full report was never made public. But the investigation convinced Green that the faculty at Brookwood was "left-wing," that three faculty members had served on the board of advisors of the New York City Communist Workers' School during the 1927–1928 school year, and that A. J. Muste supported Communism. "Radical doctrines," Green declared, "permeated the curriculum."[43]

In August 1928, after the Executive Council had digested Woll's report, the Council announced its intention to advise all unions to disaffiliate from the school. It did so on October 29, and the AFL convention of that year approved the action. Many unions resisted the move, arguing that Brookwood should at least have a hearing.[44] From Green's point of view, however, Brookwood had to be silenced because it represented growing internal opposition that could prove embarrassing to the AFL marketing campaign.

For Green, Woll, and the Executive Council, academic freedom was not at issue in the case of Brookwood; the right of the Executive Council and the convention to maintain exclusive control over the formation of the AFL policies was the only concern. The Brookwood faculty who perceived workers' education as a means to achieve gradual reform of trade unionism threatened this control. Add to this the AFL's suspicion of intellectuals and Green's actions are more easily understood. As Green said later, the AFL will not give money to "any institution that ridicules our policy and undermines the work of our leaders."[45]

Thus throughout the 1920's, Green made many appeals to advance labor's interests. By pointing to the AFL's patriotism, its opposition to radicalism, particularly Communism, and its commitment to free enterprise, Green consciously courted the support of the middle class. But the moral dimension of industrial relations remained the basis of his marketing campaign. Religion always informed his thought and actions. At no time was his religious idealism more apparent than when he crusaded to increase the prestige of the AFL by succoring support from religious organizations.

From the early days of the Federation, many labor officials addressed local churches during conventions, but Green went further, hoping to enlist the active support of religious bodies. Green appealed to Catholic, Protestant, and Jewish groups, urging them to make a study of labor problems and AFL policies. As he told a packed Carnegie Hall audience in September 1926, "it is inconceivable that the Church could remain indifferent to the spiritual and material needs" of working people.[46] Exactly what type of support Green expected from church groups was unclear. He did not expect them, for instance, to take a stand "upon the question of open-shop or closed-shop or upon technical trade matters."[47] At times it seemed that Green simply wanted church bodies to recognize the legitimacy of organized labor in the same way it recognized organized capital. But at other times he called for more active involvement on the part of the churches in capital-labor relations. He often argued that "the Church prescribes a formula . . . for the solution of all problems and all controversies which arise between employers and employees."[48] Whatever support he ultimately hoped to receive from religious bodies, it was clear to him why the Church must support organized labor: "The seeds of the Gospel cannot take root in the soil of human poverty."[49]

Thus the AFL was a beautiful package: AFL workers were efficient, concerned about eliminating waste and increasing productivity; they respected the "rights" of employers and did not question managerial prerogative; they were patriotic Americans devoted to the free enterprise system; and they did not condone radicalism of any sort. Green had added a heavy dose of moralism to the package, and he expended a great deal of energy selling it across the country.

And yet no employer wanted to buy the package. The whole approach failed miserably. Among employers who already recognized AFL unions, union-management cooperation was a disaster outside of a few well-publicized cases. The Naumkeag Steam Cotton Company of Salem, Massachusetts introduced a cooperation plan in 1927. The United Textile Workers and several Northern mill owners established "joint councils." In 1928 the Rocky Mountain Fuel Company, fourteen years after the bloody Colorado strike, entered into a cooperative arrangement with the United Mine Workers that proved successful for a time. The Printing Pressman, the Street Railway Employees, and the Hosiery Workers also worked out a few cooperative agreements with employers. But, on the whole, very few employers were interested in cooperation and many of those who did implement plans quickly abandoned them. Few industrialists had any desire to extend the boundaries of collective bargaining.[50]

Green's salesmanship proved even less appealing to firms that did not already possess collective bargaining agreements with AFL unions. The serious deficiencies of the AFL strategy were most visible in the two organizing drives the Federation conducted in the late 1920s. As we have seen, the militancy of Southern mill operatives had stirred the fighting spirit of AFL members, many of whom urged an aggressive organizing campaign. Yet driven by the logic of cooperation, Green refused to support strike action. Southern workers, who expected financial aid and a commitment to militancy, quickly became disillusioned with the AFL.

In retrospect, the auto campaign (1926–1929) was from the start a lost cause. First, the question of which AFL affiliates would have jurisdiction presented a serious obstacle. Green pressed for the organization of all workers into a single industrial union, but craft union leaders on the Executive Council refused to waive their jurisdictional claims over potential union members. A compromise was reached at the January 1927 session of the Executive Council, one which later would be applied to the organizing campaigns of the 1930s. All production workers were to be temporarily organized into federal labor unions (local unions chartered directly by the Federation), and then later parcelled out among the various craft unions. Auto workers themselves vehemently opposed this policy and demanded in its place the creation of an industrial union.[51]

Second, auto workers in the 1920s lacked the militancy found among textile operatives in the South. The intense anti-unionism of employers, the

large surplus of unskilled labor in Detroit and other centers, and dissatisfaction with federal labor unions all diluted militancy. The auto workers'
relative quiescence reinforced the belief common among craft unionists
that mass-production workers were unorganizable.[52]

Finally, Green's moralistic leadership killed whatever chance of success the AFL had. Applying his strategy of gentle persuasion, Green, on
September 10, 1926, asked Max S. Hayes, editor of the *Cleveland Citizen*,
to determine Henry Ford's attitude toward union-management cooperation:

> Could you learn if it would be possible for the American Federation of Labor
> to establish contractual relations with the Ford Motor Company along coop-
> erative lines . . . ? Could you find out if it might be possible to arrange a
> conference to be composed of responsible representatives of the American
> Federation of Labor and the Ford Motor Company where a frank, full, and
> free discussion might take place?[53]

Several months later, Green officially launched the campaign by issuing a
"challenge to Henry Ford" in the *American Federationist*: "We have
brains as well as brawn, give us a chance to mobilize the creative ability of
workers and cooperate with management." Green hoped that Ford would
become a "manager of men, cooperating with them in a quest for better
methods and better results."[54] Green issued a similar "challenge" to General Motors.[55]

Green honestly expected Ford and GM to respond. He did not even
assign organizers to auto centers until June 1927, and even then he told
them to counsel against strikes.[56] A little over one month later, the chief
organizer, Paul Smith, wrote Green complaining that organizers were already discouraged because no progress had been made. Green suggested
that instead of concentrating on the recruitment of workers, organizers
should devote their energies to persuading employers "to try collective
bargaining."[57]

Green could not comprehend the refusal of Ford and GM to confer
with him. His belief that he could, through rational argument and moral
suasion, convince these militantly anti-union companies "to try collective
bargaining" revealed incredible naivete. His faith in the public image
campaign of the AFL clouded his understanding of reality. By the end of
1929, Green was virtually the only AFL representative trying to organize
the industry, an effort fated to fail.[58]

As we have seen, the efforts of the AFL under Green to sell itself to
industry was a failure. The package Green had created was attractive
enough, but union-management cooperation did not interest firms that
already recognized AFL unions, nor was it a sound basis for an organizing
drive. The decline of many unions in the 1920s and the hostility of

employers made the strategy of the AFL in the 1920s understandable, if not justifiable. Lack of funds, declining union membership, craft union domination, and Green's moral vision all shaped AFL policy. But while one may applaud the creativity Green showed in the public relations campaign, one must question why, after experiencing nothing but failure, Green clung to the strategy. Indeed, not only did Green maintain his confidence in the plausibility of union-management cooperation, he convinced himself that the new strategy was working.

As early as January 1927, Green wrote a friend that "Leaders of industry as well as representatives of labor are understanding more and more that industrial strife and industrial war mean waste and injury while constructive cooperation and constructive effort mean increased production, better wages, and better profits."[59] At the 1927 AFL convention, Green told delegates that the outstanding achievement of labor in the past year had been the success of cooperation.[60] By 1928 the Executive Council shared Green's delusion. In its report to the convention, the Council declared that "At no time in its history has the trade union movement had greater influence in industrial circles. The constructive policies which we advocate and follow challenge the attention and respect of employers in this country and abroad ... "[61] One year later, Green made a similar claim, even in the face of the collapse of the auto drive.[62]

Green also claimed that AFL's wage policy was a success. On Labor Day, 1926, Green asserted that "The declaration of the American Federation of Labor upon the theory of wages exploded the long-accepted line of reasoning regarding wages."[63] While many interested onlookers applauded the new wage policy, public reception hardly merited such jubilation. Yet Green made similar speeches on every Labor Day until 1930. His Labor Day message of 1927 claimed a "most amazing" change in the attitudes of "employers as well as of financial an commercial interests" toward recognition of labor's contention that "high wages make for prosperity."[64] Were one to follow only Green's speeches and press releases, one would have believed that the AFL was also making great strides toward realizing the five-day week.[65]

Green and the Executive Council, one historian has written, were "whistling in the dark."[66] In full retreat against the employer offensive, the Federation claimed victory even as it ran away. But in Green's case claiming victory represented more than a strategem to keep up courage. First, Green felt a great deal of pressure as Gomper's successor, and he found it difficult to face the fact that the organization he revered was declining under his leadership. Second, Green firmly believed that trade unionism had entered a "second phase," one characterized by rationality rather than force, and he could not face the prospect that unions would once again find militancy necessary.[67] Green was morally committed to the cooperationist strategy, and it would take more than AFL losses in the 1920s to convince him that the strategy was unworkable.

Compared to the abominable efforts of the AFL in dealing with employers in the 1920s, the Federation's rather limited ventures in the political arena were a partial success. Some labor observers expected a shift in AFL policy under Green toward greater involvement in politics. Green, after all, had been a member of the Ohio Senate and a champion of progressive labor legislation. A professor of economics at Ohio State University, M. B. Hammond, expressed the view of many upon Green's election when he wrote to the new president that, although Gompers had been a great man, "his opposition to the legislative route was, in my opinion, out of harmony with the tendencies of the times." Hammond believed that Green could better "appreciate that labor can gain some things by legislation which it cannot expect to secure by collective bargaining."[68]

But for those who held such expectations, Green's performance in the 1920s must have been a disappointment, for the AFL's legislative and political aspirations did not change significantly during the first years of his presidency. The reason for this, of course, was that Green saw himself as simply the executor of the will of Executive Council. His personal views on political action were of small consequence. The role of the president, as Green saw it, was not to initiate policy, only to carry it out.

The AFL did support certain types of legislation. It continued to press for the abolition of child labor, something for which it had fought since its founding in 1886. The child labor law Congress passed in 1916, which forbade the shipment in interstate commerce of goods produced by firms with employees under the age of fourteen, had been declared unconstitutional nine months after its adoption. In 1922 the Supreme Court struck down a similar law passed by Congress in 1919. Thus when the proponents of restrictions against child labor recognized that such laws had little chance of surviving, they threw themselves behind a drive for a constitutional amendment to outlaw the employment of children. The amendment passed both houses of Congress in 1924 by more than the two-thirds majority required, despite the opposition of the American Farm Bureau Federation, many industrialists, prominent members of religious organizations, and leading educators who saw the amendment as an attempt to subvert states' rights and assert federal control over minors.[69]

Against these formidable opponents, Green led the AFL in an energetic campaign to secure ratification of the amendment by the states. Green quickly revealed a strong personal interest in the issue of child labor, and he called on labor organizations to prepare for a difficult fight. "The campaign against the amendment is perhaps as throughly organized as any in the interests of special privilege has ever been." Labor and other friends of the amendment, he wrote, "must bestir themselves and devote their full energy to the task of educating the public and the newspapers." Education would be effective, he believed, because many farmers and other opponents had been duped "by the greedy employers." Manufacturers' associations, chambers of commerce, and textile employers were guilty of "vicious propaganda" which could be counteracted only by education.[70]

As with most issues on which he held strong opinions, Green employed two arguments against child labor: the economic and the moral. The economic argument against child labor was as old as the Federation itself. As Green put it, "Each child who works is taking the place of an adult worker who supports a dependent family."[71] Although unemployment did not become a major concern of the AFL until 1929, the Federation refused to sit back and allow children to displace organized adult workers. Particularly in the textile industry, child labor was an obstacle to union growth.

But for Green, the moral argument was even more compelling:

> It is a natural right for all children to be free from bodily toil and the crushing discipline of time . . . . It is inhuman to take a child from its mother's care, love and protection and place it by a hazardous piece of machinery to perform manual labor. It is criminal to maim and cripple these little ones. It is a sin against Heaven to earn a profit from the fatigue of an undeveloped, undernourished girl or boy.[72]

Here was the cry of a deeply religious father of six against one of the most overtly exploitative aspects of industrial capitalism. Green did not want to abolish capitalism by any means, but he did hope to effect a radical change of heart among employers so that capitalism would become less profit-oriented and more humane.

Unfortunately, Green's endeavor to abolish child labor in the 1920s proved unsuccessful. The opposition was too powerful and organized. Manufacturing interests, educators and others who opposed the transfer of authority from the states to the federal government, and religious groups who opposed any governmental control over the child-parent relationship, combined to defeat the drive for ratification. By 1929 only five states had ratified the amendment; by 1932, thirty-five states had rejected it. Thus the AFL proved politically too weak to induce government to protect children in the labor market.[73]

What success Green had in the legislative field came in the AFL's most ambitious crusade of the decade—the drive to secure relief from the labor injunction. As applied to labor disputes, court injunctions threatened to restrict severely the use of the strike and the boycott. In its most virulent form, the injunction was combined with the yellow-dog contract to effectively prevent unions from organizing. And while the injunction had always been a thorn in labor's side, the problem was acute in Green's first years as president because employers resorted to injunctions more often in the 1920s than any previous decade.[74]

As always, Green was careful not to make the anti-injunction movement appear too radical. "Every good citizen must have a reverential regard for our form of Government, our institutions and particularly for the courts of our land," Green lectured. "In denouncing injunctions, as used in labor controversies, we are not striking at the courts as institutions. We are pointing out their defects and we are protesting against favoritism and injustice."[75] But because Green was well aware of the ill-effects of the labor injunction, he, along with other members of the Executive Council, was adamant that some protection be found. And as usual, Green's arguments were those of a moral crusader. "We propose to fight against judicial error and judicial wrong until we succeed in maintaining our equality before the law and in establishing the sanctity and sacredness of human rights as paramount when they clash with the right to own property and to use and enjoy it.[76]

On December 12, 1927, Senator Henrik Shipstead of Minnesota placed a bill in the Senate's coffers. Shipstead was not terribly interested in his own bill, and had introduced it as a favor to his old chum, Andrew Furuseth, president of the Seamen's Union. Furuseth had actually written the bill himself. The bill read: "Equity courts shall have jurisdiction to protect private property when there is no remedy at law; for the purpose of determining such jurisdiction, nothing shall be held to be property unless it is tangible and transferable, and all laws and parts of laws inconsistent herewith are hereby repealed." Furuseth's line of reasoning was similar to the logic behind the labor section of the Clayton Act of 1914—that labor was not a commodity and was not subject to the jurisdiction of the equity courts.[77] A subcommittee of the Senate Judiciary Committee, chaired by Republican George Norris of Nebraska, heard testimony on the bill in February and March 1928. Since no one besides Furuseth and his legal counsel appeared to defend the bill, it never made it out of the subcommittee. A February 7 conference of 125 AFL and railroad brotherhood officials revealed that even a majority of labor leaders opposed the Shipstead bill. Some believed the bill would prove as ineffectual as the Clayton Act, while others considered the language too vague to merit labor support. Thus when Green appeared before the Congressional subcommittee, he vociferously denounced yellow-dog contracts and injunctions, but he could not endorse Furuseth's bill.[78]

After the subcommittee hearings, Senator Norris, with the aid of expert advisers, drew up and introduced a substitute for the Shipstead bill. Some of the most prestigious legal minds in the country either actively aided Norris in the preparation of the substitute or supported it before the subcommittee: Felix Frankfurter, Roscoe Pound, Francis Sayre, and Donald Richberg. The Senate subcommittee reported favorably on the substitute bill, but the Judiciary Committee failed to act on the bill before the Senate adjourned for the 1928 presidential election.[79]

Green immediately expressed interest in the Norris substitute, but the 1928 AFL convention proved unwilling to abandon the Shipstead bill. Green was now in a quandary. Personally in favor of the substitute, he could not support it without convention approval. The Executive Council decided the matter for him by setting up a committee, headed by Matthew Woll, to consider both bills. In June 1929, Woll's committee recommended acceptance of the Norris substitute. The AFL convention that fall witnessed a heated debate between Woll and Furuseth, who still clung to the Shipstead bill. But, as Green told Furuseth during the convention, "enough time has been wasted" on that piece of legislation and the report of the Woll committee was carried with Furuseth alone dissenting.[80]

Securing AFL support for the Norris bill had caused problems enough, and making it law promised to prove much more difficult. The new President, Herbert Hoover, however, unwillingly aided labor's cause by nominating Judge John J. Parker for the Supreme Court on March 21, 1930. Parker, a circuit court judge from North Carolina, had earlier alienated labor and progressives across the country in his notorious Red Jacket decision of 1927, which effectively barred the UMW from organizing West Virginia coal miners.[81] Upon Green's urging, the AFL launched an aggressive campaign against Parker's confirmation. International unions and individual unionists flooded senators with telegrams and letters. Green appeared before the Senate Judiciary Committee on April 5, 1930 and argued that Parker had "a judicial and mental bias in favor of powerful corporations and against the interests of the people."[82]

Partly due to the AFL's campaign, Parker's appointment encountered massive opposition. On April 11, Green wrote Hoover suggesting that he withdraw Parker's name. Hoover was outraged. He replied that Green was mistaken about Parker's sympathies and was "doing great injustice" by campaigning against him. Hoover even defended Parker's decision in the Red Jacket case! Green remained unconvinced, and on April 16 wrote Hoover that Parker would "carry the point of view he expressed in the Red Jacket Consolidated Coal and Coke case to the Supreme Court if his appointment would finally be confirmed."[83]

When the Senate rejected Parker by a vote of 41 to 39 on May 7, 1930, Green claimed it as "a victory for justice, righteousness and human rights." "It will confirm the faith of the plain people in American institutions."[84] More specifically, the debate on Parker focused national attention on injunctions and yellow-dog contracts, creating widespread opposition to them. Just two weeks before the Senate's rejection of Parker, the Judiciary subcommittee reported favorably on the Norris bill. But the full Judiciary Committee voted 10 to 7 against it on June 9. The bill remained pigeonholed for a year and a half.[85]

Green made the fight against injunctions the paramount issue for labor in the congressional elections of 1930. The AFL's nonpartisan political committee, Green said, "would concentrate its fire against the men who voted for the ratification of Judge Parker for the Supreme Court" and support those who favored the Norris bill.[86] In part because of the Federation's vigorous activities, the 1930 congressional elections did bring changes in the Senate Judiciary Committee and produced a more favorable climate for labor in Congress as a whole. On March 11, 1932, the Senate passed the Norris bill by an overwhelming majority. Representative Fiorello LaGuardia of New York introduced the bill into the House, which passed it on March 8. Hoover's signature made the Norris-LaGuardia bill law on March 23.[87] The act was one of the most progressive pieces of labor legislation passed up to that time. It severely limited the use of injunctions in labor disputes and signalled the eventual extinction of the yellow-dog contract.

But there was little hoopla in the office of the AFL president upon passage of the act. The *American Federationist* ran only one short story summarizing its content.[88] Green issued no statements about a new era being established in industrial relations. The act was labor's greatest legislative achievement in the 1920s, but Green was not jubilant. By this time the depression was in full swing, and signs of labor unrest could already be seen.

III

Weathering The Depression:
1929–1935

A s long as wage rates for organized workers continued to rise, as long as a handful of experiments in union-management cooperation still existed, and as long as a few employers favored the shorter work week, Green could maintain that the AFL's cooperationist strategy was a success. He could deceive himself and try to convince others that a majority of employers were steadily moving toward the Christian cooperative ideal, that they were beginning to act in accordance with human values rather than naked self-interest, and that they were coming to recognize their long-range interest in bolstering mass purchasing power.

The Great Depression shattered this illusion. Green was slow to realize it, but the depression proved clearly that AFL policies had failed and that employers did not regard their interests as being identical to labor's. Extensive wage cuts and layoffs revealed that self-interest, not morality, determined corporate policy. As the economic crisis deepened, Green continued to preach the gospel of cooperation. When at last his patience was exhausted, Green composed sermons predicting imminent class warfare and social revolution. He even made veiled threats about a general strike and a labor party. But militancy violated every precept Green held dear. Green's dilemma was resolved by the AFL rank-and-file, who forced him and the Executive Council to turn to the federal government for assistance. Once forced to appeal to the state, Green proved to be an effective lobbyist. Yet he always maintained the hope that capital and labor could find a cooperative solution to economic adversity.

Just weeks prior to the collapse of the stock market, Green's Labor Day address bubbled over with enthusiasm as he cheerfully reported that the number of strikes was declining every year, that the organization of the unorganized was proceeding smoothly, and that "collective bargaining is coming to be accepted more and more as a preventive of labor disputes." "To give labor's victories in detail would fill pages," he continued. "It is sufficient to say that labor is progressing at a greater speed than for any year in the past, that it knows what it wants and is aware of the way to secure it, and that it will grow in numbers and in strength every year in the future."[1] The crash of the stock market did not shake his confidence. He closed his eyes to the growing seriousness of the situation just as he had closed his eyes to the failure of AFL policies in the 1920s.

On November 21, 1929, President Hoover called to the White House leaders of labor and industry for a conference with the pretentious title of "Conference of Continued Economic Progress." In the morning the president met with such giants in industry as Alfred P. Sloan, Jr., Pierre du Pont, Henry Ford, and Owen D. Young. At a separate meeting in the afternoon, Hoover conferred with Green, William Hutcheson of the Carpenters, John L. Lewis, John P. Frey, Matthew Woll, and other labor officials. Although Secretary of the Treasury Andrew Mellon and other conservatives had called for deflationary tactics, Hoover sought to convince both groups of the need to maintain high wages to bolster consumer purchasing power. Although the president did not receive the labor-industry agreement he hoped for, Hoover was satisfied that the employers at the conference, "on their individual behalf," would oppose wage reductions. Ford even announced a wage increase for workers at his plants immediately following the conference. Green and the other labor officials, of course, needed no encouragement to accept the president's advice. In return for the employers' pledge not to reduce wages, Green and the others agreed that "no movement beyond those already in negotiation should be initiated for the increase of wages."[2]

Green left the conference fully persuaded that the president's conference had prevented the crash from leading to depression. He released a statement to the press claiming that the ill-effect of the stock market collapse "has been successfully overcome." Industry's intention to maintain wages, he argued, would "serve as a guarantee against widespread unemployment."[3] Green's outlook for the year 1930 was as cheerful as ever.

Green's trust in the morality and vision of employers was, as usual, misplaced. Even though many businessmen shared Hoover's commitment to the high wage doctrine, economic reality would force them to act otherwise. As demand dropped, production also fell and decreased the amount of work available. Many of the smaller firms initiated wage cuts and layoffs as early as 1930. Progressive businessmen resisted the traditional response to hard times and undertook work-sharing schemes to maintain employment. But as demand continued to plummet, even the large firms could not hold the line. U.S. Steel's announcement of a ten percent wage cut effective October 1, 1931, began a wave of retrenchment throughout industry generally. In July 1931, there were an estimated 8 million people out of work. By March 1933, 15 million were unemployed, one-third of the labor force.[4]

Growing joblessness exacted a heavy toll on trade union membership. The number of organized workers declined from 3,442,600 in 1929 to 2,973,000 in 1933. Had the Mine Workers, the United Textile Workers, and the ILGWU not already lost so many members during the 1920s, the decline would have been much greater. The construction trades were the hardest hit, losing 336,300 members in four years. The transportation and communication unions also suffered severely. In this climate, individual unions struggled only to maintain their membership; organization of the unorganized was out of the question. And along with the decline in membership came the attendant problems of depleted treasuries and loss of political influence.[5]

If AFL failures in the 1920s could persuade neither Green nor the Executive Council to abandon their fruitless marketing strategy, the devastation of the depression forced them to. A few years of depression made a mockery of Green's approach. The few existing experiments in union-management cooperation were abandoned. The labor banks collapsed. And the AFL's wage policy became meaningless in the face of declining productivity. In short, there was little left to sell.[6] At a time when employers turned to massive layoffs and wage cuts to salvage their concerns, Green's call for cooperation to increase productivity and the payment of high wages seemed ludicrous. Nevertheless, it was only with the imminent collapse of the AFL itself and the pressure exerted by the rank-and-file that Green and the Council abandoned their sales campaign.

Green's reaction to the first years of depression roughly paralleled the reaction of President Hoover. Being a staunch Democrat, Green did not vote for Hoover in 1928, but the economic outlooks of both men were surprisingly similar. As Secretary of Commerce, Hoover had urged businessmen to cooperate voluntarily in an effort to reduce waste and restrain competition. Hoover preached high wages and the need for massive consumer purchasing power. The role of government in Hoover's scheme was to provide information, the facilities to mediate differences between employers, and to demonstrate the advantages of cooperative capitalism. Unlike most of his Republican contemporaries, Hoover did not condemn trade unionism. He applauded the AFL's wage policy and the Federation's emphasis on cooperation and efficiency. Hoover's policies won him the support and the friendship of the two prominent Republican trade union leaders, William Hutcheson and John L. Lewis.[7]

Both Green and Hoover responded to the economic crisis as educators. In their addresses, both men hoped to convince businessmen that their long-term interests would be best served by avoiding wage cuts and layoffs. Green's role as educator was made necessary by union weakness, but it also grew out of his conviction that cooperation between labor and capital was still viable. Businessmen must be convinced, not coerced, to see the light of economic truth. Green shunned harsh criticism of employers in the early months of the depression. He talked humbly with them. "No person abusively denounced and criticized," Green wrote, "is in a good frame of mind to sit down and work out an agreement."[8]

The analysis of the depression presented by Green and Hoover was essentially correct. Wealth in American society was distributed inequitably because wages had not kept pace with productivity. As the gap widened, the home market for manufactured goods shrank. And because there were more goods being produced than the public could consume, prices began to fall. Many progressive businessmen understood this but could do nothing about it. Without a market for their goods, industrialists were forced to cut back production. When wage cuts and layoffs resulted, both Green and Hoover were at a loss as to what to do. Hoover proved himself to be doctrinaire, rigid and uncompromising in his attitudes toward federal intervention in the economy; Green was finally able to adapt.

Because Green believed that capital-labor cooperation was a moral imperative, he found it difficult to forsake the AFL's conservative strategy. And as the depression became acute, he devised a number of arguments to cajole employers into maintaining high wages and full employment. First, he continued to lecture businessmen on the need for consumer purchasing power. Second, he told employers that they were morally responsible for their workers' welfare. Third, he warned employers that their policy of retrenchment might lead to social revolution. And fourth, he threatened the use of labor action to resist layoffs and wage cuts.

Green reasoned that since every firm depended on the investment of both capital and labor, employers had an equal responsibility to both groups of investors, stockholders and workers. "Who would say," Green asked in the *American Federationist,* "that responsibility to those who invest their lives is a less serious obligation than responsibility to those who invest their wealth?"[9] Employers had no more right to pay substandard wages or dismiss workers than they had to appropriate the capital investment of stockholders. Firms that paid dividends while laying off workers and reducing wages violated Christian precepts. After U.S. Steel imposed its first major wage reduction in 1931, Green charged that it was "nothing less than rake-offs engineered for the benefit of stockholders."[10] When the Ford Motor Company announced in July 1930 that it would close for two weeks, Green asked, "Why has Ford or any other employer the right to shift responsibility for incomes of his employees to local charity organizations or merchants?"[11] By March 1931 Green was asking "What moral right has an industry to lay off workers as it would dispense with power?"[12]

Unless businessmen repented and accepted their social obligations, Green warned, America faced the possibility of social revolution. Green hoped to change employer practices by warning that large-scale unemployment bred revolutionary sentiment. As early as July 1930, he told delegates at the Sheet Metal Workers' convention that "there is nothing so disastrous to the social order as unemployment, which provides a fertile field for discontent and even revolution."[13] Green's warnings became increasingly shrill as unemployment mounted. On July 14, 1931, at the International Longshoremen's Association convention, Green wailed that unemployment in America had "brought on a serious condition of social unrest and industrial discontent."[14] That same month he told employers to "Face Fundamentals." He asked if they had the "courage" to raise wages and refuse layoffs, "or will we drift until revolution forces action?"[15]

When particularly upset, Green threatened militant labor action. Toward the end of Hoover's administration, Green began to counsel workers to employ every weapon at their disposal to resist layoffs. In an early 1932 interview with *Nation's Business*, organ of the U.S. Chamber of Commerce, Green said that labor would no longer wait for voluntary action by industry to redeem humanity "from the lawlessness of human greed," and was prepared to use force if necessary to "compel the plain remedies withheld by those whose malfeasance caused our woe."[16] The 1932 AFL convention witnessed perhaps the greatest fighting speech of Green's career. An exasperated Green declared that labor's patience with industrial management was at an end and that labor would not hesitate to use "forceful methods" to bring about full employment.[17]

The *New York Times* condemned Green's speech the following day, and bemoaned the fact that Green had forgotten his usual "spirit of moderation" and "proper sense of responsibility."[18] In response Green proclaimed that he was a peaceful man, and yet employers steadfastly refused to listen to his proposals. "Nothing was done," he said, and "now we are meeting in the congress of labor to seek a solution of our problem. What do they expect us to do? To sit still? The fighting spirit of the labor movement is aroused. We are going to fight . . . with our entire economic strength."[19]

Green never felt comfortable wearing the mantle of a class warrior, however. Militancy violated everything he stood for: Christian brotherhood, social harmony, a concert of interests. The plight of working people in the early 1930s often infuriated Green and led him to make militant speeches, yet he never abandoned the principles of Christian cooperation.

Indeed, it was ironic that Green's burst of militant rhetoric came just when he received the Theodore Roosevelt Distinguished Service Medal for his efforts in establishing "industrial peace." When James Garfield, president of the Roosevelt Memorial Association, presented Green with the medal, he praised him for facing "the citadels of industry" armed only with the desire for peace.[20] And Green's acceptance speech revealed far more about his attitudes toward labor militancy than anything else he muttered in the desperate year of 1932. "The cause of industrial peace," he began, "must ever appeal to the judgment and sentiment of all who believe in human well-being and social justice. Strife, class hatred and industrial war are wasteful and destructive. They represent the basic elements of force and are the antithesis of reason, judgment and cooperation."[21] That a person committed to such views would call for militant strike action shows just how desperate things were for the AFL in 1932. And it was the problem of unemployment, above all, that would force Green and the Executive Council to abandon the traditional policy of voluntarism and turn to the state for assistance.

Green believed that the primary responsibility for both the cause and the cure of unemployment rested with industry. By stabilizing production, employers could do away with seasonal unemployment. And Green humbly asked employers to respect labor's rights by not introducing new technology that would displace large numbers of workers. "Labor believes there is enough intelligence in industry so that technical change need not be marred by a human scrapheap."[22] The entire unemployment problem, Green told employers, would be solved if industry learned to cooperate with labor. Both labor and capital could work together by introducing the one component of the AFL's marketing strategy to survive the depression: the five-day week. The shorter work week would become, for Green at least, the cure-all for unemployment in the early years of the depression. "The kernel of the unemployment problem, the chief question which manufacturers and labor have to face is this: should we dismiss an ever-increasing number of workers, or should we shorten the hours of work?"[23] In the 1920s Green asked employers to introduce voluntarily the shorter work week; by 1932 rank-and-file pressure forced him to turn to the government to achieve this end.

Green asked very little of the federal government in the fight against unemployment in the years prior to 1932. To combat technological displacement, he meekly asked that the federal government set up an agency that would serve as "a clearing house of information for displaced workers."[24] This was suggested not as a cure, but as an aid to help workers locate the dwindling number of jobs in their respective fields. He also called on the government to gather accurate statistics on unemployment in the 1930 census. Finally, he asked Congress to initiate "a constructive and scientific program for timing public works," arguing that specific public works projects should be available during periods of massive unemployment.[25] His plea for a system of public works in times of depression was no more than a restatement of the recommendations of President Harding's unemployment commission of 1921, of which Hoover was the guiding spirit.

Even before the depression, Green chose his words carefully when discussing unemployment compensation. Having no desire to advocate any program not endorsed by the Executive Council, Green argued that while some form of unemployment compensation was necessary, it was a concern of unions and employers, not government. He doubted the efficacy and justice of the compensation plans of the Photo Engravers, Printing Pressmen, Brewers, and others in which the union alone footed the bill. Instead he praised the ILGWU's unemployment compensation plan in which both union workers and employers contributed to a benefit fund.[26]

Thus Green's attitudes toward the problems of unemployment and relief were decidedly conservative. He did not envision an active role for the state other than information gathering, unemployment exchanges, and public works on a small scale. Along with Hoover, he shared the conviction that labor and capital could resolve their differences through joint and voluntary action. With the onset of depression, however, employers proved they were not interested in cooperation, and Green and the Executive Council moved haltingly in the direction of political action.

The slowness with which Green and the Council turned to the federal government was primarily a result of the AFL's long-standing aversion to state intervention in labor affairs, but it was also due to the AFL's political weakness in these years and the unfriendliness of government toward organized labor. As long as Washington turned a deaf ear to the AFL's limited political objectives, Green could not envision an expanded role for the state.

Hoover's selection of William Doak as Secretary of Labor in 1930 reinforced the AFL's voluntarism. In November 1930, James J. Davis resigned as Labor Secretary to assume his seat in the U.S. Senate. The AFL regarded the Department of Labor as its sole voice in the federal government. Davis, who occupied the post of Secretary under all three presidents in the 1920s, belonged to the Iron, Steel and Tin Workers. His predecessor, William B. Wilson, who served under Woodrow Wilson, was a member of the United Mine Workers. Samuel Gompers had been instrumental in the creation of the Department of Labor in 1913. Thus Green had every reason to expect that Davis's successor would be an AFL member. He confidently asserted that "The A. F. of L. is . . . the American labor movement. . . . The officers and members of this organization believe that the Secretary of Labor, sitting in the President's cabinet, should be a man that understands the American labor movement, its problems and the thought and mind of labor."[27]

At an Executive Council meeting in January 1930, Green promised Frank Duffy, secretary of the Carpenters, that if Davis won the primaries he would endorse the Carpenters' president, William Hutcheson, for Secretary of Labor and talk to President Hoover personally on his behalf. In June Green informed Duffy that he "was not favorably impressed with the reaction of the President . . . to the suggestion that President Hutcheson be appointed or that someone associated with the American Federation of Labor should be selected to serve as Secretary of Labor."[28] Nevertheless, Green visited Hoover at the White House soon after Davis announced his resignation and submitted the names of five AFL leaders who would be acceptable to labor: Hutcheson, John L. Lewis, Matthew Woll, John P. Frey, and John Alpine, president of the Plumbers.[29]

Again Green was rebuffed. When Hoover declared that he was considering William Doak for the post, Green wrote the president an angry letter, declaring that he would oppose Doak's appointment because Doak was a member of the Brotherhood of Railway Trainmen, which was not affiliated with the AFL.[30] On November 28 Hoover named Doak Secretary of Labor. "I have the highest respect for Mr. Green and the American Federation of Labor," Hoover explained, "but Mr. Green's enunciation that appointments must come from one organization in fact imposes upon me the duty to maintain the principle of open and equal opportunity and freedom in appointments to public office."[31] Hoover may not have been an enemy of the AFL, but he was not a close friend.

The AFL's lack of influence on Capitol Hill was painfully apparent when the Federation tried to secure passage of Senator Wagner's unemployment bills. In April 1928, Senator Robert F. Wagner of New York introduced three bills to relieve unemployment that were remarkably similar to Green's proposals. One called for improved methods of acquiring statistics on unemployment, another for a comprehensive system of unemployment exchanges, and a third for advanced planning of public works. All three bills received official AFL support. Because 1928 was a presidential election year, the bills received little attention. They languished in a committee pigeonhold until the beginnings of the depression compelled the Senate to pass them in April 1930. From the Republican dominated House, however, the only bill to emerge was the one dealing with statistics, which Hoover signed on July 7, 1930.[32] Green was outraged. The federal government, he said, "has neglected its part" by adjourning without passing the Wagner bills.[33]

According to Wagner, Hoover's attitude toward his bills ranged "from indifference to active opposition."[34] Hoover espoused the same general concepts embodied in the bills, but he did not believe that additional legislation was necessary. Legislation would only focus attention on the depression. As the crisis became acute and Hoover refused to act, Wagner reintroduced his public works measure on January 19, 1931, and it quickly passed both houses. Hoover reluctantly signed it on February 9, 1931.[35]

The third measure, dealing with unemployment exchanges, encountered more serious opposition from the House, the Administration, and particularly Secretary of Labor Doak. The Federation put forth a massive lobbying effort in support of the unemployment exchange bill. Local unions and state federations flooded Congress with telegrams. Green addressed a long letter to Congress detailing the reasons why the Wagner bill should be passed, and he made sure that every representative received a letter with his signature on the morning of the final vote in the House. The effort proved successful, and the House passed the bill by a large majority. "Labor concentrated all its efforts in support of the Wagner bill," Green said with satisfaction, "and after three years of constant effort finally prevailed upon Congress to enact the measure into law."[36]

Green's elation was short lived, however, because Hoover vetoed the bill in March 1931. Hoover claimed that he was preventing a "serious blow to labor," but Green condemned the veto message as "unconvincing and unacceptable."[37] Green had an extremely limited expectation of positive federal involvement in economic affairs, and Hoover had done nothing to give him encouragement. Rank-and-file pressure, not government encouragement, would force Green to seek legislative solutions to trade union problems.

As did most labor officials, Green opposed a state directed system of unemployment insurance. His reasoning, at least on the surface, reflected a narrow trade union outlook on social legislation. At the 1931 AFL convention, he cautioned that a government administered program was an unsafe policy that would "pull at our vitals and destroy our trade union structure."[38] Later, before the ILGWU's 1932 convention, he explained that upon "the question of unemployment insurance, the A. F. of L. is not so much opposed to the principle as it is jealous of its own protection and its own life. We don't want to exchange our birthright for a mess of pottage."[39] What worried Green and other AFL leaders was that unemployment union members might have to accept jobs alongside nonunion workers or lose their unemployment benefits. Unemployment insurance also threatened to shift worker allegiance from the union to the government. For most AFL leaders these arguments can be viewed as an attempt to safeguard their craft fiefdoms, but Green had no such fiefdom to protect. He spoke with conviction. For Green, the AFL represented the only hope for workers to achieve high wages and middle-class respectability. Any legislation that posed a threat to the AFL therefore, no matter what benefits were promised, had to be defeated.

Green also argued against federal unemployment insurance on the grounds that employers alone, not all taxpayers, bore responsibility for the suffering of those out of work. Unemployment, he argued, "results from the failure of industries openly to assume their responsibility toward workers who participate in creating the good name and reputation of those industries." The fact that some industries spent part of their earnings on charities was "an indirect recognition" of their obligation to the unemployed. "Because industries have not openly and honestly accepted their responsibility for regular payment of incomes to all working together in production they have been able to shift many of their problems upon public and private relief agencies."[40] Federal unemployment insurance would be simply another way of abdicating responsibility.

Green was also concerned that unemployment insurance threatened the morale of American workers. Work alone made them proud, and "the dole" would sap their pride. Furthermore, by making workers wards of the state, insurance threatened their independence. In making this argument Green sounded more like an official of the National Association of Manufacturers than a labor leader. He told a Rutgers University audience in June 1931 that "In consideration of any plan of compulsory unemployment relief the American organized worker regards the preservation of his individual liberty and freedom as of primary importance."[41]

Despite Green's opposition, the movement for unemployment relief within the ranks of labor grew by leaps and bounds between 1930 and 1932. At the 1931 AFL convention, the state federations of California, Illinois, Pennsylvania, and Wisconsin urged the AFL to support a federal program of relief. The Railway Clerks, the Machinists, the Teamsters, the Iron Molders, and the Textile Workers were some of the unions that also pushed for an AFL endorsement. Equally important, Daniel Tobin of the Teamsters and W. D. Mahon of the Street Railway Employees, two powerful figures in the Federation, broke with the voluntarists on this issue. Those favoring some form of compulsory insurance garnered over 11,000 of the 30,000 convention votes in 1931 and *New York Times* labor correspondent Louis Stark predicted that the anti-voluntarists would capture the 1932 convention if economic conditions did not improve.[42] Opponents of compulsory insurance still dominated the Executive Council, however, and Green expressed their outlook at the convention. "Our duty," he declared, "is plain, and that is, first of all, to protect the movement that we love and represent." Yet even Green braced himself for the inevitable.

If the next convention passed a resolution in favor of compulsory insurance, he would abide by its will. He told the convention that "we are rapidly travelling" toward an endorsement, but "the time has not arrived."[43]

Just nine months after the 1931 convention, the Executive Council directed Green to draw up a plan for government-sponsored unemployment insurance. This sharp reversal in AFL policy startled many but was easily understood. AFL leaders had not abandoned their commitment to voluntarism; they had succumbed to rank-and-file pressure. Sentiment was already strong in 1931 and the disastrous winter of 1931–1932 created a mandate for action. The Mine Workers endorsed a compulsory measure in January and the New York State Federation came around in February. The pressure from below could no longer be resisted. Ironically, employers also exerted pressure on the Executive Council. Gerald Swope of General Electric, a company dependent upon mass consumption, met with Green and Woll in the spring of 1932, urging them to change their attitudes toward insurance.[44]

The 1932 AFL convention accepted the Council's recommendation following a short debate. After the vote, Green declared that the AFL would never be quite the same again. "We have been irresistably forced to take new positions, to pursue a flexible policy and adjust ourselves to the changed order."[45] Voluntarism was not dead, but rank-and-file pressure had led to a significant change in policy, as John P. Frey wrote to a friend less than two months after the 1932 convention. As Frey saw it, "a number of the members of the Executive Council were in rather strong opposition (to unemployment insurance) but did not care to state their position because of the popular movement which has developed in favor of this utterly impossible and visionary program."[46]

If the debate on unemployment relief forced Green to reassess his commitment to voluntarism, his determination to implement the shorter work week substantially transformed his attitudes toward government involvement in the economy. As early as 1930 Green suggested that the only viable means of dealing with unemployment was the universal introduction of the five-day week and the six-hour day to spread work among more people. "We have arrived at the period of the history of our nation and our industrial progress," Green told delegates to the 1930 AFL convention, "when the institution of the five-day week in all industries outside of the service industries should be immediately inaugurated."[47]

By the time of the 1932 convention, Green's cure-all for unemployment, the thirty-hour week, had met with nothing but rejection from industry. A Bureau of Labor Statistics' survey made earlier that year showed that only 5.4 percent of the nation's employers had adopted a five-day week for even a part of their workforce.[48] It was thus in a mood of desperation that Green picked up the gavel. The convention witnessed a showdown on voluntarism between the Executive Council and the delegates, whose ties were closer to the grass roots. The Council's report urged a six-hour day and a five-day week but did not call for legislation. Green submitted this report to the Committee on the Shorter Work Day, which refocused the proposal to conclude that since competition made it virtually impossible for individual firms to adopt the thirty-hour week, "we instruct our Executive Council to take all necessary steps toward having proper legislation . . . presented to the incoming session of Congress for their consideration and adoption."[49]

Green now faced a momentous decision. He could side either with the Council's initial proposal or the Committee's final report. A ringing endorsement of either option from Green, in all likelihood, would have carried the convention. At the moment of truth, however, he waffled. Green lacked the will to oppose either the Council or the Committee, which represented the majority sentiment among delegates. Instead, Green abdicated responsibility by hiding behind a flourish of rhetoric and a discussion of technicalities. Shorter hour legislation was the obvious remedy for government employees and "those governed by interstate commerce legislation," Green began. For other workers in the private sector, the situation was "more complex." Green referred to "what seemed to be insurmountable difficulties."[50] Perhaps these "difficulties" had to do with the constitutionality of any proposed legislation, but Green did not elaborate.

Green's mutterings failed to dissuade delegates, who voted in favor of the committee's report. Nevertheless, there was some confusion as to the type of resolution adopted. On the day following the vote, a delegate from Illinois declared, "I don't believe this Convention has reached a unanimous feeling about the question of legislation. I am quite sure a very large number of delegates are not conscious of the fact that we did adopt a resolution in favor of legislation to regulate hours of labor."[51] Voluntarism was dying "not with a bang but a whimper." Popular sentiment had overcome the Executive Council's inability to adapt to changing economic and political conditions. And delegates had endorsed legislation for shorter hours not because of Green, but in spite of him.

Less than a month after the 1932 convention, on December 21, 1932, Senator Hugo Black of Alabama introduced legislation into the lame duck 72nd Congress that would have outlawed the transportation of goods produced by firms "in which any person was employed or permitted to work more than five days in any week or more than six hours in any day." Shortly afterward, Representative William Connery introduced similar legislation in the House. The AFL immediately threw its weight behind the legislation. Even the hardline voluntarists on the Executive Council spoke in favor of the measures. The committee hearings in both houses divided along labor-industry lines, with employers opposing the bill on the grounds that it was unconstitutional. The proponents of business self-regulation, however, had lost the initiative. Industry's inability to cope with the depression had given the upper hand to those who proposed shorter hour laws as a means of dealing with underconsumption.

Before the House Labor Committee, Green gave the bill his "personal and official approval," but he balked at the suggestion that a minimum wage provision be included. The convention had instructed him to forgo the voluntarist approach to hours, but he had no authority and no desire to abandon the AFL's traditional opposition to wage legislation, except for women and minors. When a committee member explained that a minimum wage might prevent the shortening of the work week from leading to a reduction of income, Green told him to "Pass your bill and let us handle the question of wages."[52] Green still adhered to the view that workers could win higher wages through collective bargaining than through minimum wage guidelines.

The lame duck session of Congress failed to vote on the Black-Connery bill, but the special session of the new 73rd Congress moved quickly, once convened by President Roosevelt. The new Congress and the new president had a mandate for action, and the only positive legislation under consideration was the shorter week bill. When industry could not present a viable alternative, the Senate passed the bill on April 6, 1933. Hoover had declined to take a stand on the bill, but Roosevelt had to. If the measure passed the House without his support, he would find himself in the unpleasant situation of enforcing a recovery program which he had played no role in formulating. Roosevelt and many of his advisers thought the bill unconstitutional and economically unsound. Secretary of Labor Perkins, however, believed the bill would stimulate recovery if amended to provide greater flexibility. With some reluctance, Roosevelt agreed to back her efforts to alter the bill in the House.[53]

The scene was set for a battle between Green and Perkins at the House Labor Committee hearings, which resumed in April 1933. Perkins agreed with the principle behind the bill, but she considered the thirty-hour maximum too rigid, and proposed a flexible scale of between thirty and forty hours with a maximum eight-hour day. She also recommended a minimum wage provision. In the unionized sector of industry, tripartite boards with labor representation should fix minimum wages. Green made the first of many concessions to the Roosevelt Administration when he told the Committee that the AFL would accept Perkins' suggestions on the sliding scale for hours. But he adamantly refused to budge on the question of minimum wages for male workers. Minimum wages, he explained, would "tend to injure the efforts of the bulk of labor to raise their living standards, to bring about increases in wages."[54] Green expressed interest in the tripartite boards, but insisted they were unworkable unless workers were members of independent trade unions. He therefore suggested an amendment: "Workers . . . shall not be denied by their employer the free exercise of the right to belong to a *bona fide* labor organization and to collectively bargain for their wages through their own chosen representatives."[55] This proposed amendment was one of the earliest expressions of a legislative guarantee of the right to organize, a guarantee that would later be embodied in Section 7a of the National Industrial Recovery Act and ultimately in the Wagner Act.

Green won this battle against the Administration but lost the war. Despite the opposition of industry, the House Labor Committee on May 10 voted favorably on the Black-Connery bill and acceded to Green's wishes on almost every particular. The bill even included a provision granting workers the right to organize and bargain collectively.[56] President Roosevelt killed the bill's chances, however, by failing to support it. He was troubled by widespread employer hostility to the measure, for he wanted the cooperation of both labor and industry in any recovery program. When Roosevelt began to push for an Administration substitute, the Black-Connery bill was buried in the House Rules Committee. Shorter hour legislation was never seriously considered after the passage of the National Industrial Recovery Act, although Green continued to argue its necessity throughout the 1930s.[57]

Roosevelt's failure to support Green's cure-all for economic ills perturbed the AFL chief, but Green had a warm regard for the new president and supported him in the 1932 campaign. Green would have backed almost any Democrat in a presidential contest, but he was particularly impressed with Roosevelt. In August 1930, Green had written Governor Roosevelt of New York, expressing his delight with Roosevelt's outstanding record of progressive legislation.[58] Even though Green personally rejected Roosevelt's support of unemployment insurance, he had endorsed Roosevelt's campaign for the governorship in the fall of 1930.[59]

Despite the fact that Green personally favored Roosevelt in the 1932 election, the Executive Council, to no one's surprise, maintained its official nonpartisan political policy in the campaign. Many historians have cited this as a sign of dogged adherence to outmoded policies that left the AFL immobilized and unable to jump on the Democratic bandwagon, let alone the Socialist.[60] While there is a great deal of truth in this criticism, there were valid reasons why the AFL did not endorse Roosevelt. First, powerful members of the Executive Council were Republicans and second, the Democratic platform was not enticing enough to warrant a change in policy.

William Hutcheson of the Carpenters, Matthew Woll of the Photo Engravers, and John L. Lewis of the Mine Workers were all ardent Republicans who supported Hoover in 1932. Hutcheson, in fact, served as chairman of the labor committee of the Republican National Convention. These men could not be ignored in AFL circles, and they would have resisted strenuously any attempt to endorse the Democratic candidate. When Daniel Tobin, Teamster president and chairman of the labor division of the Democratic National Convention, wrote Green in October 1932 complaining about Hoover's horrendous labor record and asking Green to "go a little deeper" before proclaiming AFL neutrality, Hutcheson responded in a letter to Green condemning what he regarded as Tobin's "attempt to use the federation for the dissemination of. . . grossly untruthful statements."[61]

If the hostility between Hutcheson and Tobin demonstrated the organizational necessity of maintaining a nonpartisan stance, the AFL's dissatisfaction with the Democratic platform's labor planks reinforced the traditional policy of neutrality in presidential elections. Indeed, the Executive Council denounced both the Democratic and Republican platforms. The Democratic convention had refused to declare in favor of either collective bargaining guarantees or the shorter work week. As did Hoover, the Democratic party recognized the political weakness of organized labor and ignored its major demands. On September 8, 1932, while addressing the closing session of the New Jersey State Federation of Labor, Green warned that "when the men and women represented in the federation believe that the interests of the workers can be best served through the organization of an independent political organization, they will adopt such action."[62] That Green, a life-long Democrat, should threaten the formation of a third party was an indication of his disgust with the Democratic platform in 1932.

The AFL and its affiliate unions made very few contributions to Roosevelt's campaign in 1932. Green maintained an official silence throughout the campaign. Thus in his speeches, Roosevelt gave little attention to labor issues and focused instead on currying the favor of farmers and progressive Republicans. And upon his election, Roosevelt did not feel indebted to the labor movement.[63] His first action concerning labor would come as a shock to Green, who believed a friend had been elected to the White House.

Soon after the election, construction of the new Department of Labor building began, and Green followed Hoover as speeches were made at the cornerstone setting ceremony. The new building, Green said, would be a symbol of "the importance, genius, dignity and service of organized labor" and a recognition of the vital position of labor in the economic life of the nation.[64] At this time Green no doubt believed that, with Hoover's defeat, the AFL stood a good chance of having one of its officials appointed Secretary of Labor.

Green's hopes were well founded. Of the five candidates under consideration, three were AFL men: Daniel Tobin of the Teamsters, A. F. Whitney of the Railroad Trainmen, and George Berry of the Printing Pressmen. On December 19, 1932, Green led a small party of AFL leaders to Albany where they met with Roosevelt and urged him to appoint Tobin. Green handed the president-elect a petition signed by international officers, representing 98 percent of the total AFL membership, backing Tobin's bid.[65]

Hoover's selection of Doak had antagonized the Federation, Green told Roosevelt. The AFL hoped to cooperate with the new Administration, and the selection of Tobin would help establish good relations. After the meeting, Green informed Tobin that the meeting had been encouraging. Roosevelt "responded that he had cooperated with the American Federation of Labor for twenty years . . ," Green wrote, "and that he was determined to work with and to have the cooperation of the American Federation of Labor for the next four years." Green added that Roosevelt's comments "could be construed as favorable to your appointment."[66]

Thus Green was aghast when Roosevelt, in late February 1933, appointed Frances Perkins, former Industrial Commissioner of New York, to the post. Green immediately responded that labor would "never become reconciled" to her appointment and suggested that labor had been given another slap in the face.[67] He later wrote Tobin a letter of condolence and expressed his rage over the selection of "some college professor who learned about labor from textbooks."[68] A Democrat had at last been elected to the White House, but Roosevelt seemed no friendlier to the AFL than Hoover had been.

Green's hopes were never lower than in March 1933. The new president had rebuffed him. The Federation he revered was crumbling under the weight of depression. Membership continued to decline, union treasuries emptied, and the partial abandonment of voluntarism had yet to yield any tangible returns. Furthermore, Green had realized that Christian cooperation bore scarce resemblance to the reality of capital-labor relations.

Within two months, however, Green was more excited about AFL prospects than ever before. The difference was the National Industrial Recovery Act (NIRA). To Green NIRA was a godsend. By guaranteeing labor's right to organize and by compelling labor and capital to agree on industrial codes, NIRA promised to establish by governmental decree the only basis for true prosperity—cooperation. For Green and for many others, NIRA rekindled hopes that the relations between employers and workers could be established on a basis of morality and mutual respect.

Roosevelt offered NIRA to Congress on May 17, 1933 as a substitute for the Black-Connery bill. Title I of the proposed legislation would suspend anti-trust laws for two years, allowing employers to draw up industry-wide codes, with the aid of government and labor, to regulate production, wages, and hours. The codes would be submitted to a proposed National Recovery Administration (NRA), which would have the power to amend, approve or disapprove a code. NRA would also be empowered to license companies, a power designed to force recalcitrant employers to comply with the codes by forbidding them access to interstate commerce. The only required code provision was Section 7a, guaranteeing workers the right to organize and bargain collectively.[69]

Labor's influence in the drafting of Section 7a has long been a matter of contention. At one time or another, credit has been given to Matthew Woll, John L. Lewis, William Hutcheson, and William Green. In early 1933, Lewis and Phillip Murray of the UMW appealed to the Senate Committees of Finance and the Judiciary to enforce workers' right to organize.[70] In April Green wrote an article in support of such legal recognition and in early May, as we have seen, he secured the adoption of an amendment to the thirty-hour week bill providing for the enforcement of the right to organize.[71] Available evidence does not support the conclusion, however, that Green or any other labor leader played a major role in the actual drafting process. Nevertheless, the AFL's lobbying effort in behalf of the Black-Connery bill showed that the Federation's political power was increasing and could no longer be easily ignored, and the Executive Council had made abundantly clear in a public statement that the AFL would not endorse NIRA without a guarantee of collective bargaining.[72]

Green did secure amendments to Section 7a once hearings on the bill began. The only AFL representative to appear before the House Ways and Means Committee, Green proposed that after the guarantee of the right to organize, Section 7a should include a provision stating that workers "shall be free from the interference, restraint, or coercion of employers of labor or their agents, in the designation of such representatives or in self-organization or in other concerted activities for the purpose of collective bargaining or other mutual aid or protection." Green also pressed for a closed shop clause and for a clause stating that "no employee and no one seeking employment shall be required as a condition of employment to join a company union, or to refrain from joining a labor organization of his own choosing."[73] Green thus hoped not only to clarify the right to organize, but also to strike a blow at the company union and give legal recognition to the closed shop. If the amendments were accepted, Green concluded, "Labor will extend to this proposed legislation its full, complete, and hearty endorsement."[74]

Green had little to say about that part of the bill pertaining to the inclusion of minimum wage provisions in the codes, a direct assault upon voluntarism, except to comment that "based upon the stabilized substantial foundation created in industry, standards with respect to hours, wages and conditions of employment can be established and this in turn will bring a revival of business."[75] Green's approval of the minimum wage provision was the result of a private agreement between the AFL and the U.S. Chamber of Commerce. The Chamber pledged to accept Section 7a if the Federation accepted the minimum wage provision.[76] But the AFL's abandonment of voluntarism on the question of wages was more apparent than real. Green and other AFL leaders gave way on minimum wages only because they were confident that unions would play an important role in the determination of codes.

On May 26, 1933 the House of Representatives passed NIRA, including Green's amendments, by a vote of 325 to 76.[77] The bill faced greater opposition in the Senate, however. The National Association of Manufacturers (NAM), which had not been a party to the AFL-Chamber of Commerce agreement, led the employer offensive against Section 7a before the Senate Finance Committee between May 22 and June 1. NAM spokesman James A. Emery charged that Section 7a violated the principles of individual liberty by coercing workers to join unions. Green retorted that while NAM was "willing that its members shall exercise the right to organize . . . under the protection of government," it was not willing to accord labor the same right.[78] The vote on Section 7a in the full Senate pitted the friends of organized labor against its enemies and on this occasion, labor emerged victorious by a vote of 46 to 31. The president signed NIRA on June 16, 1933.[79]

Green was exhilarated. He heralded the passage of Section 7a as "revolutionary."[80] Not only would the protection of collective bargaining serve to increase wages and working hours, thus lifting the nation out of depression, but it would also establish, under government auspices, a working relationship and mutual understanding between capital and labor. Employers who had refused to act in a Christian manner toward their employees would now be under federal pressure to do so. "The act rests upon the principle," Green wrote in the *American Federationist*, "that Labor is a partner in industry and has a right to participate in the decisions and duties of industry and that the spirit and practice of cooperation are essential to the best interests of all."[81]

The president appointed General Hugh S. Johnson, a former member of the World War I War Industries Board, as NRA administrator. Johnson would receive the aid of three advisory boards, representing labor, industry, and consumers. Secretary Perkins appointed the members of the Labor Advisory Board: Green, John L. Lewis, John P. Frey, Rose Schneiderman of the Women's Trade Union League, Sidney Hillman of the Amalgamated Clothing Workers, Father Francis Haas of the Catholic Welfare Council, and Leo Wolman, an economist from Columbia University. Since the NRA had to approve all codes, labor representation on the advisory board seemed to insure fair codes.[82] Green's high expectations were expressed in an editorial in which he characterized the code-making process as a "covenant" between employers and workers.[83] He believed that the codes would institute the thirty-hour week and increase wages, thereby solving the problem of unemployment and increasing consumer purchasing power.[84] His high hopes, however, led only to disillusionment.

Labor faced problems from the outset in realizing its goals under NIRA. First, the deputy administrators, who had the greatest influence in the formation of the codes, were drawn from the ranks of business and sympathized with industry's outlook. Second, the Labor Advisory Board was just that—an advisory board. It could condemn codes but not prevent their acceptance. Third, the codes could not be enforced. The only weapon at the disposal of the NRA was the licensing provision, and Johnson, unsure of the act's constitutionality, refused to invoke the penalty. Since Johnson voluntarily abdicated the only power at his command, he was forced to rely on public pressure and moral suasion. Codes drawn up by industries and reviewed by deputy administrators sympathetic business interests were incapable of reflecting labor's demands. In the unionized sector of industry, most unions were too weak to oppose the will of industry in the formation of codes. According to one historian, unions "had no leverage with which to exert influence upon Roosevelt and an industry-oriented NRA deputy administrator and staff."[85]

Every one of the codes fell short of Green's expectations. The first code, drafted by the cotton-textile industry, in which unions were virtually absent, increased wages and shortened hours of labor, but not enough to please Green. The industry recommended a minimum wage of $11 per week in the South as $12 per week in the North and proposed a maximum work week of forty hours. Green called for a thirty-hour work week and declared that the lowest possible minimum wage should be $16 in the North and $14 in the South. Despite Green's protests that it would not lead to significant reemployment, the forty-hour work week was maintained. And only at Green's insistence did employers agree to abolish child labor in the industry and raise the minimum wage to $13 in the North and $12 in the South. The minimum wage remained so low that employers could easily afford to do away with child labor. Green voiced these same objections to every code reviewed. Minimum wages were set too low to bolster mass purchasing power and maximum hours were set too high to combat unemployment. In almost every instance, his protests were ignored.[86]

The degree to which industry dominated the code-making process was best illustrated in the automobile industry. The National Automobile Chamber of Commerce (NACC), the automobile manufacturers' association, held little interest in the price-fixing and production-limiting opportunities offered by NIRA. Unlike many industries, the problems of the auto industry in 1933 were not those of overproduction and price-cutting, and manufacturers had already standardized trade practices to the degree they believed necessary. Furthermore, auto makers had already implemented a share-the-work plan and paid relatively high wages, so they could argue that an auto code was not necessary to aid in the recovery of their industry.[87] Most galling would be the acceptance of Section 7a, which posed a direct threat to their traditional open shop policy.

The NACC submitted a code that specified an average thirty-five-hour work week, although individual employees might work forty-five hours, depending on the location of the plant. Concerning Section 7a, the proposed code perverted the original intent of the law by stating that "the employers in the automobile industry propose to continue the open shop policy heretofore followed and under which unusually satisfactory and harmonious relations with employees have been maintained. The selection, retention and advancement of employees will be on the basis of individual merit without regard to their affiliation or non-affiliation with any labor or other organization."[88] NRA Administrator Johnson met with auto industry representatives and assured them that he was "sympathetic with the industry's point of view."[89]

Green, as Labor Advisory Board representative, opposed almost every aspect of the auto code at the pre-hearing discussions. He argued correctly that the minimum wage level was actually lower than that already being paid and that the maximum hour provision did not improve on the share-the-work formula. He also attacked the open shop clause as a violation of the "spirit" of NIRA.[90]

At the public hearings in Washington on August 18, 1933, Green led the assault on the auto code in his dual capacity as advisory board representative and AFL president. As he had done at other code hearings, Green not only condemned the proposed code, he also detailed an AFL code proposal as a substitute. And as he had done at all other hearings, he suggested a thirty-hour work week for all automobile production workers. A thirty-five-hour work week would be permissible, he said, only if workers were paid time-and-a-half for all work over thirty hours. Armed with a mountain of facts, Green further contended that the proposed maximum hour provisions industry offered would not increase employment, which was supposed to be the intended effect of the code. Indeed, the thirty-five-hour work week would actually be higher than the industry's average of 32.7 hours the Bureau of Labor Statistics reported. To reestablish the employment level of 1929, even the thirty-hour work week would not suffice if production remained constant. If production increased 100 percent, Green argued, "a work week of 29.2 hours would still be required to secure the desired amount of re-employment."[91]

Green also demonstrated that the wage provisions of the proposed code were inadequate to increase mass purchasing power and thus violated another objective of NIRA. Green suggested a minimum wage for factory hands of 60 cents per hour. According to his calculations, this rate would be only slightly higher than the average hourly wage paid to unskilled labor in the industry between 1928 and 1929, when employees worked longer hours. A high wage rate was essential if workers were to receive an income "sufficient to maintain tolerable standards of living."[92]

A large part of Green's testimony concerned the qualifying language the NACC had tacked on to Section 7a. His arguments revealed the wide gulf between the AFL's and industry's interpretation of labor's right to organize and bargain collectively. In order to establish "true" collective bargaining in industry, Green argued, employees must be given the right to form an organization self-governing in internal affairs and independent of management. The organization must be industry-wide and should be affiliated with the AFL. It must then negotiate a contract with representatives of industry that both parties were willing and able to enforce. The auto code itself, Green reasoned, could never be enforced if such an employee organization did not exist. And since the auto manufacturers themselves had prevented the growth of "true" collective bargaining in their industry, the federal government was obligated to promote its establishment.[93]

Practically every one of Green's proposals was ignored. The NACC made small concessions in regard to wages and hours. And an objection by Donald Richberg, general counsel for NRA and second in command to Johnson, persuaded employers to drop the open shop declaration, although the individual merit clause remained. Green was fully conscious of the dilemma: the AFL's weakness in the industry precluded a strong voice in the code-making process. As he griped in a letter to an AFL organizer in autos, the paucity of organized auto workers had "greatly interfered with a forceful and influential presentation" of labor's demands.[94]

On August 26, 1933, the day NRA officials handed Roosevelt the auto code for his signature, Labor Advisory Board members, with Wolman absent, met in conference to ponder the individual merit clause. The board agreed to accept the code "with the understanding that no section or sentence contained therein modifies, qualifies or changes Section 7(a)" and that the merit clause did "not establish a precedent to be followed in the preparation or acceptance of any other code."[95] When other industries inserted individual merit clauses in their code proposals, Green announced that the NRA would "court disaster" by accepting them.[96]

In autos and in almost every industry, employers were not cooperating to the extent Green hoped. Yet Green always attempted to present the codes in a favorable manner to workers. Nothing in the auto code modified Section 7a "in any way," he wrote his organizer in the industry, and discharge of employees for union activity violated the code provisions. "Let no one deceive automobile workers by misrepresentation and false statements," Green continued. "Their right to organize has been clearly established."[97] In an *American Federationist* editorial, he asserted that the minimum wage provisions in the codes would raise living standards for many workers and the maximum hour provisions would help to stabilize employment.[98]

Despite industry domination in the code-making process, Green's expectations of NIRA revealed the extent to which his attitudes toward government intervention in the economy had changed. By mid-1933 Green appealed to the federal government to meet objectives that only a few years earlier the AFL held to be the exclusive domain of collective bargaining: higher wages, shorter hours, and the organization of the unorganized. Indeed, Green envisioned a role for the NRA that went far beyond the intentions of General Johnson. Johnson had no desire to use NRA to promote the organization of the unorganized or to alter in any significant way the wage and hour policies of powerful employer associations.

Since the NRA did not provide machinery to deal with labor disputes or to interpret Section 7a, the Roosevelt Administration had to improvise. On August 5, 1933, Roosevelt created the National Labor Board (NLB) to "consider, adjust, and settle differences that may arise through differing interpretations" of Section 7a.[99] Headed by Senator Wagner, the NLB included three representatives from both industry and labor: Gerald Swope, president of General Electric, Louis Kirstein, general manager of William Filene Sons Company, and Walter C. Teagle, president of the Standard Oil Company of New Jersey, on the side of industry; Green, John L. Lewis, and Leo Wolman representing labor.

The NLB, however, lacked a specified procedural formula and lacked enforcement power. Its power rested entirely on what Wagner called "public sentiment," and its success depended on the voluntary cooperation of employers and unions.[100] Nevertheless, in its first three months, the NLB settled 88 percent of its cases in the field, resorting to decisions in just eight cases. Such success was possible because the NLB had yet to confront formidable open shop companies in basic industries such as steel and automobiles. The NLB also had yet to make an unequivocal interpretation of Section 7a. Once the NLB had to take a stand on the proper interpretation of Section 7a, its principal weaknesses were exposed: employers and labor representatives could not agree on a definition of the right to organize and bargain collectively, and the board could not enforce its decisions.

The honeymoon of the NLB ended in December 1933, when it was called upon to decide on the Weirton Steel and Edward G. Budd Manufacturing cases. On September 7, 1933, 92 percent of the employees at Budd, which made auto bodies and frames, participated in company-sponsored elections and created a company union. When the company told the approximately one thousand AFL federal labor union members that it "could not recognize the American Federation of Labor inasmuch as Budd has employee representation," about 1500 Budd workers struck. In December the NLB ordered Budd to hold new elections or appear before the board. Budd refused to comply. The NLB then turned the case over to the national compliance director of the NRA in the hope that he would "withdraw the Blue Eagle from Budd and order the cancellation of all his Government contracts." When neither happened, the deficiencies of the NLB were painfully apparent.[101]

Ernest Weir was a powerful independent steel magnate, chairman of both Weirton Steel and National Steel, the nation's fourth largest steel firm. Weir defied an NLB order to hold representation elections under procedures specified by the board, and instead held elections under the rules of his employee representation plan. The NLB requested the Justice Department to prepare legal proceedings. Eighteen months later, when the Supreme Court declared NIRA unconstitutional, these proceedings were still unresolved.[102]

Green was a vocal supporter of the NLB and liked the fact that it rested upon the voluntary cooperation of labor and capital. But the Weirton and Budd cases infuriated him and proved, once again, that Christian cooperation was a far cry from the reality of capital-labor relations. Green admitted later that he wanted to "pillory Mr. Weir as a public enemy" and decried the destruction of "the faith that . . . workers have in the Government and in the National Labor Board."[103] The problem of the NLB, so far as Green was concerned, was that it could not enforce its decisions against such men as Budd and Weir and that it failed to come to grips with the proper interpretation of Section 7a. He charged that "the Board has been consistently forced to straddle the real issue in many cases, and the real issue is that of union recognition for collective bargaining."[104]

By the end of 1933, Green had all but abandoned his faith that industry would reform itself. He wrote in despair that "The habits and practices of autocratic control are so deeply rooted in many industries" that they would allow their workers the right to organize "grudgingly or only under compulsion."[105] Green was slowly recognizing that the government-labor-capital partnership in which he placed such faith required the coercive power of government to be effective. Green shunned coercion as a violation of Christian precepts, but employers, through their disregard of the intent of Section 7a, through their unwillingness to allow their workers to organize, had denounced cooperation and proven that they would respond only to the force of law.

Senator Wagner's Labor Disputes bill, introduced in 1934, was an attempt to rectify all the deficiencies of the NLB. It sought to strengthen the right to organize, outlaw the unfair labor practices of employers, and create a new labor board empowered to hold elections and enforce its decisions through the issuance of cease and desist orders. While Communists and employer associations testified against the bill, Green testified on its behalf before the Senate Committee on Labor during hearings in the spring of 1934. Wagner's bill, Green argued, was "essential to the purposes of the National Recovery Act."[106] In Green's view, the principal aim of NIRA was to increase mass purchasing power and reduce unemployment. Section 7a was vital to this process, for by organizing into independent trade unions, workers would be in a better position to resist layoffs and secure higher wages. Yet Section 7a could not be effective unless backed by a board with broad enforcement powers. The Labor Disputes bill was thus crucial to the recovery program.[107]

President Roosevelt did not endorse Wagner's bill, and he killed its chances when he issued an executive order to create the National Labor Relations Board (NLRB) and terminate the NLB. The executive order gave the new board power to order and hold elections, yet it permitted employers the option of having the board's election orders reviewed in the circuit court of appeals.[108] Further, the executive order did not define unfair labor practices or the right to organize. Green protested bitterly. The Labor Disputes bill must be passed "if the working people of the nation are to be accorded the right to organize and bargain collectively as provided for in Section 7(a)." He considered the president's action "a keen disappointment."[109]

The NLRB created by the executive order was a failure. Employers continued to refuse to comply with its decisions. This failure prompted Senator Wagner to reintroduce his Labor Disputes bill in revised form in February 1935. And the new Congress elected in November 1934 proved receptive. Wagner's revised bill replaced the vague statements of Section 7a with a specific and comprehensive statute outlawing unfair labor practices, such as company unions; provided for a permanent and powerful NLRB; and gave legal sanction to the right of an employee majority to select collective bargaining representatives for the whole group.[110] Green played a leading role in securing passage of the Wagner bill in both houses of Congress. After Roosevelt signed the bill on July 5, 1935, Green declared that he was "confident that it will prove itself the Magna Carta of Labor of the United States" and claimed that it would "make the workers of the nation economically free."[111]

Three days after the passage of the Wagner Act, the Supreme Court declared NIRA unconstitutional in the landmark Schechter decision. Green was outraged. Although he often complained about the limits of labor's input to the codes, Green had been one of NIRA's strongest supporters. In his 1933 Labor Day speech at Akron, Green had tried to dispel worker hostility to the wage and hour provisions in the codes by saying that NIRA was still in the "experimental stage."[112] After a September 11, 1933 meeting of the Executive Council, Green declared that his faith in NIRA "amounted to passion."[113] At the 1933 AFL convention, Green told delegates that "it is clear that the Recovery Act is sound in principle, that it must succeed, for the reason that its failure means a chaos that the nation cannot stand."[114]

In an *American Federationist* article published just prior to the Schechter decision, Green summarized the achievements of NIRA. First, the act had "given millions of workers the legal right and the courage to organize for the first time in their lives. It has made them feel like free men for the first time in their lives." Second, although the wage provisions were not all that labor hoped for, "what has already been accomplished in lifting the minimum rates (of pay) out of the depths to which they have been driven in 1932 and 1933 is a real achievement." Third, the NIRA "has established beyond question the soundness of the principle of reduction of hours as a means of bringing about reemployment." Fourth, the NIRA had gone far toward destroying "long established evils" in industry such as child labor, sweatshop conditions, and homework. He concluded:

> It would seem to me in all fairness that if there is any group in the industrial life of the nation which might with justification feel that the NRA has been a failure, it would be labor. We have not received all we hoped for; the collective bargaining provisions of the Act have not been enforced; minimum wages established in the codes are too low; the hours fixed in the codes have been too long to re-absorb into industry all the millions of unemployed. . . . Labor has not been given the place in the determination of code provisions nor in the administration of those provisions which it had every right to expect, and which it did indeed expect.

Nevertheless, Green continued, labor was not "impatient." The AFL recognized that "social progress is a slow and unending task and that no worthwhile venture should be abandoned until there has been every opportunity for a thorough trial."[115]

The Supreme Court, however, abruptly ended the experiment. Still, Green refused to abandon the hope that federal legislation would save the AFL. He immediately began to campaign for a thirty-hour-week bill and social security legislation.[116] Yet Green now recognized that labor's right to organize into independent trade unions would not be handed to him on a silver platter. The labor-government-capital partnership had revealed serious defects, and Green saw that labor must assert its own economic power to uphold its rights and bring about a return to prosperity. "In the absence of the stabilizing influence of N.R.A.," Green concluded, "workers and industries look for help only through union organization."[117] Thus we now turn to Green's efforts as an organizer.

IV

Organizing The Unorganized
Under Section 7a:
1933–1935

"W E ARE WITNESSING a sight," Green told delegates to the 1933 AFL convention, "that even the old, tired veterans of our movement never saw before. From every city and every town and every hamlet ... the workers are marching, organizing, keeping step, coming with us into the great American Federation of Labor." Workers were joining the AFL "because they realize that there is a new day and a new deal," and there is nothing, Green concluded, that "is going to stop them from coming in."[1]

Green's remark was only half true. Workers were exhibiting a desire to join trade unions to a degree unprecedented in American history. The promise of Section 7a of NIRA, coupled with the despair born of years of depression, fostered a widespread and militant demand for unionism among unorganized workers across the country. But very few of the workers demanding unions joined and remained in the AFL. Among the most serious impediments to successful organizing by the AFL in the years 1933–1935 were continued employer resistance to independent unions, the failure of the federal government to interpret and administer Section 7a as it was originally intended, the opposition of the craft union majority on the Executive Council to organization along industrial union lines, and Green's refusal to support militant rank-and-file action to secure union recognition and collective bargaining rights. This latter factor, heretofore ignored by labor historians, proved to be one of the greatest obstacles to successful organizing in the early 1930s and helped give rise to an opposition movement within the Federation that eventually became the Committee for Industrial Organization (CIO). Green's commitment to industrial peace and cooperation between labor and capital alienated great numbers of mass-production workers who were willing to join the AFL but who did not share Green's social gospel outlook.

With the passage of NIRA imminent, Green dashed off a letter to the presidents of all affiliated unions. "Labor must be alert, prepared and ready," he told them, "to take advantage of every opportunity which presents itself, through this legislative proposal, to organize, to bargain collectively, increase wages and reduce the hours of employment." He called for a meeting of the presidents on June 6, 1933 at AFL headquarters to "plan an organizing campaign, the sort of an organizing campaign which will cover all industries and the workers employed in all lines of industry."[2]

The meeting took place as scheduled, and the union presidents authorized Green to conduct an organizing campaign, but preparations for the type of massive drive Green envisioned were not made. No large-scale, cooperative drives to establish unions in the basic industries, such as the auto and Southern textile drives of the 1920s, resulted from the meeting. The reasons were clear enough. Many, if not most, union heads were struggling to maintain membership in their own organizations, and they were unwilling and, in most cases, unable to commit money and organizers for campaigns in the unorganized sector until prosperity returned. Others, such as John L. Lewis of the UMW and David Dubinsky of the ILGWU, gambled their meager treasuries on organizing drives among workers within their own jurisdictions. If any organizing was to be undertaken in the mass-production industries, the meeting in effect told Green, it would have to be conducted by the AFL president without substantial assistance from the internationals.[3]

Green understood the inability of affiliates to mount a massive drive, but he also understood the vital role that trade union organization could play in the recovery program. The Executive Council had declared as early as 1931 that the organization of the unorganized would insure that the benefits of industrial production would be more equitably distributed and thus help avert "periodic breakdowns" in the economy.[4] Green believed that under NIRA organized workers would have greater leverage at code hearings and be in a better position to secure higher wages and shorter hours, thus attacking the root cause of the depression: underconsumption. Green therefore took it upon himself, without substantial support from the affiliates, to organize workers in the basic industries. This was an awesome task to be sure, and much more awesome than Green anticipated.

Much like President Roosevelt, Green expected organizing under NIRA to be peaceful, lawful, and cooperative. He had neither the resources-nor the stomach for militant campaigns. Success for the type of campaign Green envisioned depended upon the cooperation of government, industry, organized labor, and the mass of workers. Government would have to implement NIRA fairly and honestly, aiding workers in their quest for organization and punishing recalcitrant employers. Employers would have to succumb to the dictates of federal law and allow the unionization of their workforce. And Green expected the unorganized to be undaunted in their desire for unions, yet peaceful in their approach.

Unfortunately, the campaigns were neither cooperative nor successful. First, the federal government often implemented Section 7a in such a way as to hinder organizing work. The early labor boards had little success with recalcitrant employers, and they subverted the original purpose of Section 7a by sanctioning company unions. Second, mass-production industries did not abandon their long-standing hostility to unions. Blacklisting of union leaders, industrial espionage, and company unions remained in use. Third, rather than devote its resources to organizing the unorganized, the AFL wasted precious energy on the issue of jurisdictional rights, a question that would subsequently split the Federation. Finally, unorganized workers, growing impatient with the impediments to organization, committed the unpardonable sin (in Green's view) of militant action. The lack of cooperation among contending interests brought Green's campaigns in mass-production industries to a virtual standstill by early 1934, but not until some measure of success had been attained.

Green did not perceive the seriousness of these obstacles. Nor did he consider the lack of adequate finances or the dearth of AFL organizers to be insurmountable difficulties. His optimism had two sources: Section 7a of NIRA and the unprecedented outpouring of union sentiment among the rank-and-file in the basic industries. Armed with these weapons, Green believed that the organization of the unorganized would ultimately succeed. The lack of finances and organizers meant only that local labor officials would have to assume much of the responsibility for organizing work. The enthusiasm of local officials, not money, would lead to success; their patience, not their concerted economic power, would bring results. "If the whole membership of our local unions were fired with zeal for spreading the gospel of unionism," Green wrote in July 1933, "the organizing problem would largely be taken care of."[5]

Since the obstacles to organizing were similar in each mass-production industry, a detailed look at one campaign will serve as an illustration of Green's efforts to organize the unorganized in the years 1933–1935. The automobile industry has been selected because Green regarded it as the "battle front" of union recognition and because it received greater attention from the press.[6]

Green selected William Collins to head up the organizing drive in autos. Collins arrived in Detroit on June 21, 1933 with instructions to organize workers directly into federal labor unions (FLUs). Other organizers, who devoted only part of their time to the auto industry, were sent to South Bend, Indiana, Cleveland, and Wisconsin. In cities where organizers could not afford to be sent, Green left responsibility for organizing to city centrals. Despite the fact that when Collins arrived in Detroit no FLUs existed among auto workers, Green entertained high hopes for the campaign. He expected that by the time public hearings were held on the auto code, workers would be sufficiently organized to send their own representatives.[7]

"The door of opportunity to organize is open to the worker for the first time in the history of the country," Collins told auto workers in a campaign circular.[8] A great deal of hullaballoo attended the campaign. Handbills, plant meetings, and rallies spread the union message. Collins even sent a sound truck through the streets of Detroit. Despite the fanfare, the early results were far from impressive. Although Green issued a large number of FLU charters, including six in Detroit alone, Collins glumly wrote AFL headquarters on August 5 that he had collected initiation fees for only about one thousand workers. Collins cited continuing unemployment, fear of association with unions, and the "determined underground opposition" of employers as reasons for the less than spectacular results.[9] So little progress had been made that when code hearings for the industry began on August 18, Green alone spoke for auto workers. Without a significant number of workers organized, auto manufacturers and code authorities could virtually ignore labor's demands and insert an individual merit clause.

As if continued employer resistance and defeat at the auto code hearings were not enough, the auto campaign met serious resistance from within the AFL. As early as July, Green began receiving complaints from craft union leaders concerning violations of their jurisdictions. The Boilermakers, the Metal Polishers, and the Machinists were only the most vocal among craft unions to insist that Green respect their jurisdictional boundaries. Arthur Wharton, president of the International Association of Machinists (IAM) and perhaps the most outspoken of the craft unionists, wrote Green in July complaining that the AFL organizers were trespassing on the IAM's turf by placing machinists in the auto industry in FLUs. "I trust," Wharton wrote Green, "that you will see the importance of getting out a circular letter which will remove this misunderstanding."[10]

Green understood a basic truth that most of his associates on the Executive Council and most of the international union presidents failed to grasp: workers in mass-production industries, if they were to be organized at all, had to be organized along industrial lines. Not only had technological progress blurred and often erased craft distinctions in the basic industries, but the very nature of the job had made these workers mass-minded. Before the start of the 1926 campaign in autos, Green and the Council had settled on the federal labor union as a compromise between the workers' desire for an industrial union and the jurisdictional rights of craft unions. The FLU, which had been one of Gompers' favorite recruiting devices, placed all workers in a particular plant, regardless of skill, into a single union. Thus, temporarily at least, FLUs were of an industrial character. After the organization of the industry was complete, skilled workers would be placed in their appropriate craft unions. Without instructions to the contrary, Green placed all new recruits in FLUs. As he wrote his old chum Max S. Hayes in July 1933:

> You know enough about these mass production plants to know and understand that no success can attend any organizing effort unless these workers are organized into Federal Unions. The craft lines have practically been wiped out because the workers employed specialize and thus the services of the rounded-out skilled machinists and other skilled workers are not required. We can only succeed in organizing these workers . . . by forming Federal Unions, embracing within them all the workers employed in different industries.[11]

FLUs were not the optimal solution to difficulties encountered in organizing. First, Green employed this device in part as an attempt to circumvent the jurisdictional issue, which it did not do. Second, even though the monthly dues for FLU members were significantly lower than dues paid by members of international unions, a much greater percentage of their dues was sent to the AFL. Even so, FLU members were not entitled to strike benefits unless the union had been in good standing for at least one year. FLU members were painfully aware that they paid more to the Federation and received less in return. Third, an even more serious defect of the FLUs was the lack of coordination between them. Each FLU had a direct relationship with the Federation, but no relationship with other FLUs in the same industry. The difficulty of joint action among FLUs explained in part the strong desire among mass-production workers for international charters as early as 1934.[12] Despite the deficiencies of the FLU, it was a viable organizing device and was not in itself a significant reason for the failure of the automobile campaign.

As AFL president, Green could not violate the charter rights of any affiliate. A union's charter was akin to a contract made between the union and the Federation. But Green was aware that if craft unions prevented the use of FLUs, organizing work in mass-production industries would be severely restricted, if not stalled altogether. He therefore sought to appease Wharton, in a letter to him dated August 2, 1933, stating that FLU members over whom the IAM claimed jurisdiction would be parcelled out at some future date. The Federation had no intention of violating jurisdictional rights of individual unions, Green continued, but in the present campaign it was "for the moment" impossible to respect these rights in every instance.[13]

Had Green directly confronted Wharton and other craft union officials with the real issue—that craft unionists were endangering the success of major organizing drives because they laid claim to a handful of men in basic industries who had little or no desire to join their organizations and whom the craft unions expended little or no energy to organize—it is most unlikely that he could have continued as AFL president. Green could not order craft unions to forsake their jurisdictional claims over these workers, for he understood that a man could serve as AFL president only if he recognized that he had "no power to compel any union or person to do anything."[14] To act otherwise would invoke the wrath of the Executive Council, from which his powers were derived. Lacking the power to dictate policy, Green was essentially involved in a juggling act. It was his role to balance all interests and keep everyone relatively satisfied. Green had little sympathy with the complaints of craft unionists in this instance, but he had to soothe their rage with assurances that their rights would not be violated, while at the same time pursuing the only workable strategy: placing all workers in FLUs.

The issue of initiation fees and monthly dues compounded the dilemma of jurisdiction. The IAM charged between $5 and $20 for initiation and $1.75 in monthly dues. FLUs levied only a $2 initiation and $1 per month in dues. Auto workers willing to join the AFL found FLUs attractive not only because their structure was that of an industrial union, but because they were far less expensive than international unions. The economy of the FLUs was another point of friction between craft leaders and Green at this time. Wharton wrote Green on August 8, 1933 and all but demanded that he issue a circular letter to all state federations, city centrals, and AFL organizers instructing them not to organize machinists into FLUs. Wharton was convinced that Green did not appreciate "just what we are facing when we go into a mass meeting outlining our program and then have a representative of the A. F. of L. get up and tell the mass meeting that they can all join the Federal Labor Union for $2.00."[15]

Much to his credit, Green did not bother to respond to Wharton's whining over the issue of fees and dues. He recognized that the IAM was not conducting a drive of its own in the auto industry, that sentiment among machinists in the industry strongly favored industrial unionism, and that the FLU was the closest approximation of an industrial union acceptable to the Executive Council. Wharton brought his case before the Council, which met in session between September 6 and September 15.

Wharton wailed that workers organized by the AFL interpret FLUs as industrial unions, and again demanded that Green issue a circular to insure that no toolmakers, die-sinkers, maintenance men or machinists were placed in FLUs. Green, forever on his best behavior before the Council, did not protest. "The jurisdictions of the national organizations will be protected," he promised.[16] But as other craft union heads came forward to demand that their charter rights over workers in the auto, steel, rubber, aluminum and other basic industries be safeguarded, Green momentarily lost his composure and gave vent to his own views. He fumed that Council members were jeopardizing the organization of millions of workers by their jurisdictional bickering. He warned that critics within and without the labor movement would forever condemn the AFL if it failed to organize mass production workers.

> Unless we take them (mass production workers) in we will be denounced all over. They charge us with being dead, preventing the workers from getting in when they are breaking down the doors to get in, and there are a lot of people in our own movement hammering the life out of us because we do not do more. It has been a most trying situation for me. . . . We are charged as though we are doing all we can to keep workers out. If this policy is to be reversed for the moment we cannot go ahead and organize workers respecting all craft jurisdictions.[17]

This was probably the first time Green formally questioned the desire of Council members to organize the basic industries.

Jurisdictional jealousies, coupled with employer intransigence, led to the collapse of the auto drive in early 1934. Collins ruefully reported to the Executive Council on January 31, 1934 that the drive had stalled. Few if any workers attended FLU meetings in Detroit, Lansing, Pontiac, and Flint, the principle auto centers in Michigan. Employers usually fired those who did show up. The incipient union of auto workers, Collins was forced to admit, had been "destroyed."[18]

To say the least, organizing auto workers under NIRA was not proceeding as smoothly as Green had hoped. Employer resistance remained as determined as ever, and the government, by accepting an industry-dictated auto code, had undermined Green's plan for a cooperative drive. Fortunately, the obnoxious auto code was to expire on December 31, 1933, which again raised Green's hopes. This seemed a golden opportunity to establish a fair code and resuscitate the drive. He promised FLU members in autos that he would meet the situation "as forcefully as circumstances will permit."[19] Green hoped to establish labor representation on the NRA code authority, create a joint labor-industry board, and above all, effect the removal of the individual merit clause.

The auto manufacturers, however, maintained the upper hand in bargaining strength. As mentioned in the last chapter, the auto companies needed the NRA less than the Administration needed the cooperation of the auto industry in the recovery program. This was the deciding factor in the NRA's acceptance of the National Automobile Chamber of Commerce's proposal to extend the code without modification until September 4, 1934. Green protested vehemently. In response, NRA Administrator Johnson told Green that the code had not been in effect long enough to "constitute a real test" and that the merit clause was a "purely academic issue."[20] Again Green's hopes for true cooperation and assistance on the part of the federal government had come to naught. Quite correctly, Green drew a lesson from the decision to extend the code without modification. In a letter to auto workers he declared that "it is not alone the law which is going to help us. We must depend very largely upon our own efforts."[21]

In private, however, Green expressed grave doubts as to whether auto workers could achieve union recognition and collective bargaining rights through their own efforts. FLU membership in autos was simply too small to wage a strike or even threaten one. "We are in no position yet," he admitted in January 1934, "to demand collective bargaining." Green's prescription for success was to have the FLUs "prepare the way by frequent conferences with employers, by strengthening our position in every possible way, (and) by keeping the union as much before the employer as possible."[22] Yet when unionists began to assert themselves in a more militant manner, Green would denounce their actions and again look to the government for assistance.

The FLU rank-and-file, new to unionism and beginning to express dissatisfaction with the cautious policies of the AFL president, were not as convinced as Green that they could not secure their demands. At least they were willing to try. Many believed that the choice lay between militant action or death of their FLUs by attrition. Talk of a strike could be heard among workers in Michigan. AFL strength in the industry, limited though it was, was centered at the Buick and two Fisher Body plants in Flint and the Hudson local in Detroit. At these plants union members were under constant fire from employers. Not only did the companies refuse to deal with the FLUs in any capacity, they actively suppressed unions by discharging leaders and by spying on their meetings. In response, these four FLUs informed General Motors and Hudson on March 4, 1934, that unless the companies granted union recognition, reinstating those fired for union activity, and raised wages twenty percent, they would call a strike.[23]

The threat of a strike created fear in Green's heart. Not only did he believe that the auto FLUs were too weak to win a strike against corporate giants such as GM, but by temperament, Green much preferred a negotiated peace, one that would involve the government, and one that might lead to concessions from industry. In this instance Green underestimated the strikers' chance of success, but he had no stomach for a militant struggle. He retained his hope for the peaceful and cooperative organization of industry.

At the insistence of President Roosevelt, the National Labor Board, a body established under NIRA, promised the disgruntled unionists a hearing of their grievances, and the strike was postponed. GM and Hudson, however, refused to meet with union representatives or hold an election. Fearing that a labor-management confrontation in autos might retard recovery, Roosevelt stepped in and negotiated a settlement between March 21 and 25.[24] Green attempted to sway the president's sympathies by issuing a public statement four days before the negotiations began. "We shall do all we can to avert the strike," Green declared, "because we do not wish to see the President's recovery program hindered or halted by an industrial disturbance of such far-reaching proportions."[25]

Green's assurance of the AFL's commitment to the recovery program counted for little against the influence of the auto industry, and Roosevelt's settlement proved to be a severe blow to labor. Announced on March 25, 1934, the settlement provided for a tripartite Automobile Labor Board (ALB), composed of one industry, one labor, and one "neutral" representative, and authorized to review cases of discrimination against union members. Although the ALB would be part of the NRA machinery, it would be divorced from the NLB and be responsible to the President alone. The settlement fully endorsed the industry's position on Section 7a. On the crucial issue of collective bargaining, the President in effect defied the NLB by rejecting majority rule and exclusive representation and endorsing proportional representation. Contrary to the position of the NLB, the settlement stated that employers were obligated to "bargain collectively with the freely chosen representatives of groups," and if a plant had more than one "group," each one would have "total membership *pro rata* to the number of men each group represents."[26]

Since proportional representation denied exclusive bargaining rights to the majority union and permitted legal recognition of company unions on the basis of proportional strength, employers were thrilled with the settlement. Somewhat surprisingly, Green also defended the settlement—at first. Green could have used the threat of a strike, which had the potential of paralyzing the industry at the peak of the busy spring season, as a powerful weapon in negotiations with the industry. Instead, his opposition to strikes, except as a last resort, and the flattery of being involved in a White House settlement led him to endorse the president's actions and thus undermine the rank-and-file efforts to improve conditions in the industry. Green's willingness to squelch rank-and-file unrest is not surprising if one keeps in mind the lengths he would go to avoid strikes. Above all, Green was relieved that the strike had been averted. As he told the Executive Council two days after the settlement was announced, if FLUs in the auto industry

> could secure a settlement which provided for recognition of the right to collective bargaining and for a settlement of the grievances of the auto workers, it would be far better to accept such a settlement than to run the risk of (a) strike in the automobile industry at the present time. We did not secure an ideal agreement or one that represents the full hopes and aspirations of the workers. The President intervened, urged acceptance of the settlement, and in order to avoid the conflict, the agreement proposed was accepted.[27]

Rank-and-file response both to the creation of the ALB and Green's role in the settlement was immediate and hostile. "Everybody said we got sold down the river," an auto FLU member recalled.[28] According to the president of the A.C. Spark Plug FLU, the settlement broke the morale of the unionists "and where there was hope there is now only fear and despair."[29] The March 25 settlement and its failure to improve working conditions in autos discouraged workers who had rallied to the banner of the AFL when the likelihood of a strike promised dramatic changes in their status.

Not only had Green failed to secure a satisfactory settlement, not only had he been totally unable to obtain any sort of cooperation from industry, but it was also becoming painfully apparent that Green was losing the confidence of the rank-and-file. FLU membership declined dramatically after the settlement. In March the auto FLUs held 32,501 paid-up members, but by June the figure had dropped to a dismal 18,244.[30] More important, according to historian Sidney Fine, those who remained "increasingly came to believe that they had made an almost fatal mistake in failing to strike and in agreeing to the settlement and the establishment of the A. L. B."[31]

Green, always ambivalent about the use of economic force, was losing touch with rank-and-file sentiment, and he would become increasingly alienated as the tide of worker militancy mounted in the summer of 1934. In the early New Deal days, Green had applauded and even encouraged the militancy of unorganized workers, but he quickly became concerned over the number of strikes and the willingness to resort to force to achieve labor's goals. What pleased Green about labor activity in the New Deal was the widespread urge to take advantage of Section 7a and join the AFL; what troubled him was workers' impatience when government and industry resisted their efforts. "I freely admit that I glory in the fighting spirit of the working people," Green stated in September 1933, "but it seems opportune to counsel conservation of effort and wisdom in all our actions."[32]

Green's ambivalence toward labor unrest was rooted in his boundless hopes for NIRA and his deep-seated social gospel convictions. NIRA, Green believed, made it possible for workers not only to join unions under government sanction, but it also made possible, theoretically at least, the resolution of all disputes between labor and capital at the conference table rather than on the strike field, a goal which Green pursued since his early days in the UMW. "Through the administration of the NRA instrumentalities have been created for the adjustment of industrial differences," Green declared in a public statement issued on September 30, 1933. "The new machinery, of which the National Labor Board is foremost . . . contemplates the fair settlement of labor controversies without necessity for resort to strikes."[33]

For Green, therefore, NIRA represented the highest ideal in capital-labor relations: the transcendence of force. The significance of this promise cannot be overestimated. Green dedicated his life to securing for American workers a middle-class lifestyle and middle-class respectability, and he firmly believed that his goal could not be achieved through labor militancy. Workers, banned together in unions, could achieve their goals only if industry accepted them as partners, at least junior partners, in the production process. Militancy might secure economic gains, but respectability and acceptance were privileges that rested on a moral relationship between labor and industry. Militancy meant the failure of morality. Time and again Green lectured that "The use of force in industrial relations is always a confession of failure."[34]

The essence of Green's failure to organize mass-production industries between 1933 and 1935 was not that he attempted to organize workers in accordance with his social gospel ideals, but he refused to abandon his moralistic approach even after it had proven itself bankrupt. He had doubts about the course he was taking at times. And he huffed and puffed when industry refused to cooperate, but he never endorsed strike action when there existed a possibility of successful mediation. Green's ambivalence toward rank-and-file militancy placed him in a curious position. on the one hand, he was highest ranking elected official in the largest, most established labor organization in the U.S. at a time when millions of workers sought the benefits of trade unionism. On the other hand, he became increasingly alienated from rank-and-file sentiment. More and more he found himself acting not as a labor leader, but as a mediator between labor and capital. He tried to secure for workers the most favorable legislation from Congress; he reasoned with employers in the hope that they would moderate their anti-union position; and he devoted himself to restraining a restive working class. He placed himself between labor and capital, endeavoring to prevent class warfare.

His role as mediator proved untenable. It was based on the false premise that the interests of labor and capital were identical and that employers were susceptible to moral suasion. It could only be maintained by sacrificing the interests of workers, by failing to unionize mass-production workers, and ultimately by splitting the AFL itself. Green was a decent and moral man, but he did not address realistically the issues confronting organized labor in the 1930s.

The Toledo Auto-Lite strike of April–May 1934 best illustrated how Green found it necessary to oppose workers' interests in the name of industrial peace. The Toledo FLU, No. 18384, was organized in somewhat different fashion than most others. For no apparent reason, the local accepted workers in all the city's auto plants, including the three parts plants—Electric Auto-Lite, Bingham Stamping and Tool Company, and Logan Gear Company. On February 23, 1934, FLU members staged a walkout after management refused to grant their demands for union recognition and a ten percent wage increase. Five days later, the strike ended when workers agreed to a vague management commitment to negotiate a new contract. In early April, however, Auto-Lite declared itself unwilling to negotiate with the FLU and ordered the business agent off the premises. The union thereupon issued a strike call for April 12. Unlike the February walkout, only a minority of the workers responded, allowing Auto-Lite to maintain operations by hiring strikebreakers.[35]

Green, of course, opposed the strike call. He offered no support to the strikers and later chastised the secretary of the Toledo Central Labor Union, Otto Branch, for "failure to prevent a strike action when conditions were unfavorable."[36] Unable to obtain assistance from the AFL, the FLU turned to A. J. Muste's leftist American Workers' Party, which proceeded to organize mass picketing and rally public support behind the strikers. By the middle of May, public sympathy was fully behind the strikers and Green was worried about the possibility of a general strike in Toledo. In a letter to the Central Labor Union, he expressed his fears that labor unrest would cause "great injury" to the labor movement and cautioned that a general strike was a "serious matter and should not be ordered. . . ."[37]

In spite of Green's desire to contain the strike, public sympathy grew and the strike dragged on. Less than a week after Green mailed his letter, ten thousand people gathered in the streets of Toledo in a parade of solidarity. Police tried to maintain order, but when a deputy beat an unarmed elderly man in full view of the crowd, a pitched battle ensued. For three days the "Battle of Toledo" raged, pitting police and their tear gas and shotguns against strikers and their supporters. While naked, violent class conflict consumed Toledo, Green remained in Washington, silent and disapproving. In an emotional letter to one of his organizers dated May

25, Green confessed that events in Toledo were beyond his control and "I hardly know what to do in this situation at the present moment."[38]

Green's position was both ludicrous and pathetic. By not supporting the strikers, he had shown himself to be completely out of step with rank-and-file sentiment in unions directly under his control. In setting himself up as a mediator between labor and capital, Green had in effect deserted the strikers, who nevertheless won. Although not all of the strikers' demands were met, the FLU negotiated a contract that recognized its status as a collective bargaining unit at the three parts plants. For many FLU members and workers across the country, the Toledo Auto-Lite strike was yet another example of Green and the AFL "selling them down the river."[39]

There were numerous and sound reasons why unionists chafed under Green's leadership. First, AFL policy was too cautious concerning the use of economic muscle. Green appeared far too conservative at a time when workers were becoming increasingly defiant. Second, many unionists balked at the tight control Green exercised over the FLUs, dictating policy and squelching rank-and-file input. Third, many resented the organizers Green appointed and believed organizers should be chosen from the ranks of auto workers. These grievances were bound together in a rising sentiment for an autonomous union of auto workers. By the spring of 1934, this sentiment was too strong to ignore.

Green finally succumbed to pressure by proposing a national conference of auto workers to discuss "a specific constructive program."[40] Green had no intention of chartering an industrial union at this time. Not only would craft unions block the issuance of an industrial charter, but Green believed that no charter should be issued at all until auto workers demonstrated the capacity to erect a self-sustaining organization that could act as an autonomous union. Indeed, Green set up the conference in part as an effort to convince auto workers that they were not as yet prepared to establish an international union.[41]

Green instructed Collins to plan the conference in order to set up a national council that would act as an advisory agency to the AFL's chief organizer in the industry. Collins worked out the details of Green's plan. Eleven members would serve on the council, which would convene only when desired by the chief organizer. The council would advise the organizer on matters of strategy and would also serve as an information-gathering agency.[42] Certainly a far cry from an international union, the proposed council would at least be a step forward in the coordination and unification of the FLUs.

On June 23 and 24, 1934, 127 delegates representing 77 locals met in Detroit. The procedure was hardly a model of democracy, for Collins handpicked committee members, including members of the important resolutions committee, to insure that his proposal received favorable consideration. Several resolutions were offered calling for an international union, but no one should have been surprised when Collins' proposal emerged as the majority report of the resolutions committee. Green himself attended the conference and chose the time just before the vote on Collins' proposal to speak to the delegates. He expressed sympathy for their desire to form an international union and said that he, too, wanted to establish one "at the earliest possible moment." But that moment would not arrive until auto workers proved capable of establishing "a permanent self-sustaining organization." And since FLUs in the auto industry contained no more than 18,000 paid-up members, "a slower approach" might be more fruitful.[43] Partly because of Green's speech, or perhaps in spite of it, Collins' proposal passed by a vote of 77 to 50.[44]

The June conference may have placated some, but for many rank-and-file auto unionists it served only to increase their alienation from Green and the AFL. According to Wyndham Mortimer, president of a Cleveland FLU, a Communist, and later to be a leading figure in the United Automobile Workers, half of the conference was little more than "a mutual admiration orgy, in which Bill Green and the Executive Council were depicted as being only slightly lower than the Deity Himself." It was necessary, Mortimer continued, "to sell the Executive Council to the delegates, and to convince us that our only salvation rested with this self-perpetuating, craft-minded group of bureaucrats, who were planning to steer us up a long blind alley. They were offering us the shadow but not the substance of an international union."[45]

Upon the rejection of proposals to form an independent union, twenty-five delegates bolted the meeting. Three locals, including Detroit's powerful Hudson local, left the AFL altogether within three weeks after the conference and established an independent federation, the Associated Automobile Workers of America (AAWA). An even more important group of disgruntled unionists proved to be those in the Cleveland FLUs, who chose to remain in the AFL. Shortly after the June conference, auto unionists in this city set up, without AFL authorization, a Cleveland District Auto Council to push for the creation of an international union along industrial lines that would be controlled directly by the rank-and-file. Mortimer was the guiding spirit behind the formation of the Cleveland council. At their first major conference, held in September 1934, over forty delegates unanimously approved Mortimer's resolution to work toward the creation of an industrial, international union. Delegates took the opportunity to assail Green and AFL leadership in general, labelling Green's efforts to avoid strike action "sabotaging efforts."[46]

Green instinctively recognized the threat posed to his leadership by the Cleveland Auto Council. Movements toward the formation of an international union without his consent and in defiance of the June conference could not be tolerated. Green, the Executive Council, and the Metal Trades Department all issued orders calling for the Cleveland council to disband.[47] In response, Mortimer wrote Green: ". . . please be informed that your protest and order to disband is hereby rejected."[48]

Green remained convinced that auto unionists were as yet unprepared for an international charter, and he refused to side with the growing rank-and-file movement. Time and patience, he still believed, would allow the inexperienced FLU members to cultivate effective leadership and establish a "self-sustaining" organization. Further, he could not see how the creation of an international union would solve the difficulties of attracting auto workers to the AFL or of securing collective bargaining agreements with auto manufacturers. In a letter of November 26, 1934 to an FLU president, Green wrote:

> You seem to think that the establishment of a national or international union . . . would solve all your difficulties and bring about a perfect, ideal state. Please accept this prediction from one who has had training in a wide field of organizing work. When a . . . union of automobile workers is formed, you will still find that an ideal state has not been reached; that condemnation will be indulged in by impetuous members, that serious internal problems will be presented, and fights of the most bitter kind will take place between those who seek to secure and exercise control over the international union.[49]

Looking back on the tumultuous history of the United Automobile Workers, Green's remonstrance was right on the mark, but at the time it did nothing to dissuade auto unionists. His plea for patience meant little to the growing number of FLU members who, in a call for another Cleveland District Auto Council conference, opposed "the false policies pursued by the top officialdom of the A. F. of L.," particularly its condemnation of strike action and its reliance on "strike-breaking boards."[50]

By late 1934 Green's drive in autos was a shambles. His early hopes for a peaceful campaign with the cooperation of industry, government, and the unorganized seemed little more than a bad joke. Cooperation was not working, and a new approach was needed. Green began receiving telegrams and letters from organizers telling him that there was "no hope" of inducing General Motors to bargain "honestly" and that it would require "swarms of men" or a strike to bring Ford to terms.[51] On November 13, 1934, Francis Dillon, who had replaced Collins as the AFL's chief organizer in the industry, wrote Green urging a new and "intensive organizing campaign" that would include the flexing of union economic muscle.[52] Green apparently agreed. After weeks of foot-dragging, Dillon told reporters at the end of January 1935 that Green would make a grand speaking tour of auto manufacturing centers between February 17 and 24.[53] The day before his departure, Green hinted that his excursion was an attempt to guage the sentiment among auto workers for a general strike. On the surface, it appeared that Green was abandoning cooperation and donning the garb of class-warrior. He hailed his trip as "a grand drive for the complete organization of auto workers."[54]

Green's first stop was the Cleveland Metal Trades Temple on the afternoon of Sunday, February 17, where he addressed 6000 workers. Dillon, who accompanied Green, fed rumors of militant action when he told delegates that "we are here to see if you are prepared to move out and stay out when the order comes."[55] Green and Dillon made similar speeches in Toledo, St. Louis, South Bend, and finally Detroit, where Green's address was broadcast on national radio. During his speech in Detroit, Green received wild applause when he suggested that if auto workers wanted a strike, and their grievances could be settled in no other way, the AFL would support them.[56]

As a result of the trip, the National Council conducted a strike vote among FLUs asking workers whether they would authorize the AFL president to call a strike if the auto manufacturers refused to accede to union demands for union recognition and collective bargaining rights. The National Council, stressed that Green alone would be authorized to call a strike.[57] While the vote was being taken, Green wrote the Automobile Manufacturers' Association and each major auto company requesting conferences between management and the AFL. In every instance, Green's request was politely turned down. Alfred Reeves, vice-president of the AMA, argued that since the AFL represented only "a small minority" of workers in the industry, the AFL had "no just claim to be the spokesman for the auto workers generally."[58] Green could hardly quarrel with this judgment, since in his estimation the auto FLUs at this time contained only 20,000 dues-paying members and an equal number of unemployed members who did not pay dues. Nevertheless, he responded to Reeves by threatening that if the AMA and auto manufacturers refused to discuss a settlement, the Federation would be forced to stand behind any action the FLUs might decide to take.[59]

On April 9, 1935, Dillon announced the results of the strike vote: almost every one of the 176 FLUs in the industry voted to empower Green to call a strike whenever he deemed one necessary.[60] The industry, the workers, and the public were all waiting for Green to issue the strike call. Green's speaking tour, his press releases, and the strike vote had all set the stage. But the strike call never came. Green never issued the call for a militant showdown between workers and the industry. In fact, he never intended to issue the call. A close examination of his statements revealed that all Green's intimations of a general strike were intended only to strengthen the AFL's hand in bargaining with employers. In the words of one astute auto executive, all the militant talk was part of an "A. F. of L. sales promotion campaign."[61]

As early as February 7, 1935, Green informed an FLU president that a general strike in autos was not being seriously considered.[62] During his address at Toledo on February 17, Green bluntly told the workers of his real hopes. "We must follow constructive lines in our organizational work. We want to establish cooperation in industry."[63] In Detroit on the 23rd, he told the press that "We are thinking and working in terms of peace. . . . "[64] He later explained to the Executive Council that the auto workers wanted "to engage in a general strike but I stopped that. I said, you are in no position to engage in a strike."[65]

Whether or not Green actually uttered those words to a group of workers, his statement to the Executive Council revealed his sincere opinion. Green believed that FLU membership in autos was simply too small for the AFL to engage in a successful strike. Thus historian Sidney Fine does not find it "surprising" that Green believed a general strike "would be a disaster" for the FLUs. Fine chides Green, however, for not recognizing "the potentiality of the strike as an organizational device."[66] According to Fine, even had the strike failed, the aggressiveness shown by the AFL would have attracted new members. From Green's perspective, of course, militant action could not be employed as a mere "organizational device." Engaging in class warfare, and thus throwing morality out the window, was to be avoided if at all possible. Perhaps Green may have abandoned his moral precepts temporarily had he believed the AFL had a chance of defeating General Motors, Chrysler, or Ford, but considering Green's commitment to industrial peace, it was hardly surprising that Green did not look upon a general strike as a tool to recruit new members.

Green's trump card—the strike threat—had been played without reaction from employers or the federal government. His bluff had been called. Fortunately, the workers responded. On April 23, 1935, without Green's authorization, workers at the Toledo Chevrolet plant walked out. Perhaps sensing that the possibilities for a cooperative campaign, for the time being at least, had been exhausted, Green was willing to back the strikers. Unlike the Toledo Auto-Lite strike one year earlier, Green immediately endorsed the strike.[67]

The crux of the difficulties at Toledo sprang from the FLU's demands for a signed contract and exclusive bargaining representation status, a demand almost impossible to attain under the Automobile Labor Board's proportional representation formula. The Toledo Chevrolet plant was the sole manufacturer of transmissions for both Chevrolet and Pontiac, and a successful strike at Toledo could paralyze Chevrolet operations. The vulnerability of Chevrolet led General Motors Executive Vice-President William S. Knudsen and Chevrolet President Marvin E. Coyle to meet personally with FLU leadership at Toledo on April 22. After only one day of negotiations, when GM refused to give exclusive bargaining status to the AFL, the strike began. Unlike the Auto-Lite strike, the Chevrolet strike was virtually free of violence and free from the influence of Musteites and other radicals, although several members of the strike committee were themselves leftists.[68]

Dillon rushed to Toledo and immediately took command of the strike. His actions offended many and endeared no one to the AFL cause. Although an April 29 union mass-meeting resolved that all GM locals should go out on strike until signed contracts were secured, Dillon, believing that few locals possessed enough strength to challenge GM, sought to localize the conflict. Some locals in other cities did walk out in sympathy with the Toledo strikers, but most declined to do so without Dillon's consent.[69]

Dillon also angered unionists by supporting a compromise that would have allowed the Labor Department to conduct a poll among strikers to determine whether they were willing to accept a company proposal, made on the first day of the strike, and return to work. The proposal dealt with wages and other grievances but did not budge on the central issue of exclusive representation and a signed contract. Even Green wrote Dillon of his "apprehension" concerning the poll, but he refused to intervene.[70] Strikers voted down the proposal by more than two to one.[71]

Negotiations between GM and the strikers resumed on May 11. The company improved its offer in regard to seniority and wages, but refused to accede to the principal demands. Strike leaders opposed the new offer, but Dillon threw his weight behind it and called a union meeting for May 13 to vote on it. Before the vote was taken, however, a resolution from the floor was introduced and carried that permitted only strike committee members to address the audience, a move that specifically excluded Dillon. Dillon angrily countered this move by declaring that the union was no longer part of the AFL. Faced with this threat, the strikers withdrew the resolution. When the business agent of the FLU, Fred Schwake, told strikers of the gains embodied in the company's proposal, the strikers moved to accept the agreement and return to work by a vote of 732 to 385.[72]

Green and Dillon regarded the settlement as the best possible under the circumstances. "For the first time in history," Green wrote in the *American Federationist,* "one of the major automobile manufacturing concerns has agreed to recognize and meet with a spokesman for its employees."[73] Militant auto unionists, however, saw in the agreement a further example of AFL conservatism squandering another golden opportunity. As FLU member Joseph Wood declared, "a wonderful opportunity was muffed at Toledo."[74]

The Toledo Chevrolet strike of 1935 had numerous and significant consequences for the AFL's campaign in autos. First and foremost, it further undermined the AFL's tenuous hold over organized auto workers and increased the prestige of rank-and-file militants who demanded an industrial union. Even though Green did not play an active role in the strike, he still bears partial responsibility for the continued erosion of rank-and-file confidence. Despite numerous complaints about Dillon's conduct of the strike, Green left his chief organizer in full command. Soon after the settlement, the Toledo FLU passed a resolution condemning Dillon's performance and urging Green to remove him. Green found the charges against Dillon "false and without foundation," and refused to take action against him.[75] Opposition to Dillon mounted in Toledo and other auto centers to the point where it became a serious point of contention when the AFL finally staged a convention to form a national automobile workers union.[76]

Second, the strike crippled the ALB. The board's proportional representation formula had been a major cause of the strike, and neither strikers nor employers looked to the board for satisfaction during the course of the conflict. The ALB, along with the rest of the NRA machinery, would be declared unconstitutional by the Supreme Court on May 17, yet at least according to one historian, "It is doubtful whether the A.L.B. could have long survived the Toledo strike even if NIRA had not been declared unconstitutional, since even the employers now had some doubts as to its effectiveness."[77]

Third, the strike compelled Green to call a constitutional convention to form an international auto workers' union. The debate over the issuance of a charter to auto workers had come to head in early 1935. The 1934 AFL convention directed the Executive Council to issue charters for unions in mass-production industries and to manage their operations for a provisional period. On February 1, 1935, representatives of the National Council for autos brought the issue of an international union before the Executive Council. The overriding issue concerned the jurisdictional boundaries to be accorded the auto union. To no one's surprise, the craft union presidents immediately declared their opposition to an industrial charter. The Machinists, the Electrical Workers, the Plumbers, and the Bricklayers each laid claim to a portion of the workforce, and William Hutcheson of the Carpenters backed them by declaring, "I do not believe that we should give them (auto workers) a charter so broad that they could go out and claim any employee that might be employed by these automobile manufacturers."[78]

Green countered the arguments of the craft unionists with a sensitive description of the need for an industrial charter. Even though his conservative tactics had alienated him from rank-and-file auto workers, Green understood their desires and the necessities of organization far better than the majority of men serving on the Council. "The automobile industry," Green began, "presents the most perfect and highest development in mass production. . . . The workers are brought into this industry in large numbers *en masse,* they are employed *en masse,* they work together as cogs in a great machine. . . . Is it not reasonable to conclude that as a matter of fact men who are not regarded as skilled workers, men who are not required to exercise skill, but are required to perform a repetitive operation day in and day out would begin to think in mass terms? They become mass minded. . . . I must confess that I have come, you will come, and all of us will come face to face with the fact . . . that if organization is to be established in the automobile industry it will be upon a basis that the workers employed in the mass production industry must join an organization *en masse.* We cannot separate them."[79]

John L. Lewis, recently elected to an expanded Executive Council, was in complete agreement with Green concerning the jurisdictional question, but rather than attempt to reason with the narrow-minded craft union heads about the necessity of an industrial union charter, Lewis wanted to postpone all chatter about jurisdictional rights until the industry was fully organized. He recommended that a charter be issued "at once" and the referral to the Executive Council of "questions involving overlapping jurisdiction."[80] Craft unionists, of course, rejected Lewis's motion. They were unwilling to leave the all-consuming question of jurisdiction to some future date.

The impasse in the Council was overcome when George Harrison, president of the Railway Clerks, proposed an amendment to Lewis's motion. Harrison suggested that the charter include "all employees directly engaged in the manufacture of parts (not including tools, dies, and machinery) and assembling of those parts into completed automobiles but not including job or contract shops manufacturing parts or any other employee engaged in said automobile production plants."[81] Lewis opposed the amendment and declared that any jurisdictional restrictions at this point would hamper organization of the auto workers. Green agreed with Lewis, but in a particularly revealing statement declared that, even though he was committed to industrial unionism and believed that any other approach would lead to failure and embarrassment, he would follow the policy agreed upon by the majority of Council members. "Whatever you do I will try to carry out but I will be the target of criticism and I know we will fail."[82] After all the wrangling, Harrison's amendment passed by a vote of twelve to two, with Lewis and David Dubinsky of the ILGWU opposed and Green, as chair, abstaining.[83]

Green had finally been authorized by the Council to establish an international union in autos. Because of declining enrollments in FLUs, Green hesitated to fulfill his instructions, but the partial success of the Toledo strike helped convince him that auto workers were capable of managing their own affairs. Two days after meeting with Dillon on June 17, 1935, Green polled FLU members on their attitudes toward the creation of an international. He then issued a call for a constitutional convention to begin August 26 at Detroit.[84]

Green had just cause for apprehension over the upcoming convention. The two key issues—leadership and jurisdiction—had been decided for him by the Executive Council. By maintaining a semblance of centralized control over the proposed auto union through the appointment of its officers, the Council hoped to discourage the rank-and-file unrest that proved so embarrassing to the AFL's conservative approach. Council members had also safeguarded their interests by excluding skilled workers from membership in the proposed union. Green was willing to execute the Council's instructions, yet he realized that the mass-minded auto workers would not be satisfied with the charter. In the weeks prior to the convention, Machinists' President Wharton constantly reminded Green of his obligation to respect he decision of the Council. This type of pressure made Green uneasy, and he worried about the problems "I know I am going to be confronted with" at Detroit, but he nevertheless assured Wharton on August 25 that "I will endeavor . . . to protect and preserve the interests of your International Union."[85]

Delegates from 65 of the 148 auto FLUs gathered in Detroit to establish the International Union, United Automobile Workers of America, the AFL's first international chartered in the mass-production sector of the economy. Dillon presided. One of his first acts was to select a committee "with the honor and responsibility of proceeding to Suite 1863 of the Fort Shelby Hotel and there conveying to the president of the American Federation of Labor your desire to usher him to this convention hall." As the committee escorted Green into the hall, a chorus sang "How Do You Do, Mr. Green?" Dillon then extolled Green's leadership abilities and his achievements as a labor leader.[86]

After spending several minutes basking in the warmth of this praise, Green, as diplomatically as possible, told the delegates of their restricted charter and that he would select their officers. He attempted to soften their reaction by concluding with a platitude that could well describe his life's work. Life demands "adjustments," he told the delegates, and "we must find a basis of accommodation."[87] George Lehman, chairman of the committee on constitution and laws and an ardent AFL supporter, immediately moved to accept the charter as presented by Green. A number of delegates protested and called for a charter to organize all workers "in and around automobile or parts plants." Wyndham Mortimer probably was unaware that he was expressing Green's true convictions when he rose to tell the delegates that "the craft from of organization fits into the automobile industry like a square peg in a round hole."[88] Before the vote was taken on the charter, delegates unanimously voted to accept a resolution stating that, if the charter under consideration was adopted, the jurisdictional claims of craft unions would lead to the "gradual disintegration" of the UAW. This resolution did not call for the rejection of the charter, however, and according to the convention proceedings, the charter, with all its defects, was accepted "with but few dissenting votes."[89]

The other issue, that of leadership, gave rise to even greater acrimony than the question of jurisdiction. The Executive Council had stipulated that the AFL president would designate the officers of the new union for a temporary period. Green had apparently come to believe that this instruction would not create much opposition, since in the weeks prior to the convention, conservative members of the National Council had written him, indicating their desire to see Dillon installed as UAW president.[90] On the first day of the convention, the resolutions committee moved that Green appoint Dillon president. The committee also moved, however, that all other officers be elected by the convention. At this point the president of the South Bend FLU, Carl Shipley, moved that all officers be elected by the delegates and that all candidates be members of the UAW, which would have excluded Dillon. Green then picked up the gavel and, addressing the delegates as "my dear boys," tried to persuade them that Dillon was the best choice for the presidential slot. "Where can you find a man more capable, more trained . . . wholehearted and sincere, than honest Frank Dillon?" Green then ruled Shipley's motion out of order and called for a vote on Dillon's candidacy. Despite Green's backing, the convention voted 164.2 to 112.8 against Dillon.[91]

Three days of behind-the-scenes negotiations convinced Green that compromise was necessary if the delegates were to accept Dillon. Only the fierce opposition of the Toledo FLU, which could not forgive Dillon for his conduct of the Chevrolet strike, prevented acceptance of the original motion of the resolutions committee. Militants would later charge that Green at one point offered to allow delegates to elect all their officials if Dillon was kept on as an advisor. Green denied that he ever made such an offer.[92]

Despairing of compromise, Green used his authority from the Executive Council to impose leadership on the UAW on August 29. Dillon will be president, Homer Martin of the Kansas City FLU will be vice-president, and Ed Hall of the Seaman Body plant in Milwaukee will be secretary-treasurer, Green declared. No longer was Green willing to compromise with the contentious delegates. "There is no necessity of any vote of approval or disapproval," Green informed the stunned delegates. "It is the declaration of the Executive Council. . . . You can't bargain with the Executive Council because that is the higher tribunal."[93]

After Green had finished, voices of protest rose from the floor, particularly from the Toledo delegation. Green told the delegates that all protests should be taken up with the Executive Council, and then pronounced that the newly formed UAW was a "happy family."[94] Under instructions from the Executive Council to appoint leaders, and believing that Dillon was the best man for the job, Green had no choice but to run roughshod over the majority sentiment of the convention. Thus even as Green responded to rank-and-file pressure for a union charter, he succeeded in further alienating auto unionists from the AFL cause.

More than two years of organizational work had finally resulted in the creation of an auto workers' union. Yet despite the hoopla at AFL headquarters, the Federation's campaign in the auto industry must be considered a dismal failure. On the eve of the constitutional convention, the total dues-paying membership of the auto FLUs was 22,687. This estimate may have been somewhat conservative, and it did not include the approximately 20,000 members who did not pay dues. Nevertheless, after more than two years of effort, the AFL had enrolled no more than 5.4 percent of the 421,000 wage earners employed in auto manufacturing and parts plants as of June 1935. The failure of the AFL's campaign was even more glaring if one considers that in Detroit, the heart of the industry, the AFL had organized just 2197 workers. At the gigantic Ford plant at River Rouge, only nineteen workers were AFL members. Equally important, auto workers had been able to secure only sixteen signed contracts, eight of which had been negotiated by the rebellious Toledo FLU.[95] Yet another indication of failure was the fact that most of the workers affiliated with the AFL had little respect for the policies and leadership of the parent body. By any measure, Green had blown a marvelous opportunity to organize auto workers in the early years of the New Deal.

A similar opportunity slipped through Green's hands in the rubber industry. To a much greater extent than even the auto workers, rubber workers flocked to the banner of unionism with the passage of NIRA Section 7a. Thousands of rubber workers in Akron, Ohio, where three of the four largest rubber companies were located, had joined AFL FLUs even before August 2, 1933, when Green's chosen organizer for the industry, Coleman Claherty, arrived in the city. Green's choice of the conservative Claherty, similar to his selection of Collins and Dillon, created a great deal of friction when Claherty attempted to organize workers suffused with militancy. Rubber workers soon became disillusioned with Claherty and at least one writer who followed developments in Akron, Louis Adamic, believed that the initial surge of unionism declined largely because Claherty preached "patience and faith" while "Rubber Barons" founded company unions and refused to negotiate with independent FLUs. "The new union members demanded action from the AFL," Adamic wrote. "Action to stop speed-up. Action to get wage-cuts back. Action to protect union members from discrimination." Claherty, however, "stalled and talked and called meetings and made promises. . . . "[96] Indeed, Claherty's favorite expression was that "Rome was not built in a day," which reflected a temperament greatly at odds with the rank-and-file's sense of urgency.[97]

The Executive Council's requirement of September 1933 that skilled craftsmen be parcelled out among the sixteen internationals claiming jurisdiction in the rubber industry also hindered the AFL's drive. Untutored in the politics of jurisdiction that craft organizations practiced, rubber workers showed little respect for craft union boundaries. Even after they had been parcelled out, skilled workers continued to show up at FLU meetings. FLU membership may have reached a peak of 40,000 or even 50,000, but then, as Sidney Hillman bemoaned, the AFL "started to divide those workers among the different unions claiming jurisdiction over them. As a result of that procedure, the membership of the rubber workers union fell as low as 3,000."[98]

At the Executive Council meeting of May 1935, which was to implement the 1934 AFL convention's instruction to create an international union in rubber, only Green, John L. Lewis, and David Dubinsky spoke in favor of an industrial form of organization. "I think," Green told the Council, "we should deal with this in a big broad way. . . . If we are to organize them it will call for the yielding on the part of some of the organizations . . . for the common good."[99] The craft-dominated Council, however, resolved to issue a charter to rubber workers that excluded skilled workers. Although he opposed the decision, Green promised to fulfill his instructions.[100]

A pitiful twenty-six locals, with a total membership not much greater than 3,000 workers, were affiliated with the AFL at the time of the constitutional convention, which was held in Akron on September 12, 1935. Green himself attended the convention to issue the charter. Hoping to avoid the difficulties he encountered at the UAW convention, Green began the proceedings with a lengthy lecture in which he explained why the Federation would have to retain a certain amount of control over the new organization. "[T]he American Federation of Labor must be convinced beyond preadventure of a doubt that when a new International Union is launched that it is soundly and permanently established, that it will live to serve the workers in the industry over which the International Union has jurisdiction, that it will not fail, that it will not pass out of existence. . . . " He then explained that the union's charter excluded skilled workers and warned that the new union would have to respect the jurisdictional boundaries of other AFL unions.[101]

As soon as Green finished, Salvatore Camelio, who was to assume a leading role in the new union, asked ". . . if we the delegates assembled accept this charter, does this give the President (Green) the right to appoint its officers?" Sensing a replay of the UAW convention, Green responded forcefully that "The parent body is creating a new International Union and it cannot barter with the Union that it is creating. . . . This confers upon me the right to designate or appoint your officers for a probationary period providing I think, and in my judgement it seems necessary, to do that to protect your International Union."[102]

The next day delegates voted on a resolution that would have permitted Green to appoint Claherty as president and provide financial assistance until the union became more firmly established. Delegates rejected the resolution by a vote of $45 \frac{5}{6}$ to $9 \frac{1}{6}$. Unlike the auto convention, Green made no major effort to secure support for Claherty by meeting with delegates informally. Rather, he accepted this defeat as final and told the convention:

> You have decided to refuse to request me and the Executive Council to establish and finance your International headquarters. . . . So I accept your word as final. . . . Now the convention is turned over to you. You may elect your officers now from top to bottom and you may arrange to finance your convention and your organization work and carry on.[103]

Thus the establishment of an international union in the rubber industry followed a path similar to that in autos. Workers, bristling with militancy, demonstrated a strong desire to form a union. Hoping to temper their militancy but not their desire to unionize, Green assigned a conservative organizer who failed either to win worker confidence or cool workers down, but served only to create friction between the AFL an the rank-and-file. And against his better judgment, Green executed Executive Council policy by prohibiting organization of skilled workers into FLUs, which further discouraged workers from joining the AFL. Finally, Green aggravated an already tense relationship by attempting to foist an unwanted leadership on the new unions at their founding conventions.

Since an international union with an undefined jurisdiction already existed in the steel industry, Green and the AFL front office did not play a leading role in the organization of steel workers in the early years of the New Deal. The Amalgamated Association of Iron, Steel, and Tin Workers (AA), however, was extremely weak, holding fewer than 5000 members and less than $30,000 in its treasury as of June 1933. The union's president, Michael Tighe, was referred to as "Grandmother" because of his advanced age and timidity in dealing with employers. The AA's membership was composed primarily of skilled craftsmen, and even after the passage of NIRA Section 7a, Tighe and his executive board showed no interest in organizing the great majority of the industry's workforce, which was unskilled and semi-skilled. It was hardly surprising, therefore, that by the spring of 1934 a powerful opposition group, known as the rank-and-file movement, had emerged within the union and declared itself in favor of reorganizing in the industry along industrial lines and prepared to force employer recognition by strikes if necessary.[104]

By the time of the AA convention in April–May 1934, the rank-and-file movement was strong enough to secure passage of a resolution calling for an industry-wide strike on June 16 unless all major steel producers entered into agreements with the union. As expected, the steel firms ignored the threat, and both sides geared up for an industrial war. Two days before the strike date, Green conferred with President Roosevelt at the White House and discussed with him legislation then being formulated which would enable the president to create a steel labor board. Even though Green at this time was lobbying for the Wagner bill, he agreed not to condemn Public Resolution No. 44 in public, for Green, like Roosevelt, hoped to avoid a strike if at all possible, especially one he believed the AFL had little chance of winning. The next day, at a special AA convention, Green, assuming what many delegates regarded as a "dictatorial manner," convinced a majority of delegates to abandon the strike in return for a promise that Roosevelt would create a government board to investigate and adjust complaints, conduct elections, and hear cases of discrimination against union members.[105]

The 1934 AFL convention authorized the Executive Council to conduct an organizing drive in steel, and the Council met in January 1935 to discuss the venture. As might have been expected, Green, Lewis, and Dubinsky were the only ones who supported the organization of steel workers into FLUs until a new international union in the industry could be chartered. But craft leaders expressed concern about violating the charter rights of the AA, and Tighe had let it be known that he would refuse to stand quietly by and allow the creation of a new international union in the steel industry.[106]

In an unusual show of firmness, Green then urged a campaign in steel conducted along industrial lines, regardless of the AA's jurisdiction. "I am satisfied in my own mind that the officers of the Amalgamated can not organize those workers with their own resources or with the set-up as it is, with the National organization based upon the philosophy upon which rests or upon pursuing the policy which it is pursuing."[107] Green gave vent to his personal views in this instance probably because he realized, as Lewis certainly did, that an unorganized steel industry posed a serious threat to the UMW's position in the captive mines. Nevertheless, the craft union view prevailed and the Executive Council instructed Green to initiate a joint campaign of all unions with an interest in the steel industry.[108]

Having already expressed his belief that a campaign such as the one he was instructed to undertake was doomed to failure, Green did not relish the task before him. As did many others in the labor movement, Green probably recognized that the aborted 1919 steel drive proved beyond a reasonable doubt that the joint organizing strategy could not succeed. Thus, despite the crucial need to organize steel workers, Green did almost nothing to organize them. When the staff of the AA journal wrote Green in August 1935 for a detailed description of his organizing plans, he responded brusquely that he had none.[109] In the final analysis, responsibility for the failure to organize steelworkers before 1936 rested not so much on Green, but on the moribund AA and the craft union officials' unbending opposition to an industrial union drive.

In autos, rubber, steel, and other mass-production industries, the AFL under Green had muffed an apparently marvelous opportunity to organize workers in the first three years of the New Deal. NIRA Section 7a seemed to hold such promise and the outpouring of union sentiment among mass-production workers was enough to shock even the "old, tired veterans" of the labor movement, but the AFL failed to establish itself as a major force in any of the mass-production industries. To be sure, some gains had been made. Between 1933 and 1935, Green issued 1804 FLU charters, most of which went to auto, rubber, and lumber workers. Numerous FLUs were also set up for gasoline filling station, aluminum, and radio workers. As of 1935, 111,500 workers were enrolled in FLUs, the highest FLU membership figure ever, but still only a tiny portion of the millions of employees in the mass-production sector.[110] Further, the AFL had been unable to win a signed contract with a major employer in steel, autos, or rubber. AFL efforts, then, must be considered a failure.

Some of the reasons for this failure were obvious. First, employers in these industries were the most resourceful, sophisticated, and ruthless opponents of trade unionism, and they were unwilling to open their doors to the AFL simply because the federal government passed a single piece of fuzzily phrased legislation. Second, the federal government did not attempt to use its coercive powers to force these employers to abide by the law. On the contrary, as we have seen, the government often sided with industry's interpretation of Section 7a. Third, within the AFL, the selfish practices of craft unionists who dominated the Executive Council hampered the organization of the unorganized. A fourth reason, equally important yet not so obvious, was the outmoded morality of the AFL president, who was personally responsible for conducting the drives of these years.

Throughout his career in the trade union movement, Green was a conservative accommodationist; he sought the traditional goals of trade unions—higher wages, shorter hours, and better working conditions—not through strikes or work stoppages, but through appeals based on the economic benefits of unions, moral suasion, and negotiation. His approach rested on the ability to convince employers to allow the unionization of their workforce, rather than the ability to motivate workers to unionize. He sought union gains by appealing to the reason and morality of employers, not the class consciousness of workers. This approach was nurtured during his early years in the UMW and reinforced by his commitment to the social gospel.

Green never abandoned this conservative approach. Years of constant failure could not induce him to discard attitudes toward the labor movement that had been ingrained for decades. Even his experiences during the depression years, when employers proved unable to keep the economy on a sound footing and continued to resist labor's right to organize even after the passage of federal legislation guaranteeing this right, could not dislodge these convictions. Appeals to employers based on reason and justice still held tremendous promise, Green conjectured in 1935, because the vast majority of employers were decent and fair-minded people. "The majority of employers sincerely and honestly wish to maintain decent wage standards and humane conditions of employment. They seek neither the exploitation of Labor nor the exploitation of the consuming public. They are inspired by a keen sense of justice and are influenced in all their business dealings by a spirit of fair-dealing and fair-play." The majority of employers also recognized that unions could play a key role in the economy by insuring high wages, fostering consumerism, and maintaining a proper balance between production and consumption.[111]

In Green's view, the growth of trade unionism was impeded not because employers were determined to protect their class interests, but because a minority of employers "engage in unfair trade practices, sell goods below cost, cut and slash prices, including wages, and increase hours of employment for the selfish purpose of gaining an unfair advantage over some competitor."[112] Because of their immorality, their selfishness, fair-dealing employers were forced to respond in kind if they wanted to stay in business. The actions of a few unscrupulous employers, therefore, made the organization of the unorganized a difficult proposition.

The AFL's fight to secure legal recognition of the right to organize, according to Green, was an admission that moral suasion could not induce every employer to pay decent wages and maintain reasonable hours of employment. These few had to be compelled to do what most employers were willing to do.

The passage of Section 7a seemed to insure that recalcitrant employers would tow the line in the best interests of society as a whole. Section 7a did not mean that workers could now band together under government sanction and wrest concessions from capitalists. Quite the contrary, Section 7a meant that cooperation was now an even greater possibility, that a moral relationship could be established between workers and management. This was the perspective from which Green approached the organizing drives of the early 1930s.

Green's belief that the majority of employers would allow the organization of their workforce in the name of decency and for the betterment of society as a whole was hopelessly naive and would be hilarious were it not so tragic. Employer efforts in these years to frustrate labor organization were legion. The simplest and the favorite anti-union device of employers was the company union. Soon after the passage of NIRA, the National Association of Manufacturers printed model constitutions for company unions and distributed them to employers across the country. Between June and November 1933, the number of company unions more than doubled. Few plants in steel, autos, or rubber were without a management-run employee representation plan by the end of 1933. And according to a Bureau of Labor Statistics' survey, eighty-one of ninety-six companies interviewed indicated that their company unions were formed either in response to Section 7a or the threat of trade union inroads.[113]

Much more ominous were the anti-union practices later uncovered by the LaFollette Civil Liberties Committee, a subcommittee of the Senate Committee on Education and Labor, which, between 1936 and 1940, investigated employer interference with labor's right to organize and bargain collectively. The LaFollette Committee examined only four of the most perfidious anti-union devices favored by mass-production industries: espionage, stockpiling of munitions, strikebreaking, and intimidation by armed police. The conclusion of the Committee was that management was and had been for years conducting "a colossal, daily drive in every part of the country to frustrate enunciated labor policy. . . . "[114] The number of firms employing labor spies astounded Committee members, who found espionage so pervasive they did not believe collective bargaining could be successful as long as the practice continued. To cite only one example, in the FLU for GM workers at Flint at least three of the thirteen members of the executive board were spies, including the chairman of the organizing committee. LaFollette Committee members believed that espionage was the major reason why membership of the FLU, which reached a height of 26,000 in 1934, fell to 120 by 1936.[115] If spies failed to dispel the lure of unionism, employers had stockpiles of tear gas, machine guns, gas bombs, clubs and other weapons to deal with a troublesome workforce. Between 1933 and 1937, four steel companies—U.S. Steel, Republic Steel, Bethlehem Steel, and Youngstown Sheet and Tube—each procured more tear and nauseating gas than did any law enforcement agency in the U.S.[116] The LaFollette Committee showed then extremes to which employers in mass-production industries were willing to go to meet the challenge of unionism. These were Green's "fair-dealing" employers, the ones with whom he wanted to cooperate, the ones who would accept unions after he described their economic benefits, the ones susceptible to moral suasion.

To forego voluntarily the only weapons at the disposal of unions, strikes and work stoppages, and to rely solely on moral suasion and economic arguments was nothing short of madness in the 1930s. Recalcitrant employers, who found nothing funny about independent trade unions, surely must have laughed when Green begged, as he did in October 1933: "Masters, render unto your servants that which is just and equal, knowing that ye also have a Master in Heaven." Appeals such as this made to class-conscious, powerful employers had no effect. "If we are to go forward to a better world without a transition marked by class hatred, violence and bloodshed, progress must come through . . . the voluntarily relinquishment of privilege and power by our privileged classes. . . . "[117] The mere asking of GM, Ford, Republic Steel, and other mass-production firms to relinquish voluntarily unilateral power revealed just how removed Green was from the realities of the 1930s.

The rank-and-file in the mass-production industries knew better than Green that employers responded only to the language of economic power. Green's attempt to maintain his fruitless, conservative strategy alienated large elements of the rank-and-file who responded to trade union appeals in 1933 and 1934. Green's opposition to strikes proved so discouraging to workers that most of those who joined FLUs departed by 1935. Why would a worker in autos or rubber join the AFL at the risk of losing his job for union activity if in return Green would denounce their militancy and beg on bended knee to employers in their behalf?

From Green's perspective, the militancy workers exhibited was a sign of their trade union inexperience. To a large degree paternalism characterized green's relations with the rank-and-file. His reference to delegates at the founding convention of the UAW as "my dear boys" revealed that Green, who was sixty-five years old in 1935, regarded the new unionists as youngsters who lacked education in trade union practices. When Daniel Tobin of the Teamsters asked Green at an Executive Council meeting in February 1935 to characterize the rank-and-file movement in steel, Green told him that "They are a lot of poor fellows, untrained and uneducated."[118] An experienced union member, in Green's estimation, was one who shunned class conflict, resorted to strikes only as a last resort, and always remained willing to negotiate a quick settlement of grievances. Those thousands of workers who flocked into FLUs had to be educated. In almost every instance between 1933 and 1935, Green counseled them against strike action.

From the perspective of the rank-and-file, education in trade union practices along the lines Green advocated meant being "sold out." Since Green was always ready to negotiate a quick settlement to prevent a strike, no matter how limited the gains, his policies were identified closely with those of management. Workers saw in Green's desire to maintain harmonious relations between capital and labor not an admirable commitment to Christian principles, but weakness and fear of corporate power. At a time when workers themselves were losing their fear of employer coercion, Green's call to settle all industrial disputes at the conference table fell on deaf ears. The young militants of the 1930s had not been reared on social gospel principles. They saw nothing moral about a willingness to compromise with employers who laid them off or reduced their wages at will and who refused to respect their right to organize.

The gulf between Green and the rank-and-file was not a matter of trade union objectives. Both Green and the majority of workers in the 1930s fought primarily to improve working conditions and, above all, to increase job security. Green and the rank-and-file split over strategy and tactics. The rank-and-file proved willing to employ almost any tactic to secure their objectives, while Green, with his social gospel predilections, could not countenance militancy and the breakdown of industrial peace.

Green's failure to sanction worker militancy left the door wide open to radicals to win the confidence of the workers. In the great strikes of 1934, workers followed radical leaders not because of a shared hostility to capitalism, but because radicals educated them in the use of militant tactics and gave them confidence in the power of collective economic action. The Toledo Auto-Lite strikers were certainly not all Musteites, but they welcomed the support of the American Workers' Party because this group showed them how to organize mass pickets and how to use the unemployment to help the employed. Wyndham Mortimer appealed to auto workers not because he was a Communist, but because he understood their needs and respected their militant spirit. William Green did not have this confidence in the rank-and-file. He placed his faith in religious principles.

V

A Conflict of Styles and Principles:
1932–1935

I T WOULD BE difficult to imagine two more distinct styles of union leadership than those of William Green and John L. Lewis in the 1930s. Even their physical appearance in these years was a study in contrast. The troubles that beset the Federation in the early New Deal years apparently did not diminish in any way Green's complacent demeanor. He simply did not look as though he was experiencing the most serious crisis of his professional career. At the age of sixty-five in 1935, Green looked every bit the part of the Baptist minister he had once hoped to become. Slight of stature and more than a little plump, Green had a solemn but well-fed appearance. Conservative suits, pince-nez glasses, and a gold watch chain all lent an air of respectability and trustworthiness. His well-scrubbed, rosy-cheeked, fat face, combined with his ever-present smile, gave him a sincere and submissive semblance. After thirty years as a labor official, there were no visible reminders of his struggles in Coshocton's coal mines.[1]

Not only did Green look the part of a preacher, he acted the part as well. He came across as unpretentious yet eminently honorable. Labor reporters, accustomed to more charismatic labor leaders, often ridiculed him as being bland and boring. One such journalist quipped that his posture was "as plain, as plodding, and as undramatic as his name."[2] Green spoke to audiences as if from a pulpit, exhorting them with biblical injunctions and emphasizing points with a pointed forefinger. Intended to make his audiences reflect rather than spring into action, his speeches succeeded in doing neither. Another reporter sneered that a speech from Green served only to keep "things going through dull spots of an AFL convention, when the boys wanted time for a drink, a caucus, a poker game," and still another reporter dubbed him the "All-American mushmouth."[3] Len DeCaux, director of publicity for the Committee for Industrial Organization (CIO), accurately summarized the impression Green made on even those who had high regard for him: "He was above all a respectable person; a happier fate might have made him a reverend one."[4]

By contrast, John L. Lewis was an imposing figure. Although slightly less than six feet tall, Lewis had a huge frame that made him appear much larger. He was fifty-five years old in 1935 and tipped the scales at 230 pounds. While Green's face seemed to apologize, Lewis's face seemed to threaten. His forest-like eyebrows, his deep-set eyes, and the ever-present scowl gave Lewis an ominous guise. Lewis consciously adopted his famous angry frown for he believed it suited the leader of the coal miners. As he told Frances Perkins, "Madame Secretary, that scowl is worth a million dollars."[5] Dubofsky and Van Tine have suggested that Lewis was keenly aware of his public posture and "cultivated an image of size, strength and anger."[6]

In public, Lewis swaggered and always sought to dominate. And he usually did. His oratorical skills were perhaps no greater than Green's, but he used these skills for different ends. While Green sought to soothe, Lewis pummeled his audiences. As Irving Bernstein notes, "His words were weapons of warfare, not tools of analysis or communication. As weapons they were supremely adapted to the attack—the epithet, the insult, the defamatory adjective."[7]

Beneath the comparatively superficial qualities of appearance and bearing lay world views remarkably similar and yet ultimately at odds with one another. Both Lewis and Green were committed to the capitalist system and yet both opposed laissez-faire, "dog-eat-dog" capitalism or the irresponsible, anti-social, anti-union variety of capitalism represented by the giant mass-production industries. Both Lewis and Green were committed to the improvement of labor's position within the existing economic structure. Both also believed that the success of capitalism in America was founded upon technological, innovation, which provided the source of all wage increases, and a strong labor movement, which guaranteed a more equitable distribution of income. Yet while they agreed that a strong labor movement was essential for the maintenance of prosperity, Lewis and Green held radically different views as to what a strong labor movement was and how it should be used.

Lewis's overriding concern was the acquisition and use of power. He was in fact obsessed with power. In order to subdue irresponsible capital, Lewis believed that labor must be tightly and completely organized and willing to engage in warfare on the economic and political fronts. Even though he shunned the use of the term "class conflict," Lewis often referred to labor's struggle with military allusions. He was an opportunist who was willing to use any means at his disposal, any tactic, to wrest power from the White House, Congress, and industry. Declining to ponder the distant future, Lewis focused solely on present-day demands and the means necessary to achieve them. As his biographers note, Lewis was "the complete chameleon, always ready to change colors to suit a new milieu. . . . Life was a contest to Lewis in which success went not to the best sportsman or the man who followed the rules but to the man who made his own rules and played the game according to present needs, not past rituals."[8]

Green, on the other hand, had a severely limited understanding of power. His desire to improve the lot of America's working men and women was every bit as, and perhaps even more, sincere than Lewis's, but Green was very selective in his choice of weapons. Indeed, he relied almost exclusively on the power of moral suasion. In Green's view, union gains would be secured not by the organized might of the workers themselves, but by a change of heart among employers and government leaders. The labor movement must secure the backing of public opinion and induce employers to live up to the Golden Rule. He recognized that placing capitalism upon a moral footing implied "a revolution in thinking for most of those in responsible economic and political positions" but believed it was the only strategy that could achieve permanent results.[9]

Unlike Lewis, Green did not calculate strategy based upon existing power relationships. Green's strategy was constant and was based upon what could and should be, not upon what was. Much more than Lewis, Green focused on ultimate ends, believing that labor and society in general must progress toward a Christian cooperative ideal. The strategies of class warfare, therefore, did not represent progress but rather the continuance of the rule of force and immorality.

Green was a reformer and an idealist. While Lewis appreciated the first, he had little patience with the second. Lewis was convinced that every person had a price and could be bought or bullied into submission. One need only to read his book, *The Miner's Fight for American Standard* (1925), to recognize that for Lewis, idealism was a sham that hid more base motives. One historian has concluded that since Lewis had no understanding of ideals, he "misunderstood men like Powers Hapgood and John Brophy; when they fought him (in the 1920s) because they believed him morally wrong he thought they were feathering their own nests."[10] Lewis's reaction would be the same when Green attacked him for destroying the unity of the labor movement.

Friction was bound to develop between men of such divergent temperaments and attitudes if forced to work together. And as we have seen, the working relationship between the two men while Green was secretary-treasurer and Lewis president of the UMW was hardly ideal. But even Lewis's actions in the 1920s, when he twisted Green's arm to fix the union's books, could not dispel the loyalty Green felt for the UMW. Despite their personal differences, Green was loathe to leave the union that had been his home for the first thirty-four years of his professional life. Moreover, Green undoubtedly appreciated the fact that Lewis was the first UMW president to give the union stability, continuity, and a diminution of factionalism. By his own admission Green consented to be kicked upstairs to the post of AFL president only at the instance of Lewis and the UMW executive board.[11]

During his January 1925 farewell address to the UMW, Green assured the miners that "At all times (as AFL president) I will be inspired by the fact that I can count upon your sympathy, co-operation and support."[12] But it was to be Green who came to the aid of Lewis and the UMW, using the power and prestige of his office numerous times in their behalf in the late 1920s and early 1930s. Green was the chief fundraiser during the anthracite and bituminous strikes between 1925 and 1927. Green was able to report to the 1928 AFL convention that the Federation had raised hundreds of thousands of dollars worth of food, clothing, and supplies, in addition to almost $700,000 in cash.[13] Green again came to Lewis's aid in 1929 when Union financial difficulties forced Lewis to petition the Executive Council for exoneration of part of the UMW's per capita assessment. Although the Council granted the request, the Carpenters' union strongly opposed the decision. Green then went to bat for Lewis before the Council, explaining the situation in terms the Carpenters could accept, and thus making it possible for the UMW to stay in the black.[14] One year later, Green supported Lewis's bid for the Secretary of Labor post, calling on President Hoover numerous times and expressing sincere displeasure when Lewis did not get the nod.[15]

Green's most notable service to Lewis in these years was his role in squashing a powerful insurgent movement—led by such figures as Frank Farrington, Alex Howat, John Walker, John Brophy, and Adolph Germer—that mounted a serious challenge to Lewis's control of the UMW. The center of the opposition movement was Illinois District 12, Lewis's home district and the only district in which bituminous miners were well organized during labor's "lean years." When Lewis revoked the charter of this rebellious district in October 1929, the officers of District 12 and other opposition leaders pointed to a technicality and declared that the UMW constitution was void and called for a constitutional convention at Springfield, Illinois on March 10, 1930 to reestablish the union. Lewis responded by calling for a UMW convention the same day at Indianapolis.[16]

The assemblage at Springfield, which became known as the Reorganized United Mine Workers (RUMW), resolved to ask Green's assistance in working out a formula for unity that would place William B. Wilson and Green temporarily in charge of the miners' union. But at the time the resolution at Springfield was being passed, Green was addressing the Indianapolis convention, throwing the prestige of the AFL behind Lewis, and denouncing the insurgents for the crime of dual unionism. "When a charter of affiliation is granted to an organization by the A. F. of L. . . . ," Green explained to the cheering delegates, "the A. F. of L. is under obligation to support that organization in the exercise of its jurisdictional and autonomous rights."[17] Green was Lewis's trump card at Indianapolis. While Green's actions alone did not account for the demise of the RUMW, his efforts were significant in allowing Lewis to retain control of the union. His behavior—this time on Lewis's behalf— was based upon principles he would uphold against Lewis after 1935.

One aspect of Green's role in squashing the insurgents, for instance, revealed his unflagging commitment to labor unity. John H. Waler, Green's long-time friend and president of the Illinois Federation of Labor, was deeply involved in the RUMW from the beginning. When UMW officials pressured Green to remove him from office because of his complicity in setting up the Springfield convention, Green wrote Walker on March 6, 1930 demanding an explanation. Walker replied with a long letter attacking Lewis and his conduct of union affairs. Green refused to accept this explanation for, as he wrote Walker, "the merits of the controversy" between Lewis and the insurgents was not at issue. The only issue in question was union autonomy and Walker had violated this principle by arranging the convention of a dual union. On March 20 Green demanded the resignation of his friend.[18] Perhaps Lewis never fully appreciated the tenacity with which Green attacked even old chums guilty of undermining union solidarity.

As a result of Green's various efforts in behalf of the UMW, Lewis seemed quite satisfied with Green's leadership of the Federation. As late as October 1931, Lewis called the AFL president "capable and aggressive."[19] Two years later, however, it was apparent that Lewis had grown dissatisfied with Green's conduct of affairs and even began to regret that he had boosted Green into the AFL presidency.[20] By the spring of 1935 Green and Lewis were embroiled in a bitter feud.[21] Between the years 1932 and 1935 the divergent outlooks of the two men had once again come to the force and this time there would be no compromise.

The passage of NIRA Section 7a in June 1933 was the event which created the head-on collision between the leadership styles of Lewis and Green. Both men had lobbied energetically for the insertion of a guarantee of labor's right to organize and yet Green and Lewis held diametrically opposed views as to how Section 7a could be used to benefit organized labor. As we have seen, Green heralded the passage of Section 7a as the dawning of a new era in industrial relations, a promise that government was committed to cooperation between labor and capital. The act revived his hopes that the relations between employers and employees could be established on a basis of morality and mutual respect.

Lewis saw Section 7a differently. To be sure, Lewis frequently resorted to the state in an effort to revitalize the UMW. Unlike Green, who waited for employers and the state to permit the establishment of unions, Lewis recognized that workers had to rely on their collective strength and militancy, not on the Christian spirit of employers and government officials. Only after workers were fully unionized would labor gain real political influence. The "favorable attention" labor leaders received from government and industry, Lewis was fond of explaining, "comes as a result that back of us is organization."[22] Rather than wait for a change of heart among employers and state officials, Lewis put his faith in the economic power of workers themselves.

Green feared the militancy that erupted among rank-and-file mass-production workers with the passage of Section 7a. He believed it would create adverse public opinion and destroy the chances for peaceful cooperation between industry and labor under government supervision. He regarded militancy as a reversion to the barbaric days of industrial relations and believed it could lead only to the moral and economic bankruptcy of the labor movement. Lewis harbored no such moralistic qualms. Indeed, Lewis recognized that worker militancy was his most potent weapon in negotiations with employers and government. He understood that militancy in and of itself could not guarantee success, for an inopportune strike could spell disaster. But he realized that without a militant rank-and-file, a union leader was essentially powerless. Thus Lewis welcomed the upsurge of militancy among coal miners in 1933, and he made frequent use of the strike threat to wring concessions from coal operators and the government. Conversely, Lewis used his ability to restrain the rank-and-file to maintain harmonious relations with President Roosevelt.

John L. Lewis would not allow the obstacles that overcame Green—overcautiousness, moral opposition to militancy, and respect for outmoded jurisdictional boundaries—to prevent him from seizing the opportunity presented by Section 7a and the upsurge of union sentiment among the unorganized. By the summer of 1934, Lewis had resurrected the UMW and was committed to the organization of all mass-production workers. For more than a year, he would attempt to organize them from within the AFL, using various tactics to mobilize the Federation into action. Yet Lewis placed his faith not in the AFL hierarchy, but in the increasingly class-conscious mass-production workers themselves. He was willing to support their militancy, espouse their hopes, and thus present himself as a class-conscious labor leader. He sympathized with the plight of these workers and echoed their contempt for men such as Green who advocated a partnership between labor and capital, telling them that while "labor and capital may be partners in theory, (they) . . . are enemies in fact." As Dubofsky and Van Tine argue, "Lewis caught the gut feelings of auto and rubber workers," and reinforced their determination "to battle their employers."[23]

While Green had suited Lewis's purposes on matters of crucial importance to the UMW when the union was in dire straits, Lewis had little confidence that the moralist Green was capable of conducting successful campaigns in autos, rubber, or steel. Lewis had himself often employed the strategy of cooperation; he had done so in the 1920s and would do so again in the late 1940s and 1950s. Yet Lewis pursued cooperation as an expedient; he was not morally committed to the strategy. Unlike Green, Lewis recognized that the strategy of cooperation was unworkable in the climate of the early New Deal years. Employers were too well organized, too class-conscious, too adamant in their resistance to unions. His experiences in the coal strikes and code negotiations of 1933–1934 convinced him that government officials would begin to play an increasingly important role in labor-capital relations, but he was also quite certain that only a militant, organized army of workers would compel government administrators to support unions in their struggle against management. The times called for a union leader who would pose as a class-warrior and move without hesitation to capitalize on worker unrest and thereby revolutionize not only the labor movement but power relations in the nation as a whole.[24]

Green was not such a labor leader. He did not share Lewis's sense of urgency. He did not believe the AFL was squandering the opportunity presented by Section 7a and labor's uprising. Indeed, he claimed in 1934 and again in 1935 that the AFL was making substantial progress. Certainly he saw the need for further advances, but the situation was not so desperate as to risk the destruction of the AFL and the abandonment of peaceful cooperation. Rather than risk achievements he believed labor had won by supporting the "immoral" militancy of the rank-and-file, Green stuck to his strategy of moral suasion. Green preferred to ask the Roosevelt Administration to live up to its stated ideals of promoting justice and equality rather than face squarely the fact that government in the New Deal years responded favorably to the better organized, more powerful party in any given conflict. The sound, cautious, peaceful policies of the AFL were making progress, Green insisted, and there was no need for alarm. In a speech in September 1934, Green likened the labor movement to a ship in troubled waters:

> Like a vessel sailing upon the high seas, enveloped in a fog so thick and heavy as to be impenetrable, the ship of Trade-Unionism has cut through the

waves of economic adversity along a safe and chartered course. It has not been diverted from the well-marked line of ocean travel by the siren blasts of the opportunist nor has it risked the safety of those on board by a reckless drive into the shoals of experimentation.[25]

Green's caustic reference to the "opportunist" was undoubtedly aimed at Lewis, for by the fall of 1934 Green realized that his former boss, and numerous others, were challenging his ability to lead the labor movement. Green often felt the need to defend his cautious, moralistic leadership style. Yet mere words were not sufficient to appease those who envisioned a more militant labor movement capable of organizing mass-production workers and of wielding tremendous economic and political power. The "siren blasts" of Lewis the class warrior reflected the sentiments of rank-and-file workers who chafed under Green's ineffective leadership.

If Green and Lewis represented two distinct styles of union leadership in the 1930s, craft unionists represented a third. Compared to Green and Lewis, both of whom in their own way sought the organization and advancement of the entire working class, the craft unionists who dominated the Executive Council were Neanderthals completely devoid of social vision. Daniel Tobin of the Teamsters, William Hutcheson of the Carpenters, and their cronies were interested only in the affairs of their own individual unions, which they ran as private businesses, and in maintaining control over the affairs of the Federation. The cause of Christian cooperation or the economic and political possibilities of a massive labor movement held no appeal for them. They safeguarded their interests by an inflexible adherence to the chief weapon at their disposal: the principle of exclusive jurisdiction. On this issue craft unionists refused to compromise, even at the expense of the organization of the unorganized and the unity of the labor movement.

Craft consciousness had been the guiding spirit of the Federation since its inception. Conditioned to think in terms of the skilled craftsman rather than the unskilled factory worker, early AFL leaders viewed craft unionism as the most logical approach to the problem of organization. They were certainly not unaware of the levelling influence of technology upon skill, and in 1888 Gompers had in fact suggested organization into industrial divisions. Nothing came of this proposal, however. Since the skilled worker had taken the lead in organizing, the craft union remained the dominant form of organization, even though jurisdictional lines became blurred by the advances of technology. In their struggle to increase membership, craft unions, if needed, could be quite flexible on the issue of structure. They afforded themselves substantial leeway and room to neuver in order to meet changing conditions. Thus most craft unions represented a curious blend of craft-industrial jurisdictions.[26]

Despite their flexibility, craft unions were woefully inadequate to meet the needs of an industrial working class in the 1930s. As both Green and Lewis recognized, the millions of unskilled and semi-skilled workers could not be parcelled out among the existing craft organizations. The work of an unskilled factory hand did not fit any of the existing jurisdictions. Further, mass-production workers expressed no interest in joining craft unions. They were, in Green's words, "mass minded," and demanded the creation of new and massive unions that would include all workers in a particular industry. Craft unions could not meet this demand. The Federation's compromise, the FLU, was a temporary expedient, one that did not resolve the basic issue. Craft unionists correctly regarded the erection of new industrial unions that would embrace millions of workers and wield tremendous power at AFL conventions as a threat to their continued control of the Federation. They thus put forth jurisdictional claims over handfuls of skilled workers in autos, rubber, and other basic industries to prevent the organization of all workers in each industry and the rise of powerful new unions that would assume control of the AFL.

The intellectual standardbearers of craft union ideology in the 1930s were John P. Frey and Matthew Woll. Frey, who was sixty-four years old in 1935, had been vice-president of the Iron Molders since 1900, a post he would hold until 1950. One historian has described him as "dogmatic, self-important, a snob, given to the *ad hominem* argument, an a big hater. He sincerely believed that skilled workers were better than ordinary workers."[27] Upon the death of Gompers, Frey formed close ties with other craft unionists on the Executive Council, especially Tobin, Hutcheson, and Arthur Wharton of the Machinists. These leaders successfully worked for his election as secretary of the Metal Trades Department in 1927 and president of that body in 1934 so that Frey could watch out for their interests within the Federation while they ran their own unions without interference. Frey was an arch-Republican and anti-New Dealer who was deeply committed to the protection of craft union interests.[28]

Matthew Woll was a relatively young labor leader in 1935, just fifty-five years old, even though he had already served a long tenure as president of the Photo Engravers Union from 1906 to 1929. Although the Photo Engravers had a membership of only a few thousand, Woll became an important figure in the Federation because of his close association with Gompers, and he was in fact considered Gompers' heir apparent. Woll was elected eighth vice-president of the AFL in 1919, thereby becoming a member of the Executive Council. After stepping down as president of the Photo Engravers, Woll played virtually no role in the affairs of any union, devoting most of his time instead to his post as an officer of the Union

Labor Life Insurance Company. Woll was perhaps the most talented Red-baiter in the AFL and, next to Frey, the best versed in craft union traditions.[24]

If Woll and Frey were the chief dogmatists of craft unionism, Hutcheson and Tobin were the premier practitioners. The outrageously obese William Hutcheson was sixty-one years old in 1935 and czar of the Carpenters union from 1919 until 1952. A life-long Republican, he consistently supported conservatives for office and opposed New Deal policies. Under his leadership, the Carpenters were more concerned with protecting their jurisdiction than with recruiting new members. His organizing staff initiated jurisdictional disputes with other unions to increase membership rather than working to enlist nonunion carpenters. Hutcheson ignored the unorganized while claiming jurisdiction whenever another union entered the field. A popular saying among unionists was that "God created the forests and He gave them to Bill Hutcheson." By the 1930s, long after technology had undermined much of the need for skilled carpenters, Hutcheson based his jurisdictional claims on the principle that anything ever made of wood was carpenter's work. Thus Hutcheson was continually at war with machinists, bricklayers, and other unions.[30]

Irish-born Daniel Tobin was sixty years old in 1935 and had been president of the International Brotherhood of Teamsters since 1907. The long-standing tradition of local autonomy prevented Tobin from exercising real power over Teamster locals, and Tobin devoted most of his energies to the activities of the Federation. He served as an Executive Council member from 1907 until his death in 1955, excepting only the period between late 1929 and early 1934. As did Hutcheson, Tobin refused to extend money and organizers for campaigns in the mass-production industries, for he did not want unskilled workers in his organization. He expanded his union by allowing local leaders to compete with other unions for workers already organized, while he battled other craft unions for jurisdictional rights to these workers at the national level.[31]

Tobin and Hutcheson, along with like-minded craft unionists, controlled AFL policy in the 1930s. The combined votes of the Carpenters, Teamsters, Machinists, Electricians, and the various small craft unions that invariably followed the lead of the larger unions on matters of import, represented the overwhelming majority of the convention votes. And before 1934, when the Executive Council was enlarged, only the craft union point of view was voiced in the AFL's high council. Even after it was enlarged, craft unionists retained a firm hold over its affairs.

William Green had far less in common with craft unionists than he did with industrial union advocates. Many craft unionists came from the ranks and represented the interests of urban, skilled workers on the East Coast. Their attitudes and values could hardly be expected to mesh with those of a small-town miner from the Midwest. Even after a decade of living in Washington, D.C., Green adhered to the values of small-town America. And since all of Green's trade union experience had been with an industrial union, he did not share the craft leaders' devotion to exclusive jurisdiction or their prejudice against the unskilled. Even though green had known the principal craft leaders for at least two decades, he was not close friends with any of them. Green was never a member of the inner circle of the Executive Council which largely controlled Federation policies. Since at least 1919, many of the important decisions of the Council had been hashed out at evening poker sessions held during quarterly meetings. Certain presidents of international unions who were not Council members often joined the poker sessions. Hutcheson and Tobin were regular members, but neither as AFL vice-president nor as president was Green ever a member of this elite group.[32] Surely part of the reason for Green's exclusion was personal choice, for Green did not engage in the standard activities of the sessions—smoking, drinking, and gambling—but perhaps an even more important reason was the fact that Green shared neither the close confidence nor the friendship of the craft unionists.

Unlike Green and Lewis, craft union leaders unequivocally dreaded rank-and-file militancy in the 1930s. While Green was ambivalent about the unrest for moral reasons, craft leaders had more secular and concrete reasons for their opposition. On one level, craft unionists believed that the unskilled were unorganizable. On a much deeper level, if somehow the millions of mass-production workers were in fact organized into industrial unions, the hegemony of craft unions in the Federation would be seriously threatened. Rather than squander money or risk the loss of their power, craft union leaders chose to cite union traditions and jurisdictional claims as reasons not to build industrial unions. In the final analysis, craft unionists had everything to lose and nothing to gain from campaigns in mass-production industries.

Despite the overwhelming evidence with which Green, Lewis, and others presented them, craft unionists steadfastly refused to concede that mass-production workers in fact wanted to join unions. This self-serving blindness was perhaps best illustrated when Arthur Wharton of the machinists rose at the 1935 AFL convention to ask, "Who are those people on the outside who want to come in?"[33] Another spokesman for the Machinists declared in August 1936 that the notion that mass-production workers were eager to join industrial unions was "pure bunk"; they would not join any union voluntarily and in fact could not even be driven into one.[34] Similarly, John P. Frey maintained as late as November 1935 that a large number of workers had "no irresistible desire to join a union."[35]

Also unlike Green and Lewis, both of whom had a warm regard for all working people, craft union leaders held a strong prejudice against semi-skilled and unskilled workers. Prejudice against the unskilled was perhaps the most virulent expression of craft consciousness. Tobin articulated the craft union bias against the unskilled when he declared in October 1934 that there were 135,000 Teamster members and that "they are not the rubbish that have lately come into other organizations."[36] Other craft unionists undoubtedly shared these views, but they were seldom as careless as Tobin in expressing them in public.

Craft union leaders preserved their power primarily through the enforcement of the principle of exclusive jurisdiction. Federation charters established the boundaries within which an affiliate could operate. Regardless of whether or not a particular union made an effort to organize all workers within those boundaries, no union was allowed to invade the jurisdiction of another union. Thus even though the Machinists made virtually no effort to organize machinists in the auto industry, the union was within its rights as an AFL affiliate to prevent anyone from organizing rights as an AFL affiliate to prevent anyone from organizing machinists in auto plants. Exclusive jurisdiction could thus be used as a defensive weapon by which unions protected themselves from encroachments by other unions.

Exclusive jurisdiction was also an offensive weapon; it allowed unions to compete against each other for workers at the national level. As craft lines became increasingly blurred, the Federation became a battleground of literally hundreds of jurisdictional squabbles. It was far easier for the Carpenters, Teamsters, and other craft organizations to increase membership by contesting the jurisdictional boundaries of other unions than it was to organize the unorganized within one's own boundaries. Many of the jurisdictional disputes of the 1930s were patently absurd, such as Hutcheson's demand that the Carpenters be allowed to organize aircraft workers since airplanes had once been made of wood. Again, in the fall of 1933, the Iron Workers and the Carpenters battled over which union was to have the work on elevators in the federal buildings then under construction, which to Green's embarrassment delayed completion of the new Labor Department building.[37] Much more serious disputes included the fight over whether the AFL should for the first time in its history charter a union, the Amalgamated Clothing Workers, with the same jurisdiction as one already chartered, the United Garment Workers.[38] The most divisive jurisdictional battle, of course, revolved around whether craftsmen in mass-production industries should be placed in FLUs or turned over to existing craft unions. This last battle involved a great deal more than competition over a few thousand workers; it involved the sanctity of the principle of exclusive jurisdiction itself, the craft unionists' major weapon for self-preservation and growth.

The years 1933–1935 witnessed a growing polarization of views within the AFL between craft-conscious labor officials and those favoring more militant tactics. John L. Lewis, Sidney Hillman, and other champions of industrial unionism made increasingly strident demands that the Federation set aside jurisdictional disputes, pursue a more aggressive strategy, and create a labor movement with real political and economic power. In response, their craft union opponents, who dominated the Executive Council and controlled AFL conventions, banded even more closely together to protect their interests. No one in the AFL, it seemed, was willing to compromise on the grave questions facing organized labor. No one, that is, except William Green. Just as Green intended to mediate between labor and capital, he also sought a basis of accommodation within the labor movement. As he told the Executive Council:

> I would grab at a straw to . . . preserve the solidarity of the American Federation of Labor. It has been my whole policy in life to compose differences, to find a way out of a difference or dispute. I try to do that as President . . . because I fully appreciate in this great voluntary movement we are dealing with men holding different opinions, different views and the real problem . . . is to compose differences, hold men together, because as Mr. Gompers said years ago the Federation is a "rope of sand."[39]

Composing differences between men holding such divergent views as to the future of the labor movement was the greatest challenge of Green's professional career. Yet he lacked the machinery, the leadership ability, and, above all, the values necessary to meet the challenge.

There was little question as to where Green stood on the basic issue of industrial versus craft forms of organization. That he personally continued to believe in industrial unionism in the 1930s was well known. But Green did not crusade for industrial unionism as AFL president, for he sincerely believed that his principal duty was to maintain peace and unity within the labor movement. He continued to hope that the Federation would adopt new forms of organization, but he was unwilling to sacrifice unity to achieve this goal. Moreover, while Green favored the organization of mass-production workers, he did not support militant tactics. Green thus supported Lewis's goal—industrial unionism—while rejecting his means.

Even though a primary function of the AFL presidency was the resolution of disputes between affiliates, Gompers had never established formal machinery to do so. He had relied instead on an informal network of personal relationships that aided him in maintaining relative peace.[40] Green lacked Gompers' network, which had died along with the old man, and Green possessed neither the ability nor the vision to develop his own. Unlike Gompers, Green was never "one of the boys." He kept a formal distance between himself and other Executive Council members, which restricted his ability to resolve disputes amicably and informally.

Failing to develop a personal following, Green relied almost exclusively on formal procedures to maintain harmony. He believed such legalisms guaranteed his own neutrality and assured a fair settlement of grievances, yet those formal procedures actually worked to the advantage of those already in control of Federation policy. At several key junctures during convention debates, craft unionists were able to out-maneuver their industrial union opponents, and Green, in attempt to remain an impartial mediator, unwittingly served the old guard.

An even more serious defect of Green's leadership, one that assured craft union victories, was his mechanistic view of majority rule. The primacy of the majority vote at conventions had always been a cardinal tenet of Green's trade union philosophy. He never questioned whether the majority vote at AFL conventions in fact reflected the majority sentiment of organized workers, let alone the entire working class. According to the AFL's constitution, international unions were allowed one vote for every hundred members. City centrals, state federations, and FLUs were given one vote each regardless of their size, and some were quite large.[41] Thus these latter bodies were denied an adequate voice during conventions and the sentiments of mass-production workers were never a factor in determining policy. Moreover, many unions had unit rules requiring all delegates to vote as a bloc, thus eliminating the view of delegates who may have sympathized with the industrial union outlook.

All in all, Green was a weak, unimaginative, and ineffectual peacemaker within the labor movement. His reluctance to shape policy, his dogmatic adherence to parliamentary rules of order, and his mechanistic view of majority rule—all of which he believed guaranteed his impartiality—functioned to maintain craft union hegemony. Green did not, as some historians claim, bow to the will of craft unionists solely out of respect for their power within the Federation.[42] He was not so crude or self-serving. In this and most instances during his professional career, Green's actions were lofty in purpose, but his leadership was passive at a time when only dynamic leadership could have succeeded.

Green's performance at the 1933 AFL convention revealed how the Federation president, by methodically following parliamentary rules of order, actually undermined efforts to discuss the situation openly and reach a compromise. Several resolutions on the organization of mass-production workers were introduced at the convention, and Green appointed members of both the craft and industrial camps to the committee on resolutions, hoping that committee members might resolve the dispute.

The committee met every day for six days, but rather than rational discussion, the committee sessions were marked by continuous arguing between John L. Lewis and John P. Frey. The committee finally admitted its failure to reach agreement and submitted majority and minority reports to the convention. The majority report embodied the craft union perspective on organizing mass-production workers; it stated that all skilled workers organized into FLUs must be turned over to their appropriate craft unions. The minority report was an extremely cautious statement of the industrial union perspective. It did not call for the establishment of international unions in mass-production industries; it suggested only that skilled workers in FLUs not be transferred to craft unions unless it were "practicable" to do so.

After the reports were read to the convention, Frey, in a deft tactical maneuver, immediately moved that both reports be referred to the Executive Council and that the Council call a conference of all international unions to consider the matter. If successful, this motion would have prevented the one thing craft unionists hoped to avoid: a general convention debate on the issue of jurisdiction, which could only work to their disadvantage. Since Frey's motion was seconded, Green had little choice but to ask for a vote on referral. Several delegates who supported industrial unionism then moved that a full discussion of both reports be allowed, but Green, in strict conformity with parliamentary procedure, told the delegates that the only issue now before the convention was the motion to refer, which carried by a majority vote.[43] Craft unionists had thwarted a general debate on the jurisdictional issue and had thus won the first round against industrial union proponents with the help of Green.

In accordance with the convention vote, Green duly called and convened the conference of international unions, held in Washington, D.C. on January 24 and 25, 1934. On the day before the convention began, nearly one hundred delegates from FLUs assembled in Washington in the hope that they would be able to argue the case for industrial unionism at the conference. They came prepared with concrete suggestions and a willingness to compromise, but since the convention did not specifically invite FLU members to the conference, Green did not allow them to attend.[44] By strictly adhering to the rules, Green had again squelched open and honest discussion of issues.

In his long opening address to the Washington conference, Green impressed upon the union representatives that changes were needed in AFL policies if successful campaigns were to be conducted in the basic industries. Section 7a presented labor with a marvelous chance to organize millions of workers, Green argued, but it also presented the AFL with a challenge. Unless changes were made, "in our organizing movement, in our administrative work . . . ," he warned, the opportunity would be lost forever. Although he stressed the need for flexibility and compromise, he made no specific recommendations, no proposal that moderates on both sides could rally around.[45]

The Washington conference was another victory for craft unionists. Although the committee appointed to examine the majority and minority reports stressed the AFL's dedication to organizing the unorganized, it pointed out that the conference had no authority to alter the principle of exclusive jurisdiction. At the close of the conference Green made another long speech in the course of which he warned that mass-production workers were going to organize "with or without us" and that AFL policy must be flexible enough to organize these workers.[46] Again Green had demonstrated his desire for peace and proven his unwillingness to put forth a viable compromise proposal. According to Daniel Tobin, the result of the Washington conference was that industrial unionism "was most definitely thrown on the junk pile."[47]

The intransigence of craft unionists at the Washington conference, combined with the continuing failure of Green's organizing drives in autos and rubber, fueled the movement for industrial unionism. Between January and October 1934, most of the unions that would later comprise the CIO declared themselves in favor of creating industrial unions in the mass-production industries. No less than twelve resolutions expressing industrial union sentiment were introduced at the 1934 AFL convention at San Francisco. From the Boilermakers and the Metal Trades Department came resolutions reasserting the gospel of exclusive jurisdiction and prohibiting the inclusion of skilled workers in FLUs.[48]

Green again placed members of both blocs on the committee on resolutions. Quite unexpectedly, the committee was able to agree on a single report. Perhaps Green's strategy had paid off. Perhaps by forcing industrial and craft proponents to sit down and hash out their differences, common ground could be reached. The report stated, in bare outline, the compromise Green had been intimating all along. It stated that the AFL should formulate policies which would "fully protect" the jurisdictional rights of all craft unions, but that the Executive Council should charter new unions in the automobile, cement, and aluminum industries and in "such other mass-production and miscellaneous industries" as the Council believed necessary. The committee's report passed by unanimous vote of the entire convention.[49]

Had craft unionists, still securely in control of AFL policy, voluntarily compromised on the issue of exclusive jurisdiction in order to maintain peace within the labor movement and facilitate the organization of the unorganized? Outside observers believed they had done just that. Louis Stark, labor correspondent for the *New York Times,* regarded the decision as an unqualified victory for industrial unionism; craft unions were to be protected "in their own sphere:" but all workers in mass-production industries would be organized into industrial unions.[50] The historian Charles Beard thought the AFL had taken "certain steps away from historic craft unionism in the direction of organizing workers in great industries to 'vertical unions.' "[51]

Green himself was ecstatic. The unanimous acceptance of the committee's report, he told delegates, was a victory for "calm and careful deliberation. Democracy has been in action, we have seen it here, every question adopted has been adopted in accordance with democratic rule and democratic principles." He expressed his joy over "that wonderful, historic decision," that allowed the Federation to pursue a "flexible policy" and organize mass-production workers "as solid units into this great Organized Labor Movement."[52]

Green was not alone among labor officials to regard the San Francisco decision as a momentous victory for industrial unionism. Industrial union advocates also heralded the passage of the committee's report. They were further inspired by the convention resolution to enlarge the Executive Council from eleven to eighteen members and the election of three members of their camp, John L. Lewis, David Dubinsky of the ILGWU, and George Berry of the Printing Pressmen, to the enlarged Council. Although craft unionists still controlled the Council, Lewis told the convention that he had faith the Council would interpret and implement the report of the committee as it was intended.[53]

The 1934 convention seemed to vindicate Green's approach to peacemaking. The contending forces apparently had reached a compromise through rational discourse. Craft unionists apparently had agreed to forego their selfish claims in mass-production industries. Indeed, many craft leaders complained that Frey, who chaired the committee on resolutions, had given up too much. Frey wrote a friend that presidents of some of the international unions had criticized him "on the ground that I had given away a great deal more than I had authority to do. . . . "[54] The convention revived industrial union advocates' faith in the ability of the Federation to adapt and renewed their confidence in Green's leadership abilities. Lewis had nominated Green for the AFL presidency every year since 1925, but in 1934 his speech was more glowing than ever. He spoke of Green's "unselfish devotion" to labor and called Green "a champion of democracy" and "a great leader of labor."[55] Green had every reason to rejoice that democracy, reason, and Christian brotherhood had triumphed.

Green's jubilation proved short-lived, for it soon became evident that among craft unionists self-interest continued to be a much more powerful motivation than Christian brotherhood. The 1935 sessions of the enlarged Executive Council revealed wide disagreements over the proper interpretation of the San Francisco convention report. The report did not state precisely whether all workers in mass-production industries were to be placed in new industrial unions or segregated among the crafts, and craft unionists continued to demand that Green refrain from organizing skilled workers into FLUs. And as we have seen, when the council finally issued charters to auto and rubber workers, craft unionists made certain the charters did not include jurisdictional rights to skilled workers.

The feeling of betrayal among the industrial union advocates was keen. As early as May 1935, Louis Stark reported rumors that Lewis would bold the AFL and erect a rival federation of industrial unions if craft unionists continued to obstruct the organization of the unorganized.[56] In June Sidney Hillman of the Amalgamated Clothing Workers, Francis Gorman of the United Textile Workers, and Emile Rieve of the Hosiery Workers all spoke before the Tamiment Economic and Social Institute, expressing their displeasure with Federation policies and calling for the creation of industrial unions.[57] The following month Frey confided to a friend that "There are hotel lobby rumors that unless they (industrial union advocates) can have their way we may be faced with a secession movement."[58]

Even as rumors of secession spread in labor circles, Green did nothing. He continued to espouse the ideal of unity in the labor movement, but he did absolutely nothing to promote it. During August he exacerbated tensions by cramming restricted charters down the throats of auto and rubber workers, even though the charters did not jibe with his own interpretation of the 1934 convention report. His acceptance of a limited role for the AFL presidency tied his hands, left him unable to put forth and campaign for a binding compromise, and he braced himself for the showdown he knew would come at the 1935 convention.

By October 1935, the time of the Atlantic City convention, AFL organizing drives were at a standstill. Outside of coal and the needle trades, organized labor had few concrete victories in any industry in the first three years of the New Deal. The AFL's membership stood at just over three million, a smaller proportion of the nonfarm labor force than in 1922. More company unions than independent unions had been established under Section 7a and worker militancy had all but disappeared.[59]

Green nevertheless believed the Federation was making significant progress. In his Labor Day speech of 1935, he pointed to passage of the Wagner Act, the Guffey Coal Act, and the Social Security Act as symbols of labor's growing influence in national affairs. "In addition to achievements in the legislative field," Green continued, "the organized labor movement has increased its strength in the economic field during the past year. The membership of unions has grown and our extension into mass-production industries steadily increases."[60] Green, the cautious liberal, saw no need for alarm in the fall of 1935. The Wagner Act provided a much more adequate expression of labor's right to organize than did Section 7a and, although it had not been tested by the judiciary, it revived Green's hopes for organizing work under the auspices of the federal government. Green was also relieved that the worker militancy of 1933–1934 had subsided, thus allowing him to reassert labor's goal of peaceful cooperation without fear of contradiction from the rank-and-file. Finally, the movement for industrial unionism was making progress within the Federation. The support for industrial unionism had grown tremendously between 1933 and 1935, and there was reason to hope that by 1936 or 1937, as the mass-production unions grew and as other unions became convinced of its necessity, the movement would prevail.

John L. Lewis and other industrial union advocates did not share Green's optimism. Contrary to their interpretation of the San Francisco decision, restricted charters had been issued in autos and rubber, and the steel drive had yet to begin. Over two years of organizing work had not yielded a single contract between the AFL and a major mass-production employer. Further, the most potent weapon in any campaign—worker militancy—was withering away in the face of Federation inactivity. Proponents of industrial unionism recognized that immediate and even drastic action was necessary to rescue the labor movement from the selfish interests of craft and unionists.

Craft unionists also understood the importance of the 1935 AFL convention. As early as March, John P. Frey predicted a confrontation between the industrial and craft blocs at Atlantic City. "There must be a showdown," Frey wrote to an English friend, "for it is becoming intolerable to have some International Unions determined that other International Unions change their form of organization against their desire."[61] Craft union leaders were prepared to settle the controversy once and for all while they still maintained a majority of convention votes.

That Green was unaware of the seriousness of the dispute could be seen in his opening remarks to the 1935 convention. He tried to impress upon delegates his belief that the Federation was a cautious yet liberal organization that could adapt to new situations, and he cited the 1932 convention's resolution in favor of unemployment insurance as evidence. "There are those who say that the American Federation of Labor—and I mean our enemies—occupies a rigid, static position. That is untrue. The American Federation of Labor has always followed a flexible policy, adjusting itself to the legislative, economic and social changes which have come about in a changing world. Our organization could not serve the workers or the social order unless it responded to facts and faced bravely and courageously the realities of life."[62] Having reminded delegates that the AFL was in fact capable of progressive change, Green resumed his role as impartial chairman at the convention. Again he refused to throw the prestige of his office behind a viable compromise.

Twenty-two resolutions in favor of industrial unionism were introduced at the convention and, as in 1933, the committee on resolutions could not reach agreement on them, finally submitting majority and minority reports to the convention. Of the fifteen committee members, nine, including Chairman Woll, endorsed the majority report, which called for nonconcurrence with the industrial union resolutions. The minority report, signed by the other six members of the committee, directed the Executive Council to initiate aggressive organizing drives in unorganized industries, draft unrestricted charters for international unions in mass-production industries, and issue similar charters to independent and company-dominated unions that wanted to affiliate with the AFL.[63]

After a convention debate that raged for seven hours, the convention rejected the minority report by a roll call vote of 18,024 to 10,933. Approximately thirty-eight percent of the roll call vote was cast in favor of the report, and included in this percentage were the votes of twenty-one of the Federation's ninety-four international unions. Two unions divided their votes and eleven abstained from voting.[64]

On the final day of the convention, after most of the delegates had gone home, debate resumed on the structural issue. As a delegate from the Rubber Workers launched into his arguments in favor of an industrial union charter for the rubber industry, William Hutcheson interrupted him and called for a point of order, asserting that the delegate was reopening an issue that had already been settled. Green stated that he was "inclined to support the point of order," which prompted Lewis to take the floor.[65] Lewis concluded his speech with a verbal attack on Hutcheson, arguing that raising points of order on minor delegates was "rather small potatoes." When Hutcheson defended himself by assailing Lewis's character, Lewis strode down the aisle to where Hutcheson was seated and punched him in the face. No act could have better symbolized Lewis's calculated resolve to break with the craft unionists.[66] According to at least one account, Green turned to Lewis after the incident and said, "You shouldn't have done that, John." "But he called me a dirty name," replied Lewis, whereupon Green apologized and said, "Oh, I didn't know that."[67] It is unlikely that Green and Lewis ever exchanged such words, but the story does symbolize the dilemma of the AFL president who wanted so desperately to maintain peace but was unwilling to take the positive steps necessary to do so.

As in previous years, Lewis again nominated Green for reelection. In his speech of acceptance, Green made some comments pertinent to the internal conflict. "This is an historic convention. I think I can declare that no more historic convention of the American Federation of Labor was ever held. During its deliberations . . . we have been torn by conflicting emotions; we realize, after all, that we have come through with flying colors and our ranks indissoluble and intact. . . . So it becomes our duty now to forget. The debate is over. The problems have been solved. A settlement has been made, and from this convention we must go out united."[68] Less than three weeks later the Committee for Industrial Organization was formed.

VI

Anti-Insurgent Crusader:
1935–1941

O N NOVEMBER 9, 1936, eleven high-ranking labor officials from eight unions gathered at UMW headquarters in Washington, D.C. and created a permanent Committee for Industrial Organization. The CIO named John L. Lewis as president, Charles P. Howard of the Typographers as secretary, and John Brophy, a former foe of Lewis in the UMW, as director. The ILGWU, UMW, and the Amalgamated Clothing Workers (ACW) each pledged $5,000 to enable the organization to begin activities. According to the statement of purposes issued one week after the meeting, the CIO was formed to encourage the organization of mass-production workers along industrial lines and "bring them under the banner and in affiliation with the American Federation of Labor."[1]

The CIO originally presented itself as a pressure group working for progressive change within the AFL. As such, it was neither novel nor illegal. On several previous occasions affiliates had banded together to achieve a purpose at odds with official AFL policy.[2] Yet the official statement of purpose did not tell the whole story of the CIO's formation. Most CIO founders undoubtedly viewed the new organization solely as a means to influence AFL policy, but John L. Lewis had a grander vision, and as Dubofsky and Van Tine have written, "the CIO, at birth, was Lewis."[3] Unlike the other CIO founders, Lewis exhibited little concern with the legality of the CIO in the eyes of AFL officials, nor did he care a great deal about the unity of the labor movement. From 1935 onward, Lewis remained steadfast in his purpose to make organized labor a vital political and economic force with national clout and, at the same time, to become the most powerful individual in the revitalized labor movement. Other CIO members may not have been completely aware of it at first, but Lewis was fully prepared to sever the ties with the AFL to achieve his goals. Through the successful organization of millions of mass-production workers, Lewis hoped to force craft unionists either to accept loss of control over the Federation affairs or maintain control by expelling the CIO unions and obliging Lewis to create an independent federation of industrial unions with a larger membership than the AFL. "In either case," Dubofsky and Van Tine concluded, "Lewis would become the dominant power in the national labor movement, a leader whose massive union army would guarantee him unprecedented political and economic influence."[4]

Eleven years had elapsed since Green served as Lewis's lieutenant in the UMW. Even though he had willingly deferred to Lewis's more forceful personality as UMW secretary-treasurer and, to some extent, as AFL president, green believed that in those eleven years he had established himself as a labor leader in his own right. He had set the AFL on a course of Christian cooperation, had overseen the partial abandonment of voluntarism, and despite vast differences of opinion over politics and organizing strategy, had maintained the unity of the labor movement. And from his perspective, the AFL had made great strides under the New Deal, growing from a membership of 2.3 million in 1933 to 3.2 million in 1935.[5] He believed his style of cooperative leadership was largely responsible for the passage of the Wagner Act. He was convinced that during his tenure the AFL was progressing steadily and he never doubted that, given time, the Federation would adopt policies that would make possible the organization of mass-production workers.

It was because Green understood Lewis's intentions that he recoiled in horror to the formation of the CIO. The CIO, as Green perceived it, was a Lewis plot to foist his own brand of union leadership on the entire labor movement and also undermine the power and prestige of the AFL president. Lewis had outmaneuvered Green to capture the UMW presidency in 1919–1920, and now he was making a bid to supersede Green as the leader of all organized workers. Lewis had thrown down the gauntlet and forced Green into a personal contest for control of the labor movement. The stakes were high, for if Green lost the contest, he stood to lose his prestigious position and, even more unthinkable, the future of the labor movement would be left in the hands of the militant and opportunistic Lewis and progress toward the Christian cooperative ideal would be halted.

Another factor shaping Green's reaction to the CIO was the almost mystical qualities he attached to labor unity. For Green, labor unity rested not so much on economic necessity or a sound institutional framework, but on spiritual and fraternal bonds. In an essay written soon after the 1935 AFL convention, Green warned Lewis and the industrial union bloc that nothing posed a greater threat to brotherhood than "internal strife and personal gain." Even if Lewis and the others successfully organized workers in the basic industries, labor stood to lose if the fraternal bonds were severed in the process. "For what will it profit labor to gain power and material advantages if it loses the spirit of fraternity which sees men as brothers and gives itself in their service?"[6] Locked in a power struggle of cataclysmic importance, Green determined to assert his personal authority by disciplining Lewis and preserving labor unity.

The formation of the CIO, however, did not immediately transform Green from a peacemaker to a self-righteous and vindictive anti-insurgent crusader. Indeed, until May 1936 Green sought to placate rather than punish the rebels, hoping to convince them of the value of a united labor movement. He directed most of his appeals at Lewis. Thus when he mailed identical letters of warning to each CIO member on November 23, 1935, he couched his message in terms of the UMW's internal practices and had Lewis's letter hand-delivered so that the UMW president would receive his copy before anyone else. Contrary to the opinion of Dubofsky and Van Tine, Green's letter of November 23 did not contain "dire warnings and exaggerated allegations," and he did not accuse committee members of dual unionism.[7] Green simply told them the truth—that craft union leaders would press for disciplinary action. "Some officers of National and International Unions . . . regard separate movements formed within the main structure as dual in character and as decidedly menacing to its success and welfare." Green even hinted that he believed the CIO's cause was a noble one, but he reminded its founders that all AFL members had an obligation to comply with decisions arrived at by the majority at conventions. "Those who disagree with the action of the majority are accorded the right to urge the acceptance of their point of view at succeeding Conventions."[8]

Green's missive contained nothing that CIO officials did not already know, and he certainly did not intend it to worsen relations with the industrial union bloc. It was Lewis, acting without the consent of other CIO members, who took the second step toward disunity when he responded to Green in a one-sentence telegram: "Effective this date (November 23), I resign as vice president of the American Federation of Labor."[9] This bold move put Lewis and the CIO at the center of national attention for five consecutive days, and it became increasingly obvious to Green and the AFL old guard that Lewis was indeed prepared to break with the AFL and establish a rival federation. In the words of economist Walter Galenson, Lewis "used his resignation as a means of dramatizing the split and of driving a further wedge between the AFL and the CIO."[10]

The CIO did not send an official response to Green's November 23 letter of warning. Instead, six committee members individually wrote to Green, most of them arguing that the CIO's intent was to strengthen, not weaken, the AFL. Charles P. Howard, in a typical reply, assured Green that the CIO did not intend to establish any form of dual unionism. "Quite the contrary is true," Howard wrote. "We seek to alter a policy that invites such dual organization."[11] It is interesting to note that while all responses disavowed dual unionism and upheld the legality of CIO actions, no one commented on Green's warning that craft unionists would not tolerate a permanent organization within the AFL dedicated to putting into effect a defeated minority report.

Dual union disclaimers did not appease Green. He understood that Lewis controlled the CIO, and he also knew that by early December 1935 Lewis was devising a strategy to organize mass-production workers. And Lewis's December 7 letter to Green showed his willingness to make the CIO a personal battle between himself and Green. Arguing that it was "bruited about" that Green personally sympathized with industrial unionism, Lewis told Green that he would be much happier and of greater service to workers were he to resign the AFL presidency and join the CIO. Privately favoring industrial unionism while officially opposing it made him vulnerable to criticism, Lewis told Green, and craft unionists might demand more than perfunctory support of their position. Why not "return to your father's house?" Lewis asked. "You will be welcome."[12]

Lewis's taunt infuriated Green. Not only was Lewis flirting with disunity, but he also had the arrogance to suggest that the Federation president join him in his disruptive activity. "I am governed by the laws of the American Federation of Labor," Green indignantly replied to Lewis. "The obligation I assumed when I became a member of organized labor and the responsible position I now hold require me to carry out policies adopted at annual conventions of the American Federation of Labor." And as if to make clear that he accepted Lewis's challenge to his authority, Green added, "This I will do at any cost."[13]

By the time the Executive Council met in session at Miami, Florida in January 1936, the old guard faced not simply a group disseminating propaganda, but a permanent organizing committee preparing drives and succoring support among workers in the auto, rubber, steel, radio, lumber, gas, and coke industries. No longer was the issue that of tolerating propaganda for industrial unionism, but what actions to take against a massive insurgent movement acting in direct violation of a convention decision. With Lewis absent, several members of the Council—William Hutcheson, Thomas Richert of the Garment Workers, Arthur Wharton of the Machinists, and Harry Bates of the Bricklayers—pressed for the immediate suspension of unions affiliated with the CIO.[14] Their hostility proved that Green's original warning was not an exaggeration. Like Lewis, these craft union leaders were not concerned with legal technicalities. They hoped to use the formation of the CIO as an excuse to expel the industrial union bloc.

Green soothed their rage by counseling peace and moderation. The AFL constitution conferred no authority on the Executive Council to suspend unions, he argued correctly, adding that the Council would find it difficult to instill a proper regard for Federation law and procedure among CIO adherents if the Council itself violated the law in an effort to punish them. "We are trying to conciliate and placate," Green told the hardliners.[15] Largely because of Green's coaxing, the Council decided not to suspend the CIO unions. Instead, it issued a statement calling for the immediate dissolution of the CIO, which it branded as "a challenge to the supremacy of the American Federation of Labor and . . . ultimately . . . dual in purpose and character."[16] The Council then appointed a committee, headed by George M. Harrison of the Railway Clerks, to meet with the CIO and discuss the Council's position. For the time being, Green had blunted the full force of the Council's rage.

Several events took place between the January and May 1936 Council sessions, however, that led Green the peacemaker to join with the hardliners and launch an aggressive and vindictive crusade to destroy Lewis and the CIO. The first event was the humiliation Green received at the 1936 UMW convention, which opened on January 28 in Washington, D.C. If the convention was a contest of personalities between Green and Lewis, it was certainly not an even match. Lewis, on his own turf, whipped the 1,800 delegates into a frenzy as he detailed the staggering advances the UMW had made in the past few years. Lewis was at his oratorical best when he brought up the issue of the CIO and the Council's demand that the CIO disband. At one point in his speech he howled that "all the members of the Executive Council of the American Federation of Labor will be wearing asbestos suits in hell before the committee (CIO) is dissolved."[17]

Needless to say, Lewis had created a hostile audience for Green, who addressed the delegates on the last day of the convention to argue his case against the CIO. For ninety minutes, Green bared his soul to his beloved union in an uncharacteristically candid discussion of the issues as he saw them. He described the inherent weakness of his office, telling delegates that while he had no authority to coerce affiliates, he was still duty bound "to find a basis of accommodation, to harmonize conflicting opinions." He assured them he was pressing for organization along industrial lines, and admitted that when he did, he was opposing "men who have a proprietary interest in the American Federation of Labor." Nevertheless, he argued, progress toward industrial organization was being made through the proper channels.

The CIO was wrong in principle, he continued, because it was not proper for a minority to organize after it had been defeated. All loyal union members "ought to be willing to abide by the decisions reached by the conventions in which we participate." If unionists could not do so, they had proven themselves incapable of self-government, for "self-government means the subordination of the opinion of myself and yourself to the will of the majority."

In his concluding remarks, Green warned delegates what they could expect if his peace efforts failed and Lewis established a rival federation. "Remain at home, for if you go out there will be but one result: The American Federation of Labor will remain supreme. It is so firmly established in our institutional life that storms from within and attacks from without can never move it from the solid foundations upon which it rests."[18]

When Green resumed his seat, Lewis called on delegates who wanted compliance with the Executive Council's dissolution order. Only two delegates stood up. Lewis then rephrased the question. Only one delegate rose. When Lewis called on those who would continue to support the CIO, delegates rose en masse and applauded. "President Green," said Lewis, "you have received the answer of the United Mine Workers of America to your ultimatum."[19] Heywood Broun, the newspaper columnist, aptly commented that Lewis had "knocked out William Green in precisely three minutes."[20]

Lewis had humbled Green before his own union. Green insisted, however, that he did not feel humiliated. He wrote a friend that despite being "fully conscious of the stage setting and of the psychological condition" Lewis had created, "I came away feeling quite satisfied with the results of my attendance at the meeting."[21] Yet Green was worried by the fact that Lewis's performance had further incensed craft union leaders and made peace in the AFL more difficult to maintain. He discussed his predicament in a letter to James Maloney, president of the Glass Bottle Blowers Association:

> I am doing all I can, going even beyond the limit, to maintain the solidarity of the American Federation of Labor. I am appealing to those who formed this organization . . . to accept the decision of the Atlantic City Convention and to adhere to the policies, rules and procedure of the American Federation of Labor. I know, however, from the sentiment which has been repeatedly expressed, not only by members of the Executive Council, but by officers and representatives of the International Unions . . . that an organization functioning in direct opposition to the policies of conventions of the AFL . . . will not be tolerated.[22]

Maintaining peace would prove even more difficult after the CIO's takeover of steel industry organizing. At its January 1936 session the

Executive Council instructed Green to formulate yet another plan to organize the steel industry. But the CIO countered this move before Green had a chance to canvass opinion among AFL leaders. On February 22, Lewis and Howard wrote the AFL president and promised to contribute $500,000 to a steel campaign if certain conditions were met. First, organization had to be along industrial lines. A joint campaign without a waiver of jurisdiction would be useless, they wrote, and "We therefore require assurance that all steel workers organized will be granted the permanent right to remain united in one industrial union." Second, AFL unions must contribute another $1 million to the campaign fund. And third, "a responsible and energetic person" must be placed in charge of the drive.[23] This last condition presumably meant that CIO officials did not want Green or an AA official to conduct the campaign.

Lewis's proposal suggested a new departure in organizing technique. Whereas the AFL in the campaigns of 1933–1935 depended to a great extent on local labor bodies and cost only a few thousand dollars, Lewis envisioned a massive, centralized effort costing millions. The actual organization of the steel industry would prove that even Lewis's estimate of $1.5 million was conservative. Nevertheless, Lewis was prepared to face the realities of organizing a basic industry.

As Lewis expected, the AFL balked at his proposal. Executive Council members wrote Green expressing doubt that the CIO unions could muster the $500,000 or that AFL unions could raise $1 million. Others objected to the industrial union requirement. Still others, including Daniel Tobin of the Teamsters, claimed "There isn't a chance in the world at this time to organize the steel workers."[24] And several advised Green not to respond to the CIO at all, fearing that any response might be construed as tacit recognition of the rebels.[25]

On March 2, 1936, Green announced his plan to organize steel, and estimated that "preliminary needs" would cost $750,000. He canvassed 110 unions, including those affiliated with the CIO, but received only 46 responses. The CIO unions did not respond; Twenty-nine unions could give no answer before referring the matter to the union's executive board or convention; and twelve declared their unwillingness or inability to contribute. Only five unions responded favorably, yet even they could pledge a total of only $8,625 and the services of four or five organizers.[26] Once again, the Federation had demonstrated its indecisiveness toward the organization of mass-production workers.

Anxious to get a steel drive underway, Lewis wrote AA President Michael Tighe on April 15 offering $500,000 to initiate a campaign run jointly by the AA and the CIO. At the AA convention, which began April 28, many locals urged acceptance of the CIO's offer. But Tighe wavered. He feared aligning himself with the rebel movement because such a step would threaten his position within the AFL and, even worse, meant relinquishing much of his authority to Lewis. In the hope that the AFL would present a viable counter offer, the AA sent its secretary, Louis Leonard, to visit Green at his home in Coshocton. Without the backing of AFL unions, however, the best Green could offer was thirty-five organizers and an undetermined amount of money. The "confusion" created by the CIO, Green told Leonard, was responsible for his inability to state an exact figure.[27]

Out of desperation, Leonard arranged an appointment with John L. Lewis on June 3 in Washington, D.C. At this meeting, as Leonard later told his executive board, "Lewis . . . made it very plain that the Committee for Industrial Organization had practically decided to begin a campaign of organization . . . whether they had the cooperation of the Amalgamated Association or not." The next day AA officials accepted Lewis's demands, affiliated with the CIO, and agreed to serve as an administrative unit in the Steel Workers Organizing Committee (SWOC).[28] Lewis's victory was complete. He secured complete control over the steel drive and the legitimacy conferred by the AA's charter. He had also, once again, publicly humiliated Green.

The day after the June 4 agreement, an outraged Green told reporters that the CIO's steel campaign would probably fail and, with an air of condescension, added that he and the Executive Council would therefore watch the drive with interest.[29] Lewis feigned disbelief. "It is inconceivable," Lewis wrote "Dear Bill" on June 6, "that you intend doing what your statement implies, i.e. to sit with the women, under an awning on the hilltop, while the steelworkers in the valley struggle in the dust and agony of industrial warfare."[30] This, too, hurt Green, who was always sensitive to personal criticism, especially when it questioned his manhood. More important, the seizure of the AA offered Green positive proof that the CIO intended to function as a dual organizing committee within the AFL.

A third transforming event occurred on April 2, 1936, when the CIO announced the formation of Labor's Non-Partisan League (LNPL) to rally labor support for Roosevelt's reelection. Even though a few less orthodox AFL leaders such as George Berry of the Printing Pressmen supported the League, Green denounced it was a "nucleus for a political organization" to gain the presidency of John L. Lewis. Less than three weeks after the League's formation, Green informed AFL members that LNPL was a CIO attack on the Federation's nonpartisan political policy. In order to "avoid division even in the pursuit of its political policies," the AFL had to maintain a "strict and close" adherence to nonpartisanship.[31] When George Berry asked Green to join the League, Green refused, saying that he intended "in the future as in the past to subscribe to the non-partisan political policy of the American Federation of Labor."[32]

The May session of the Executive Council marked Green's complete conversion to the hardline stance in regard to the CIO. The CIO takeover of the AA and the formation of LNPL had convinced Green that the unity of the labor movement was impossible as long as the CIO existed. "Can the American Federation of Labor sit still and allow a rival organization to function within it?" he asked Council members. Without waiting for an answer he declared that it could not "because either we will be destroyed or they will be." We cannot tolerate a "divided house." We must inform the rebels that "you are dual unionists and must either sever your relations with CIO or with AFL." And with a fierce resolve he had never exhibited when dealing with anti-union employers, he concluded by bellowing "We cannot shirk our duty."[33]

Green then sought the legal advice of Charlton Ogburn, general counsel of the AFL, on the possibility of suspending or expelling the CIO unions. In an incredible display of legal gymnastics, Ogburn assured Green that the Executive Council did have the power to hold formal hearings, consider evidence, and decide on suspension. Ogburn's opinion, of course, completely ignored the constitutional stipulations (of which Green was fully aware) that the Council could suspend a union only if the union failed to pay per capita taxes and could expel a union only by two-thirds vote of the convention. Philip Taft, the principal historian of the AFL, considers Ogburn's interpretation "pernicious," "a perversion," and "careless advice given by one who knew little of the customs and history of the A. F. of L."[34] Yet Ogburn had told Green what he wanted to hear, and with this charade of legality, Green began to move against the CIO.

Why was Green, an impeccably moral man, willing to resort to obviously illegal means to subdue Lewis and the CIO? On a basic administrative level, there was nothing exceptional about Green's actions. No union leader, including those in the CIO, dared tolerate a powerful insurgent movement within his organization. As Philip Taft has written, "most unions explicitly prohibit the existence of factions, cliques, or political parties organized to discuss union business outside official meetings. . . . [35] The illegitimacy of organized opposition was mouthed not only by incumbents seeking to maintain their tenure, but also was a commonly held belief among the rank-and-file. Thus Green was quite correct when he told the National Press Club in July 1936 that no CIO union would "tolerate for a single moment" an organized opposition "which constitutes a challenge to the supremacy of the authority of their national unions."[36]

Among CIO leaders, no one was more ruthless in his opposition to insurgents than John L. Lewis who, in the 1920's, crushed several threats to his dominance. As UMW secretary-treasurer and later as AFL president, Green had joined hands with Lewis to quell insurgency. We have seen how Green gladly assisted Lewis in 1930 to put down the RUMW. And no one ever accused Lewis of pursuing an overly legalistic approach to international dissent. Lewis destroyed his opposition in the UMW by any means possible.[37]

Even though the AFL was a federation and not a union, the illegitimacy of organized opposition rang as true in the AFL as it did in individual unions. If the Federation was to survive and prosper in a hostile environment, it could not afford to tolerate a large scale insurgent movement that proposed to unseat the existing power structure and radically alter organizational policy. As president, Green was always willing to assist individual unions when combatting opposition movements, especially Communist ones. More to the point, Green's takeover of the independent Workers' Education Bureau and his condemnation of Brookwood Labor College in the 1920s showed that he, too, firmly rejected the legitimacy of organized opposition within the AFL. The illegitimacy of organized opposition provided craft unionists with adequate justification to move against the CIO, using any means at their disposal.

Green, however, was never one to justify his actions on mundane grounds. he sought a moral rationale for combatting insurgents and believed he found one in the concept of majority rule. "No great institution can live if it is to be governed by a majority or by fractions, by those who disagree, individually or collectively, with a majority decision or majority rule," Green declared. By subverting the will of the majority, the CIO represented the rule of "force, the law of the jungle, the survival of the fittest."[38] Yet Green chose to interpret majority rule in the narrowest possible sense—conforming to the decisions of the Executive Council and conventions. As the crisis deepened, Green foolishly insisted that the only issue involved in the CIO crisis was that of majority versus minority rule.

To the extent that convention votes and Council decisions were representative of AFL sentiment, which is debatable, the Federation did adhere to democratic practices. but in a much larger sense, the AFL represented the autocracy of craft unions over the majority of American workers, who possessed little or no skill and were not union members. In such a setting, democratic procedure could easily become a tool by which craft unionists maintained their hegemony over the labor movement and thwarted the rights and ambitions of millions of workers. John L. Lewis understood the dilemma: as long as craft unionists retained control of the Federation, mass-production workers would never be organized along industrial lines; and craft unionists would continue to control the AFL until mass-production workers were organized industrially. Until organized labor became a movement that truly represented American workers, democratic procedure served as a mask for the selfish interests of the minority of skilled workers.

Moreover, in his crusade to uphold his narrow interpretation of majority rule, Green ran roughshod over the other guiding principle of the AFL: union autonomy. If democratic procedure is a necessary basis for any voluntary organization, so are the protection of minority rights and the proper observance of law and procedure. By his willingness to pervert the AFL constitution to punish Lewis and the rebels, Green undermined his moral rationale. Green's crusade against the CIO thus can be best understood as the conditioned response of a labor official to an insurgent movement expressed in terms of high ideals that had little basis in reality.

Green and the Executive Council outlined their plan of attack in conformity with Ogburn's advice. They reactivated the Harrison committee, which still had not met with the CIO, and gave the rebels a final chance to dissolve. If the rebels refused, the Council would notify the CIO unions of the charges against them, and then conduct formal hearings that would result in suspension. The Harrison committee met with CIO officials for two hours on May 19, 1936. Harrison admitted that he had no authority to negotiate, only to insist upon the CIO's dissolution. This, of course, Lewis and the others were unwilling to do. But the Council now had the answer it sought, and Green was instructed to proceed with the process of suspension.[39]

On June 20 Green summoned each CIO official to appear individually before an emergency session of the Executive Council to be held from July 8 to July 15.[40] Without exception, CIO officials spurned the summonses. Evidently, they found it difficult to believe that the Council would carry through with its threat of suspension. Despite the conspicuous absence of the accused, the "trial" of the CIO unions was set to proceed as scheduled with Green leading the cheers for suspension. Three letters from Ogburn, Dated July 8, 9, and 13, however, rained on Green's parade. Ogburn warned Green that his summons of June 20 did not establish the legal framework for suspension. Green must provide the accused unions with details of the charges and possible penalties in advance of the hearings. If he failed to do so, Ogburn wrote, the CIO unions could challenge the suspensions in court and win.[41]

Ogburn's letters jolted Council members, and at the July session for the first time there was widespread uncertainty as to how to proceed against the CIO. Many of those who had urged suspension in January now expressed fears of the possible legal ramifications. Green was taken aback, too, but he continued to press for ejection. Even if the CIO had its day in court, he argued, the AFL should suspend the CIO unions.[42] In the end Council agreed to begin the suspension process all over again, this time with greater regard for "legality." On July 16, Green "invited" the CIO union heads to appear before the Council on August 3, 1936. He included in his letters a copy of the charges and a description of the procedure to be followed at the hearings.[43]

John P. Frey drafted the formal charges agreed upon by the Council at the July session. He named twelve unions in his brief: the ACW, UMW, ILGWU, AA, the Textile Workers, the Mine, Mill and Smelter Workers, the Hatters, the Flat Glass Workers, the Oil Workers, the Typographical Union, the Auto Workers, and the Rubber Workers.[44] Frey accused each of these unions of dual unionism, "fomenting insurrection," "rebellion" against the 1935 AFL convention decision, and violation of its AFL charter. George Harrison of the Railway Clerks was the sole Council member to question the charges. He analyze each one, pointed out the lack of evidence to substantiate them, and argued that whether or not the charges were true, the Council had no authority to suspend a union. Green, in turn, felt compelled to counter Harrison's objections.[45]

Upon receipt of Green's letter of July 16 detailing these charges, CIO leaders defended themselves on legal and moral grounds. Suspension would be a breach of the AFL constitution, an illegal device to get around the requirement of a two-thirds convention majority for expulsion. They also attacked the character of the "heads of certain craft unions" who exercised "dead-hand control of the Federation" and smugly refused to meet the needs of the unorganized. In a stinging moral indictment of the craft union position they wrote that labor leaders

> have an obligation that ought to outweigh their personal ambitions, and may even call for some sacrifice of real or fancied advantages enjoyed by the crafts they represent. That obligation is to organize the unorganized for the common benefit of all who toil, whether craftsmen or unskilled. . . . In the fair and just solution of those problems rests the welfare of all our working millions and the heritage they shall leave their children.[46]

Such powerful moral reasoning had no effect on Green and the Council. On July 22, Ogburn, obviously frightened by the possible legal repercussions of suspension, wrote Green and urged him not to follow through on his course of action. In a complete reversal of his earlier position, Ogburn argued that courts would not allow suspension to be used as a means to evade the two-thirds majority convention vote for expulsion. Green, however, casually brushed aside Ogburn's warning.[47]

Council members assembled at AFL headquarters on August 3 to conclude the trial. They spent three hours listening to Frey repeat his charge and Edward Bieritz of the Electrical Workers support them. On August 4, Dubinsky of the ILGWU, who was still a member of the Council, made a final plea for restraint. He argued that several CIO unions, including the ILGWU, had a sincere desire to remain loyal to the Federation, but that suspension would compel them to tie their fortunes to the rival federation. Out of desperation, Dubinsky offered a compromise. The ILGWU would break with the CIO if a simple majority at the 1936 AFL convention, not two-thirds, resolved that the CIO was dual in character.[48]

Council members were not impressed. Hutcheson, Wharton, and John Coefield of the Plumbers derided Dubinsky's offer and attacked him for participating in the CIO. And Green, offered a final opportunity to show restraint, proved again that he intended to deal ruthlessly with the insurgents: "We were patient in January, patient in May, patient in July, we are patient now." The Council had made offers even though the CIO did not come in with "clean hands." But now the issue had become "a fight for democracy," comparable to the struggle against Fascism.[49] On the following day, with Dubinsky not voting, the Council resolved that the CIO unions were guilty of dual unionism. Green was instructed to inform these unions that if they did not withdraw from the CIO by September 5, 1936, they would stand suspended.[50]

Even in the eyes of a sympathetic observer, the historian Philip Taft, the suspension vote demonstrated "a failure of leadership that has no equal in the history of American labor." Taft attributes much of this failure to Green himself: "As president of the Federation and the man who might at this stage have prevented the action by threatening to resign, Green must bear the chief blame."[51] Yet in all fairness to Green, he had acted as a responsible labor official faced with the threat of insurgency. He had given the rebels adequate warning, and had moved against them only after he was convinced that they were operating as a dual movement. Even his support of an illegal suspension was understandable, if not justifiable, because the Federation lacked appropriate channels to deal with a large-scale insurgent movement. Given the fact that Green did not share the outlook of Lewis, he had acted as would any union official faced with a similar threat. Green will always suffer the judgment of history, however, for his failure to recognize the CIO as a progressive union movement seeking the advancement of the entire working class.

At its meeting of August 10, the CIO faced a choice. It could either accept suspension an the split in organized labor or challenge the decision in the courts. The CIO's legal counsel advised that the insurgents had a solid case, but they would have to demand seats at the 1936 AFL convention at Tampa and continue to pay per capita assessments to the AFL. There would be "no chance of our getting admitted to the Tampa convention," Lewis told his cronies, and paying per capita taxes "seems futile." Lewis recommended that the CIO "carry on and not let suspension detract from our organizing activities." By a unanimous vote, CIO officials decided not to challenge the suspensions in court.[52] Thus on September 5, 1936 all ten unions stood suspended. That same day Green, acting on his own initiative, instructed city centrals and state federations not to kick out locals affiliated with the CIO. In his mind, the trouble-makers had been ejected, and the remainder of the AFL could be main-tained intact.[53]

Green's response to the dual movement was well-conditioned and consistent. He simply followed the prescribed formula. But the CIO did not collapse. Rather, it thrived in 1936 and especially in 1937. The CIO had sufficient size and strength to launch organizing drives without assis-tance from AFL affiliates. More importantly, the CIO attracted the sup-port of millions of workers disenchanted with the AFL and was able to translate their militant desire for unionism into lasting union gains. By mid-1937 the CIO achieved amazing success in autos and steel and Lewis had displaced Green as the recognized spokesman for America's working class.

Numerous factors account for the CIO's early success in organizing mass-production workers. First, suspension freed the CIO unions from the jurisdictional barriers that hampered earlier campaigns. No longer were workers subjected to the separation of skilled and unskilled. Second, the CIO was able to raise huge sums of money for organizing drives. As opposed to the few thousands the AFL spent on the drives of 1933–1935, the CIO spent almost $1.7 million on the organization of steel workers alone.[54] Much of the funding came in the form of direct contributions from affiliates, and the rest was raised through an exceedingly high (com-pared to the AFL) per capita assessment. Third, whereas the AFL always suffered from a dearth of organizers, the CIO employed thousands of organizers drawn from affiliates, radical groups, including Communists, and rank-and-file leaders. Fourth, prolabor sentiment in Washington, rep-resented by the Wagner Act, meant that employers could no longer depend on governmental neutrality or assistance in their behalf.[55]

Yet the single most important ingredient of the CIO's success was its support of rank-and-file militancy. This, too, had been largely impossible within the Federation. By upholding his religious commitment to indus-trial peace, Green had alienated millions of mass-production workers. His values, combined with the AFL weaknesses and employer hostility, had all but crushed the worker militancy that erupted in 1933 and 1934. Indeed, 1935 and 1936 were years of relative quiescence in American factories. But with the rise of the CIO, workers again exhibited intense enthusiasm for unionism that surpassed even the upheaval of 1934. Because the CIO supported and encouraged walkouts and mass picketing, "sit-down" strikes and slowdowns, workers in the basic industries flocked into the insurgent camp. With an army of workers having tremendous confidence in collective economic action, the CIO was able to win major battles against the two most powerful anti-union employers: autos and steel.

The first significant breach in the anti-union wall around mass-production industries occurred on February 11, 1937 when General Motors, faced with the novel and immensely effective weapon of the sit-down strike, in which workers took physical possession of the plant, strong governmental pressures, and artful negotiating by Lewis, signed a contract with the United Automobile Workers (UAW). To be sure, the contract did not include a union shop provision, but GM granted exclusive representation to the UAW in the struck plants, agreed not to discriminate against union members, and agreed to rehire all strikers.[56]

Green, of course, offered no support to the striking auto workers. When the UAW appealed to the AFL for financial help on February 2, Green told reports that he had no intention of asking internationals to contribute. With more than a hint of bitterness, he added that it was "rather surprising that the United Automobile Workers now comes to an organization which it had deserted with a plea for financial aid."[57] Moreover, by insisting that the UAW's demand for exclusive representation would deny representation to the handful of auto workers in AFL craft unions, Green actually obstructed negotiations between GM and the UAW. On February 6 GM proposed a settlement that would have made the UAW the exclusive bargaining agent in the struck plants for a temporary period. Green immediately visited President Roosevelt at the White House and later telephoned him to voice his opposition to the proposed settlement. That same day Green telephoned Governor Murphy of Michigan, who was directly involved in the negotiations, and, as Green later told the Executive Council, "in a rather long and very clear and definite conversation" urged him to "yield to force and wrong." Green also sent a telegram to Murphy, telling him that any agreement in which the UAW was accorded exclusive representation would be "direct injury" to the AFL.[58]

When negotiations between the UAW and GM resumed, Governor Murphy showed Green's telegram to Lewis, who thereupon rose from the conference table and went for his coat and hat. When asked where he was going, Lewis answered that if AFL demands were to be considered, he and his associates would gladly leave and GM could settle the strike with the AFL. Lewis then proposed that Haile Selassie be invited to the negotiations since he represented as many GM workers as did Green.[59] Lewis's outrage was warranted, historian Sidney Fine was observed, because "the intervention of the AFL undoubtedly reinforced GM's determination not to yield on the issue of exclusive representation."[60]

On the day the settlement was announced, Green was happy to detail its shortcomings to the press. Indeed, his animosity toward the CIO led him to claim the agreement represented a "complete surrender" of all major UAW demands. "So far as recognition of the union is concerned, the situation is practically the same as it was before the strike was called," he erroneously told reports. "As regards the closed shop principle, the defeat is complete."[61]

CIO leaders did not overlook Green's obstructions, and the hostility Green aroused made a reconciliation between the AFL and the CIO even more unlikely. One CIO official, Van A. Bittner, indignantly wrote Green that the AFL Executive Council included "men who face this battle between the automobile workers and General Motors with only one thought in mind—to drive the automobile workers back to work so that it might be said that the Committee for Industrial Organization is a failure."[62] When the contract was signed, UAW President Homer Martin denounced Green as "the modern Judas Iscariot of the labor movement."[63] And the UMW Policy Committee condemned both Green and John P. Frey for "the gratuitous, anti-union, strikebreaking statements."[64]

An equally historic, if somewhat less dramatic CIO breakthrough in the mass-production sector occurred on March 2, 1937 when U.S. Steel, the leading bastion of the open shop, signed a contract with the Steel Workers' Organizing Committee. The victory was less complete than in autos because SWOC was named bargaining agent for its members only without any guarantee of union security. Nevertheless, the agreement was a tremendous conquest for organized labor and, unlike the GM accord, there had been no dramatic confrontations between workers and management and virtually no governmental interference immediately prior to the agreement.[65]

Green, who was in Coshocton celebrating his sixty-seventh birthday when the U.S. Steel contract was made public, again refused to concede that the CIO had won a major victory. Since the U.S. Steel agreement was negotiated peacefully without public strike threats, Green could not in this instance castigate the CIO for its methods. Instead, he condemned the CIO for its failure to "stand up" for the union shop. "Neither side . . . attempted to invoke the National Labor Relations Act provisions to determine the sole bargaining agent," he complained. "Only in such union recognition and in no other way can the cooperative industrial relationship between companies and workers be improved."[66]

On the surface, Green's reaction to the CIO's advances in steel and autos seemed to be simply a matter of sour grapes. There is undoubtedly some truth to the view that Green was unable to admit that a dual federation could succeed where he had failed. Yet a great deal more than jealously motivated Green. Above all, his need to justify Christian cooperation led him to claim the victories were failures. Indeed the overriding factor behind Green's vindictive crusade against the CIO after 1936 was his disdain for worker militancy. His entire career rested on the premise that labor would gain only insofar as all parties to the production process promoted harmony and cooperation. He considered the CIO's approach barbaric, futile, and immoral, and he steadfastly refused to believe that its tactics could ever be successful.

The CIO's use of the sit-down strike, which was of dubious legality, its tolerance of Communists, and its occasional willingness to break a contract and conduct sympathy strikes were, for Green, all signs of the CIO's immorality, symptoms of a "disease which is eating into the vitals of trade-unionism."[67] He held the sit-down strike in particular contempt and referred to it as "sabotage beyond the wildest dreams of the I.W.W." The sit-down "connotes a desire to bargain by violence, to use force in the taking of public and private property, to take the law into one's own hands. . . . "[68] Such tactics, Green argued, not only violated Christian precepts, but they also imperiled labor's standing by alienating public opinion and arousing the hostility of government. Thus even as the CIO grew in power and influence, Green regarded it as "a perversion and contradiction of all the ethical standards which Organized Labor had created and observed."[69]

The CIO's capacity to translate worker militancy into trade union gains, particularly in 1937, pointed out the fallacy of Green's approach. Cooperation had failed to secure a single signed contract with a major mass-production employer. The "immorality" of the CIO, not Green's Christian ideals, brought millions of workers into the trade union fold and made labor a force to be reckoned with in the nation's political and economic life. Green never recognized that moral suasion, in and of itself, was an ineffective tool for the advancement of working-class interests.

The CIO enjoyed remarkable growth in early 1937. The UAW followed up on its GM victory by winning a contract with Chrysler on April 6. The Rubber Workers became firmly entrenched in the rubber industry. The United Electrical Workers won bargaining rights at RCA, General Electric and other radio and electrical companies. in areas dominated by mass-production industry, the CIO met with considerable, although by no means complete, success. At the CIO conference in October 1937, the rebels claimed four million members. This figure, however, was an exaggeration, the real membership being closer to two million.[70] Nevertheless, the CIO could boast 32 international unions, 600 local industrial unions (comparable to FLUs), and 80 state federations and city centrals.[71]

Try as he might, Green could not whistle away the CIO's early success. If the Federation hoped to avoid being swallowed up by its rival, immediate and aggressive action was necessary. And to the surprise of many observers, the AFL under Green was able to meet the challenge and initiate a powerful counterattack. Only after the CIO demonstrated conclusively that unskilled workers could in fact be organized and that industrial unionism was a viable strategy did AFL affiliates adjust their organizational strategy. Without any fanfare, the Carpenters began to organize lumber and sawmill workers on an industrial basis; the Machinists advanced a "substantial majority" formula to organize mass-production workers that allowed crafts to withdraw jurisdictional rights when a clear majority of workers in a plant were eligible to join a particular AFL union; and the Brotherhood of Electrical Workers began to recruit all electrical workers regardless of skill. Faced with potentially ruinous competition, these and other AFL unions scrapped their dogged adherence to craft unionism. The CIO menace forced AFL affiliates to recognize that twentieth century economic developments required a twentieth century form of unionism.[72]

At the April 1937 session of the Executive Council, Green voiced the fears of AFL leaders as the CIO expanded:

> The country seems to be filled with C.I.O. organizers. Every town and every city, small and great, seems to be filled with organizers employed . . . by the C.I.O. I am amazed at the reports I get from our people in all towns and cities . . . advising they have ten or twelve, or five or six C.I.O. organizers active. . . . Because of these activities there has come a general demand that the Council proceed to take action. . . . [73]

Green persuaded Council members to call a special convention on May 24 at Cincinnati so that the Federation could devise a strategy for a counter-offensive. Several Council members suggested that if the AFL were to compete successfully, it would have to launch campaigns comparable to those of the CIO. Green replied that a dearth of organizers precluded such a policy for the present. "Our foes are heavily financed and we are limited." If the AFL planned to mount massive organizing drives, Green concluded, a scheme to raise money would have to be approved at the Cincinnati convention.[74]

At the well-attended special convention, delegates approved the Executive Council's recommendations to establish a "war chest" by levying an assessment of one cent per member per month; to have international unions "carry forward without limit aggressive organizing campaigns within their respective jurisdictions"; and to expel locals affiliated with the CIO.[75] Without explicitly stating so, the Cincinnati convention signaled the end of the debate over industrial versus craft forms of organization. in the ensuing civil war, both the AFL and CIO chartered craft and industrial unions alike. Some AFL unions, such as the Carpenters, Teamsters, and Machinists, emerged from the war with jurisdictions as broad or broader than those claimed by some CIO unions.[76]

The Cincinnati convention was indeed a declaration of war against the CIO. Green had been one of the most vocal supporters of war, yet he did not consider the battle cry adequate justification to abandon cooperation and morality in organizing. The convention provided him with a five-fold increase in organizing funds and allowed him to increase his organizing staff to 200. Green appointed Lewis G. Hines, a dyed-in-the-wool conservative trade unionist who shared Green's misgivings about labor violence, as his special assistant in charge of organizers. In his instructions, Green placed a ban on sit-down strikes and urged organizers to sell the AFL by pointing out to workers and employers that the Federation did not condone the CIO's "irresponsible tactics."[77]

Fortunately, many organizers and AFL affiliates paid no heed to Green's prohibition of militant tactics. many of the 477 sit-down strikes recorded by the Bureau of Labor Statistics in 1937 were led by AFL unions.[78] Green dismissed many organizers who spurned his instructions, but because he did not have the authority to interfere with the practices of individual unions, he could do nothing when affiliates violated his moral code. Indeed, the tremendous growth of the AFL in the years 1937–1941 was a result of militant campaigns conducted by individual unions. With the rise of the CIO, affiliates no longer looked to Green and the AFL front offices to organize workers for them.

Divested of most of his organizing duties, Green played the role of cheerleader for AFL unions as they battled their CIO opponents. And by the time the AFL met in convention in the fall of 1937, Green had a great deal to cheer about. The AFL had regained practically all membership losses caused by the suspensions.[79] Further, the tremendous initial surge of the CIO seemed largely spent. Defeat in the Little Steel strikes, highlighted by the bloody Memorial Day Massacre in Chicago that left ten dead, served notice on the CIO that it could expect no more quick, nonviolent victories. The strikes also demonstrated the limits of New Deal support for the insurgents. President Roosevelt wished a plague on both the CIO and Republic Steel during the strike. The UAW's attempt to organize Ford also met with armed resistance and ended in disaster. These and other CIO defeats were followed by an upsurge in unemployment. During the "Roosevelt depression" of 1937 and 1938, the number of jobless again reached eleven million. Largely as a result of layoffs, the UAW and other CIO unions lost tens of thousands of members. Because AFL unions were not concentrated in mass-production centers, they were not hit quite as hard as CIO unions.[80]

Intoxicated by AFL successes and CIO setbacks, Green expressed his desire to carry the fight against the CIO to the finish. In a ninety-minute speech to the 1937 AFL convention, delivered in the same Denver, Colorado, convention hall in which he had nominated Lewis for the AFL presidency in 1921, Green declared the AFL would build "the greatest fighting machine that was ever created within the ranks of organized labor" to drive the CIO "out of existence." Amid cheers from the 600 delegates, Green blasted the "destroying, destructive, ripping policy" of the CIO. Again he denounced the sit-down and pledged AFL loyalty to private property rights and the sanctity of trade agreements. Unlike the CIO, the AFL wanted "to avoid industrial conflicts, to promote under-standing between employers and employees," and "to win our battles in accordance with law and lawful procedure." He then asked delegates to clothe the Executive Council with authority to revoke the charters of the suspended unions: "The clock is struck. The hour is here. . . . Having appealed to them for two years to come back, you are now going to say that appeal will no longer be made."[81] By a vote of 25,616 to 1227, delegates empowered the Council to expel the CIO unions.[82]

Ironically, it was the CIO and not the AFL that responded to mount-ing pressure and initiated peace talks. By the fall of 1937, the "Roosevelt depression" and numerous organizing failures had created a spirit of com-promise in the insurgent camp. The loss of much of their influence with President Roosevelt also convinced a number of CIO officials of the need for labor unity. Accordingly, on October 12, the CIO forwarded a tele-gram to AFL Secretary Frank Morrison calling for a conference to con-sider unity.[83]

Unity talks were held from October 25 to December 21, but it seems clear that neither the AFL nor the CIO were sincerely interested in peace in 1937. In large measure, both sides agreed to negotiate only because neither party wanted to appear responsible for the breakdown of labor unity. Throughout the negotiations, the AFL demanded that the CIO dis-band prior to the settlement and steadfastly refused to accede to the principle of industrial organization of mass-production industries. The CIO could not accept these terms, for it would have meant a return to the situation existing before the CIO's formation. On the other hand, the CIO would not retreat from its position that all of its unions, some of which were newly-created, be admitted into the AFL with full rights. And in 1937, the AFL was unwilling to put its stamp of approval on dual union-ism.

Green himself must bear partial responsibility for the failure of these early unity talks because he consistently opposed all AFL concessions to the CIO. In his mind, responsibility for the "division in the house of labor must rest absolutely upon the shoulders of those who divided it through the setting up of a dual movement." He would welcome the CIO unions back into the AFL, but he would not allow them to impose any conditions on the parent organization. "We ask them to come into the open forum of debate with their opinions, their suggestions and their recommendations, and we say to them, 'If you can win a majority of the delegates to your point of view, amen, all right, but you must do it in democratic, orderly fashion and not in accordance with minority rule or the rule of the jungle.' "[84]

The failure of the peace talks led to an intensification of Green's crusade against the CIO. Declaring that it was time to "meet the challenge of the C.I.O. in a militant, determined and uncompromising way," Green terminated the services of thirty-eight AFL organizers whom he deemed pro-CIO, and systematically began to purge subordinate bodies of CIO influence.[85] As early as February 24, 1937, Green had informed state federations and city centrals that they "must decide whether they will be loyal to the parent body . . . or give support to an organization which is classified as dual and rival. . . . " He insisted that they "renew their pledge of loyalty and devotion to the American Federation of Labor and to the principles and policies which it represents."[86] The majority of these bodies dutifully expelled CIO locals.

By the end of 1937, Green began to revoke the charters of city centrals and state federations with CIO locals. When Green demanded that the West Virginia Federation of Labor oust all CIO locals, the state federation's president retorted that if all CIO locals were expelled, "the Federation would be so weak that it would be of no material benefit to the workers of the State." Green smugly reminded him that, as an officer of a subordinate body, he was duty-bound to conform to the rules of the parent body.[87] After a trial in which Green appeared in person to present charges, the state federation was reorganized. Similar action was taken by the AFL president against the Kentucky and Pennsylvania state federations and recalcitrant city centrals.[88]

On the national level, Green and the Executive Council moved to seal the split in organized labor by expelling the already suspended unions of the CIO. Before taking this step, the Council had to wait for the United Mine Workers to expel Green, thereby avoiding the embarrassing situation of having an AFL president who was a member of an expelled union. Under the UMW constitution, expulsion trials were to be held before a committee of the accused member's local union. Whatever the verdict, either side could appeal the case through subdistrict and district organizations to the UMW executive board, which served as the board of final appeal. Yet Green's local, No. 379 in Coshocton, was largely defunct. The mines were not in operation and the local was held together largely for tradition's sake. Many of its members had worked with Green at the turn of the century, and only the local's president, J. R. McCormick, who was also a CIO organizer, was willing to obey Lewis's order and try Green. The others, such as Ben Mobley, declared their intention to "stick with

Billy Green to the last." If the order to try Green was given, Mobley said, "We'll just ignore it entirely."[89] Thus Lewis was denied the opportunity to expel Green through constitutional means.

The UMW executive board, at its July 1937 meeting, considered charges that Green was "encouraging a dual union," the Progressive Miners Union. Green had, in fact, given an FLU charter to this UMW splinter group of about 30,000 Illinois miners in July 1937. Still, the UMW executive board refused to move against Green, perhaps fearing that a trial before the board would be regarded as prejudicial.[90] In a clearly unconstitutional move, the executive board referred the matter of Green's expulsion to the February 1938 UMW convention. In a four-thousand-word letter to UMW Secretary-Treasurer Thomas Kennedy, Green argued that since the convention had no jurisdiction over expulsions, he would not appear to defend himself.[91] The trial took place on the last day of the convention, but before the act of expulsion had been finalized, Green tendered his resignation.[92]

Green now found himself in the ridiculous position of having to present himself as a member of the Musicians Union, which had anticipated expulsion by issuing him a membership card on February 28, 1836.[93] "That is appropriate," Lewis quipped to the miners' convention, "Like Nero, he fiddles while Rome burns."[94]

With this absurd formality out of the way, Green and the Executive Council proceeded to revoke the charters of the suspended international unions between February and May 1938. In the cases of the Flat Glass Workers and United Mine Workers, the AFL bigwigs took further action by chartering rival unions, the National Flat Glass Workers and the Progressive Mine Workers. The promotion of the dual miners' union was inspired by Green, who carried on negotiations with this group as early as 1936. It was a vindictive act intended to antagonize Lewis. Based almost entirely in Illinois, the Progressive Mine Workers had no chance of displacing the UMW. Indeed, the AFL had to give it $50,000 just to keep it afloat and, soon after the union received its charter, thirty-six of its leaders were convicted in federal court on charges of conspiracy.[95]

In October 1938, after almost three years of independent activity, the CIO issued a call to all affiliates to meet on November 14 in Pittsburgh for a constitutional convention. Representatives from 34 internationals, 8 organizing committees, 23 state federations, 116 city centrals, and 137 local industrial unions gathered in Pittsburgh to adopt a constitution and change the name of their organization to the Congress of Industrial Organizations. Delegates elected Lewis president, Murray and Hillman vice-presidents, and James B. Carey of the United Electrical Workers secretary.[96] The split in labor was sealed.

Green had done as much as anyone to create the split in labor's ranks, and he had insured the continuation of that split by wielding the club of a self-righteous warrior. Yet he assumed no personal responsibility. His conscience remained clear. And he could see no contradiction in his Christmas message of 1938, in which he bemoaned the fact that in many areas of human endeavor "we still follow the ethical standards of 'an eye for an eye and a tooth for a tooth,' and we deal with offenders in the spirit of vengeance."[97] When it came to the CIO, Green himself had forgotten the teachings of his Lord.

Although Green played virtually no role in the AFL's organizing campaigns of 1937–1941, he spearheaded the AFL's war on the CIO in the halls of Congress and among the public. In his continuing effort to cultivate public acceptance of the AFL, Green stressed the real or supposed differences between the rival labor federations. The picture he painted of the AFL was that of a responsible, patriotic organization committed to the free market and cooperation with management; the CIO, by contrast, was dictatorially controlled, a bastion of Communists and other radicals, and a militant organization bent on class conflict and social strife. His speeches bore little resemblance to reality, but they did increase Green's popularity among the public. A Gallup poll conducted in the fall of 1938 posed the following question: "Which labor leader do you like better: Green of the A. F. of L. or Lewis of the C.I.O.?" Seventy-eight percent of those responding favored Green, whereas in July 1937, when the same question was asked, only sixty-seven percent voted for the AFL president.[98]

Green also proved to be an effective lobbyist, competing successfully against the CIO for federal favors. Much of Green's effort focused on the administration of the National Labor Relations Board. Throughout labor's civil war, the NLRB often had to choose, in effect, between the AFL and CIO when forced to determine the proper bargaining unit in an industry. Decisions made in favor of the CIO naturally prompted Green's dissatisfaction. His opposition intensified when the NLRB made several decisions setting aside AFL contracts with employers that were deemed collusive arrangements to frustrate the desire of a majority of workers to join a CIO union. For instance, in 1936 the CIO's United Electrical Workers began an organizing drive at the National Electric Products Company. Although the drive attracted a great many workers, the company refused to bargain with the CIO union and signed a closed shop agreement with the AFL's Brotherhood of Electrical Workers. The NLRB cancelled the AFL contract because it did not represent the free choice of the majority of workers.[99]

Decisions such as this one convinced Green that the three-man NLRB was biased in favor of the CIO, and he moved at once to block reappointment of the administrators. Although Roosevelt declared his intention to reappoint Donald Walkefield Smith in 1939, Green lobbied so effectively against him that his name was never submitted to the Senate. He was replaced by William Leiserson of the National Mediation Board, a man Green held in high regard. Green successfully opposed the reappointment of NLRB chairman J. Warren Madden in 1940 and greeted with satisfaction his replacement by Harry A. Millis. In 1941, Green also prevented the reappointment of Edwin Smith, thus making a clean sweep of the NLRB's original personnel.[100]

Green could hardly conceal his glee at this deft assault on the supposedly pro-CIO NLRB. And he noted with pride that the board did pursue more favorable policies under the new administration. In particular, craft groups were given a greater amount of protection against CIO charges of collusion. By 1941, Green was able to report to the AFL convention that the NLRB was now "fair and impartial."[101]

But the victory was not without cost. In his campaign against the NLRB, Green had looked the other way as AFL Executive Council members formed an unholy alliance with the House Committee on Un-American Activities, created in June 1938 under the chairmanship of Representative Martin Dies of Texas. The Committee's first notable witness, John P. Frey, made nation-wide headlines with sensational charges that Communists had captured the CIO and that the NLRB was its handmaiden. Frey and other AFL officials also assisted Dies as he took his committee on a tour throughout the country to smear ostensibly pro-CIO candidates on the eve of the 1938 elections.[102] While Green himself took no part in the campaign against such pro-labor candidates as Frank Murphy of Michigan and Elmer A. Benson of Minnesota, his official silence served to legitimize Frey's actions.

By acquiescing in the conservative assault on pro-labor politicians, Green bears partial responsibility for the 1938 election results, which significantly altered the political balance in Washington. Republicans picked up eighty-eight seats in the House and eight in the Senate. In the upcoming Congress, an alliance between Republicans and Southern Democrats would assume control over labor legislation. That Green had played even a passive role in the creation of this powerful anti-New Deal coalition revealed the lengths he was willing to go to combat the CIO and its "immorality." Green's crusade against the CIO had led to the weakening of labor's voice in Washington.

Green may have competed successfully against the CIO in national politics, but he proved unable to match the CIO's efforts to attract black workers to trade unionism. Indeed, the formation of the CIO not only exposed the AFL's incapacity to organize mass-production workers, it also exposed the AFL's shameful record on the organization of blacks. The AFL's record had, in part, fueled the enmity between the Lewis group and the craft bloc between 1933 and 1935. At the 1934 AFL convention, black workers picketed outside the convention hall. Inside the hall, black unionists introduced resolutions condemning the AFL's treatment of blacks. They complained about the eight international unions that completely excluded blacks from membership, the unions that accepted blacks but forced them to join separate "Jim Crow" locals, and the overall lack of concern about the special problems facing black workers. A. Philip Randolph, president of the Brotherhood of Sleeping Car Porters, which was composed primarily of blacks, explained that there was "widespread unrest . . . with the existing status of Negro workers in the American Federation of Labor, and with its policy toward the organization of Negro workers."[103]

Randolph proposed that the convention expel all unions that violated the AFL constitution by excluding blacks. He also called for the appointment of a committee to investigate discrimination against blacks in the AFL. The committee on organization, to which Randolph's resolution was referred, claimed that the AFL, from its inception, held all workers eligible for membership, regardless of race, creed, or nationality. Further, the committee stated that the AFL could not "interfere with the autonomy of national or international unions" and could not "say who are eligible or who are not eligible to membership in national or international unions." Nevertheless, the committee did authorize Green to appoint the investigating committee on discrimination Randolph desired.[104]

Before the strident tones of disgruntled black unionists made themselves heard at the 1934 AFL convention, Green had said little on the question of racism in the AFL. Since Green had been a member of the UMW, one of the least discriminatory unions in the AFL, some blacks had hoped that his election in 1924 would lead to changes in AFL policies. In September 1925 Green had encouraged these hopes by writing in the black journal, the *Messenger*, that the doors of the AFL were now open to blacks. Yet his article showed that blacks could expect little change. Green repeated the old argument that black workers had only themselves to blame for their exclusion from AFL unions and that they could expect to receive equal treatment only when they developed a trade union mentality.[105]

If Green's words provided little solace to black workers, his actions proved that he had at least some interest in improving their status. When the Brotherhood of Sleeping Car Porters was formed in 1925, Green worked hard to convince the Executive Council to give the new union international status. However, the Hotel and Restaurant Employees' Union, which claimed jurisdiction over the porters, blocked the Brotherhood's application. Green and the Brotherhood were forced to accept a compromise, in which Brotherhood locals received FLU charters.[106] Thus while Green was not a racist, he was unwilling to challenge the racist policies upheld by the Executive Council.

For reasons which are not altogether clear, Green waited eight months, until June 1935, to appoint the Committee of Five on Negro Discrimination authorized by the 1934 convention. Witnesses appeared before the committee and presented an impressive body of facts on the racist policies of AFL unions. One witness argued that, because of depression conditions, many workers found it impossible to travel to AFL headquarters and suggested that the committee hold regional hearings to collect additional evidence. Green, however, claimed that "there was no necessity for holding such hearings" and ordered the Committee of Five to submit its final report.[107]

It was hardly surprising that the report of the Committee of Five received little attention at the 1935 AFL convention because of the debate between craft and industrial unionists. In his determination to maintain peace at any cost, Green did not even present the full report to the delegates. Instead, he had George M. Harrison of the Railway Clerks prepare a summary. Green disallowed all discussion of this emasculated version of the committee's report until the last day of the convention, after most of the delegates had gone home.[108]

The Committee of Five's report thus went largely unnoticed by most delegates. During the short debate on the report, Green emphasized the progress made by the AFL in fighting racism. He pointed out incorrectly that 100 of the AFL's 105 affiliates accepted black members. He declared that, although he personally abhorred discrimination, he did not have the power to "say to an autonomous International union how it shall draft its laws." Randolph's proposal to revoke charters of unions barring blacks, Green continued, was unworkable. The AFL could only hope that through education racism in unions would be eliminated. Meanwhile, FLUs served the needs of black workers excluded by internationals.[109]

Green's suppression of the report of the Committee of Five convinced many blacks that the AFL would never do anything to advance the cause of black labor. Thus with the formation of the CIO, blacks abandoned hope in the AFL and threw their support to the rebels. Blacks supported the CIO in large measure because the great majority of black union candidates were employed in mass-production industries. Even A. Philip Randolph, who kept his Brotherhood of Sleeping Car Porters in the AFL, recognized the tremendous promise the CIO held for black workers. "The craft union invariably has a color bar against the Negro worker," Randolph declared, "but the industrial union in structure renders race discrimination less possible, since it embraces all workers included in the industry, regardless of race, creed, color or craft, skilled or unskilled."[110]

The CIO organizing drives in mass-production industries, by recruiting both black and white workers, brought dramatic changes in the race relations of working-class communities. At least temporarily, class consciousness supplanted race consciousness among black workers, and many whites began to protest against discrimination their black co-workers faced. While the CIO did not revolutionize the status of blacks, in its early years the CIO revealed a strong sympathy for the plight of black workers and struggled to overcome divisions in the working class based on race.[111]

As the demand for the organization of black workers shifted to the CIO, Green and the AFL once again were able to ignore the problems blacks faced and maintain their racist policies. Indeed, the economist Walter Galenson concludes that "there is no evidence to indicate that the Executive Council gave the question (of discrimination) any serious consideration" between 1936 and 1941.[112] For his part, William Green continued to assert his opposition to racist practices in AFL unions, but claimed his hands were tied because of union autonomy. Thus Green remained silent when eight black leaders appealed to the AFL's Railway Employees Department in April 1938 for action to strike out discriminatory clauses from AFL union constitutions. He failed to intercede when the Railway and Steamship Clerks Union organized white redcaps and barred black redcaps. And when the Brotherhood of Sleeping Car Porters applied for jurisdiction over the black redcaps, Green actually helped the Railway and Steamship Clerks Union in its successful effort to block the Brotherhood's petition.[113] Green was not a racist, but his unwillingness to exert his influence to put an end to discrimination made his condemnation of racism sound insincere. Few blacks found comfort in Green's declaration at the 1940 Brotherhood of Sleeping Car Porters convention that "So long as I can express myself, I shall fight against racial intolerance and hatred in America."[114]

It is an irony of history that the two men most responsible for the split in organized labor and the ferocity of labor's civil war, William Green and John L. Lewis, should both suffer a loss of personal power as a result. Dubofsky and Van Tine have carefully analyzed Lewis's fall in 1940, when Lewis threw his support to the Republican Willkie in the presidential election and kept his promise to resign as head of the CIO if Roosevelt won.[115] Although he maintained his official position, Green, too, suffered a loss of power in the wake of the civil war. Most significantly, Green no longer conducted organizing drives as he had done in the 1920s and early 1930s. Competition from the CIO forced international unions to conduct their own drives, and they no longer looked to Green to organize for them. Thus in his declining years, Green served largely as an administrator and figurehead for the Federation.

Even in these duties Green was forced to share his workload. In 1939 the Executive Council forced the retirement of seventy-nine year old AFL Secretary-Treasurer Frank Morrison and replaced him with New York Sate Federation of Labor President George Meany. In seconding Meany's nomination at the 1939 AFL convention, Daniel Tobin argued that Green, who was then sixty-nine years old, needed an officer "who will be helpful and assume the responsibilities of office. He does not need just a book-keeper. . . . The President wants a man who is able to take his place, engage in the work of the Federation, one who is able to take the platform in his absence explaining the work and the position of this Federation."[116]

Green, however, did not want such an active underling. He jealously guarded his control over all aspects of the AFL's affairs, and he had no intention of sharing his authority. As one AFL administrator, Boris Shiskin, recalled; "Meany moved a little too fast for Green, and friction developed quickly. This had the effect of encouraging Meany to push stronger. . . . " The conflict, Shiskin continued, "was not so much on substance but on the manner in which things were done. Meany wanted to make the AFL more responsive to current conditions; Green liked things the way they were."[117]

Although the relationship between Green and Meany was never overtly hostile, Green was wary of the new secretary-treasurer's ambitions. In Meany's first few years, Green gave him as little important work to do as possible. But he could not prevent Meany from making administrative reforms clearly within the jurisdiction of his post. Meany captured control over the management of the *American Federationist* and frequently complained to Executive Council members that he wanted to serve as the AFL's chief lobbyist.[118] Even though Green continued to serve the AFL as chief lobbyist until the late 1940s, he was clearly a waning star in the labor movement galaxy.

VII

War, Politics, and Death:
1941–1952

W HEN THE JAPANESE bombed Pearl Harbor, William Green was seventy-one years old. Nor was he a healthy seventy-one. The characteristic rosy glow in his cheeks and the enchanting smile were both fading, and it was apparent to many that he was simply too old and too weak to perform all the arduous tasks required of the AFL president. Beginning in the early 1940s, Green entered hospitals several times each year for checkups. Although the exact reason for these checkups was never revealed to the press, by the late 1940s it was widely known that Green had a serious heart condition. Throughout the 1940s, Green frequently returned home to the restful quiet of Coshocton for extended periods, leaving his duties in the hands of George Meany.[1]

The war year also witnessed the continuing decline of Green's influence over the affairs of the AFL. The Executive Council chose not to appoint Green to important posts on government boards, naming instead younger, more energetic officials. Increasingly, Green was delegated to less critical tasks, such as addressing union conventions to garner support for Roosevelt's defense policies, raising money for the relief of displaced persons, and publicizing the AFL's contribution to the war effort. While the powerful craft union leaders remained loyal to Green until his death, they no longer called upon the aged president to do their bidding.

By the end of the war, Green's involvement in Federation affairs was essentially passive. According to one employee at AFL headquarters, the most important activity in Green's working day in the late 1940s was his afternoon nap. No longer was Green physically capable of addressing those countless union conventions, state and city body gatherings, and other labor groups that had consumed so much of his time in years past.

Rather, he placed this dreary burden on Secretary-Treasurer Meany. No longer did he write many of the editorials that bore his name in the *American Federationist* every month. Although he continued to write on a few selected topics, the bulk of the editorials were written by more active underlings. An even more important indication that Green lacked the stamina to conduct his affairs as usual was his resignation, at the war's end, from the AFl's legislative committee. No longer would Green serve as the AFL's chief lobbyist, a role he had guarded jealously since Meany became secretary-treasurer in 1939.[2]

Rumors began circulating during the war that Green would soon retire. Despite his failing health and advanced years, Green dismissed such rumors as without foundation and insisted that he had no intention of stepping down as long as the Executive Council desired his services.[3] Why Green refused to retire in spite of his inability to perform all the duties expected of him will remain always a matter of conjecture. For labor leaders whose careers centered on amassing power, the question of why they clung to power is easy to answer. But Green shunned the exercise of economic power. He had no union army at his command. However, he did derive great satisfaction from the attempt to exercise moral influence in economic and political affairs. Perhaps Green chose not to retire because he continued to recognize the need for spiritual leadership in the labor movement, leadership that would be lost of George Meany succeeded him as head of the Federation. The union movement had always been much more than a job to him. It was a righteous cause. While the instruments of power were being parcelled out among the younger and more energetic, Green was still the figurehead and could still preach his gospel of union-ism. As late as June 1951, he wrote an editorial entitled "Unions—A Moral Force." He could still view himself as the shepherd tending to his flock.

The Second World War provided Green another golden opportunity to stress accommodation between labor and capital. In the war years, management, government, and labor cooperated on a unprecedented scale in an effort to mobilize America's resources to meet the Axis threat. Immediately after the declaration of war, Green proudly announced that the Federation would forego voluntarily all strikes for the duration, a pledge the Federation was remarkably successful in keeping. Yet, ironically, despite the cooperation of labor throughout the emergency, the war years gave rise to powerful anti-union sentiment among employers, Congress, and the general public. The Smith-Connally and Taft-Hartley Acts re-vealed that significant political forces were still unwilling to accept the existence of a strong labor movement. Christian cooperation remained an elusive dream.

Throughout his life, Green was a vocal opponent of totalitarianism in every form, whether Soviet Communism, Italian Fascism, or German Nazism. Beginning in 1933, he carried on a propaganda war against the Nazi's ruthless suppression of trade unions and persecution of Jews and racial minorities. In part because of his efforts, the 1933 AFL convention unanimously adopted a resolution that the Federation join hands with other organizations in a boycott of German goods and services "until the German government recognizes the right of the working people of Germany to organize into *bona fide,* independent trade unions of their own choosing, and until Germany ceases its repressive policy of persecution of Jewish people." Succeeding conventions reaffirmed the boycott, which lasted until 1945. Green also convinced delegates to the 1934 convention to establish a "Chest for the Liberation of the Workers of Europe" to raise funds for German and Italian workers resisting government efforts to undermine unions.[4]

But while Green was quick to denounce Hitler and Mussolini, he consistently opposed any action on the part of the U.S. government that might lead to U.S. involvement in war. He drew a sharp line between voluntary action against aggressors and the conduct of the government in foreign affairs. He insisted that the U.S. champion the cause of peace and "never again . . . become involved in a European conflict."[5] Consequently, he refused a request by Walter Citrine, secretary of the British Trades Union Congress, that the AFL pressure the federal government to impose an embargo on Japanese goods after Japan invaded China. He did support a boycott of Japanese goods, however, which the 1938 AFL convention approved. Nevertheless, he did not want to advocate policies that might lead to open hostilities.[6]

When fighting broke out in Europe in 1939, Green reaffirmed his opposition to American involvement. "Labor firmly believes that we should have no part in this European War," Green wrote. "We have had no part in its causes, and can have no responsible part in its adjustment. We want policies best calculated to keep us free of European entanglements."[7] Green shared the belief, common among trade unionists during and after the First World War, that the transformation of the economy to a war footing would inevitably strengthen the domestic enemies of labor and restrict labor's economic and political power. While the AFL had made tremendous membership advances during the First World War, the gains proved ephemeral. Cooperation with government and industry in 1917 and 1918 gave way to a massive anti-union movement after the war that depleted the AFL's ranks by almost thirty percent. In his opening address to the 1939 AFL convention, Green argued that American involvement would reverse all the gains labor had made since 1933 and should be avoided at all costs.[8]

The fall of France in June 1940 weakened Green's insistence on non-involvement. He realized that if the Nazi war machine took England as easily as it had taken France, the Axis powers would control Europe and pose a threat to American security. Aid to Britain thus could be viewed as an integral part of our national defense. All-out aid to Britain became Green's battle cry.[9]

Once committed to the defeat of the Axis powers, Green pledged the AFL's "active and cooperative support with industry and with every appropriate governmental agency having to do with the production and construction of material for national defense." In return he asked only that any government agency set up to deal with the emergency be truly representative of labor, management, and the public.[10] Thus he was outraged when Roosevelt appointed the CIO's Sidney Hillman as the sole union member of the seven-man National Defense Advisory Commission. He also protested Hillman's elevation to the post of associate director-general of the Office of Production Management in December 1940, making him second in command to William Knudsen as administrator of the entire defense production program.[11]

Despite Green's desire to cooperate with the President, Roosevelt denied the AFL (and the CIO as well) adequate representation on war agencies. One historian found that, in 1940 and 1941, "labor's influence was vastly inferior to that of management spokesmen" in defense agencies. And indeed, throughout the war years, labor exercised only "limited influence over governmental policy."[12]

Yet Green never wavered in his commitment to the president's defense policies. In addition to patriotism, one primary reason for Green's loyalty was that defense production was a boon to the nation's economy and was largely responsible for pulling the country out of depression. Eight years of the New Deal had been unable to solve the problem of unemployment, but between June 1940 and the attack on Pearl Harbor twenty months later, 4 of the 8.5 million unemployed found work. As job opportunities increased and as lucrative defense contracts boosted corporate profits, wages also began to rise.

Green was fully aware, however, that the expansion of production contained perils for organized labor. Management regarded the defense boon as an opportunity to curb unionization. The war gave business a chance to drape a cloak of patriotism around anti-union activities; to insist that "labor peace" was essential to defense production; and to attack the closed shop as undemocratic and un-American. As the employer offensive took shape, Green placed another qualification on the continued cooperation of the AFL: continued enforcement of prolabor legislation. In a 1940 Labor Day speech made in Denver, Green declared that "our National Preparedness program must provide for the maintenance of our social and economic gains. They must neither be lowered nor wiped out." The Federation would join hands with government and industry in transforming the country into an "arsenal of democracy" as the president wanted, but not at the expense of gains won by labor during the New Deal.[13]

The Administration's support for prolabor legislation became increasingly difficult to maintain, however. Although the number of strikes in 1940 represented a sharp decline from 1939 and had only slight impact on the defense program, conservatives in Congress made use of the few strikes that did occur to attack the labor movement, and a number of bills intended to limit labor's right to strike were placed in congressional hoppers. Green responded not by assailing those who impugned labor's strike record, but by pledging a no-strike policy on defense orders.[14] Green hoped to check labor's enemies by displaying the AFL's patriotism and willingness to cooperate.

Green's no-strike pledge notwithstanding, labor-management conflict intensified in 1941, when strikes occurred in virtually every industry. There were twice as many strikes and four times as many strikers in 1941 than in 1940. The employer offensive, attacks from conservatives in Congress, and the growing number of strikes all posed serious challenges to Green's leadership. Thus far he had assumed that if the AFL refrained from strikes, both Congress and industry would, for the most part, respect labor's contribution to defense production and welcome labor as an equal partner in the war effort. Now it was apparent that many in industry and government were using the emergency to attack labor, and there were many in the labor movement itself who were playing into the hands of these groups by hurting the defense effort through the use of strikes.

Varied, predictable, and ineffective were Green's responses to the impending collapse of his hopes for a cooperative war effort. He bombarded the media with an array of arguments in an effort to set the record straight as to labor's role in meeting the Axis threat. First, Green claimed that the number of strikes had been greatly exaggerated, that while a no-strike pledge could never be one-hundred percent effective, American workers lived up to their pledge "at least ninety-nine percent."[15] Second, he asserted that the vast majority of strikes that did occur were conducted by the CIO. And here Green returned to the old theme that the CIO was Communist-inspired and somehow not as American as the AFL. Even after June 1941, when Hitler attacked the Soviet Union and Communists in the U.S. became staunch defenders of the no-strike pledge, Green continued to blame Communists and the CIO for most of the strikes in war industries.[16] Third, Green tried to persuade Congress that appealing to workers' patriotism was a much more effective means of curbing production delays than limiting labor's right to strike. Infringing upon this right, he insisted, would be a step toward the forced labor of Fascist nations and actually would serve to "provoke strikes, social unrest, and destroy efficiency."[17] Fourth, Green pleaded for forebearance from AFL members, asking them to make every possible sacrifice to avoid strikes.[18]

True to form, however, Green directed most of his appeals to employers. As he had done in the 1920s and 1930s, Green was still peddling the idea that the AFL was "constructive, democratic and American." The AFL was "not hostile to business," it did not hope to interfere with "the right of employers to manage their property free from restrictions." Quite the contrary, the AFL wanted to assist employers as they sought to "earn a fair return upon invested capital." Indeed, collective bargaining agreements with the AFL unions would aid business by increasing efficiency and reducing strife. The Federation was more than willing to avoid strikes, but employers must cooperate by reducing the cause of strikes. Once employers "grant wage increases to correspond to living costs," there would be no need for industrial strife and employers and labor could then "join hands in the service of our country during these critical times."[19]

Green's propaganda war of 1941 had as much effect as his campaigns of the 1920s and 1930s—none. Employers ignored him, conservatives pressed forward with their anti-labor agenda, and the public's perception of unions began to erode. In May 1940, seventy-four percent of those responding to a national poll answered in the affirmative to the question "Are you in favor of labor unions?" By June 1941, only sixty-seven percent answered favorably. Curiously, another poll conducted in June 1941 reported that seventy-eight percent answered "no" when asked if "labor unions are helping the national defense production program as much as they should."[20] Green's media blitz was thus remarkably unsuccessful.

The no-strike pledge did not spark a cooperative war effort. Not only did it fail to create a labor-management-government partnership, it damaged the labor movement itself by dividing union leadership and the rank-and-file. Workers faced serious problems in 1940 and 1941. They confronted increases in the pace of work, extended hours, and wages that failed to keep up with mounting inflation. Locked into the no-strike pledge, Green had abdicated voluntarily the traditional means of redressing such grievances. When workers were forced to strike, they were opposed not only by employers, but often their union leadership as well. Green's appeals to workers' patriotism offered little solace to the hard pressed rank-and-file. We have seen how alienated Green was from rank-and-file sentiment in the 1930s; his position in the 1940s did nothing to close the gap.

Few events can transform a nation as quickly as attack by a foreign power. The Japanese assault on Pearl Harbor forged a unity of purpose among Americans never equalled before or since. The vast majority of working men and women joined hands with their employers in shedding traditional feelings of pacifism and isolationism and calling for the destruction of the war machines in Japan and Germany. The aged AFL president applauded the declaration of war and took to heart the fact that the Japanese, at least for the time being, had united capital and labor in a common cause. The tragedy of Pearl Harbor rekindled the dream of cooperation that had sputtered in 1940 and 1941.

Within a matter of days Green had prepared and delivered a no-strike pledge on behalf of the Federation's 5 million members. He had called for the establishment of a federal war labor board, based on the one that operated during the first World War. And he had convened a conference of all heads of affiliated unions to endorse the no-strike pledge. "Labor will produce, and produce without interruption!" Green promised the nation.[21]

As one who had shunned economic muscle throughout the struggles of the 1930s, Green had no qualms about issuing the no-strike pledge. He graciously offered labor's full cooperation to management and government as a sign of the AFL's commitment to the war effort. In return, Green asked for similar commitments. First, he urged that the government follow the example of the first World War and provide labor with adequate representation on all boards dealing with defense policy. Second, he begged industry not to take advantage of the no-strike pledge by slashing wages or undermining unions. Third, he called for peace between the AFL and CIO, a working arrangement to lessen jurisdictional conflicts. Finally, he pleaded with Congress to forgo anti-labor legislation. If all three groups—labor, industry, government—pulled together, they could not only insure an Allied victory, but establish once and for all an ethical foundation for capital-labor relations.[22]

The cooperation Green envisioned seemed to be taking place in the first few months of American participation in the war. Green led the AFL contingent to Roosevelt's joint labor-management conference held on December 17. Despite days of squabbling that forced Roosevelt to impose a settlement, all participants seemed reasonably satisfied with the creation of the National War Labor Board, which was given jurisdiction over all disputes involving labor. The Board consisted of twelve representatives, four each from labor, management, and the public. The AFL and the CIO were each asked to name two representatives. The Executive Council selected George Meany and Daniel Tobin, reflecting Green's waning influence and leading to a rash of rumors that he would soon retire. Another indication of cooperation was the virtual lack of strikes for the first several weeks, and the Senate reflected the same spirit by shelving the Smith anti-strike bill passed by the House prior to Pearl Harbor.[23]

Green recognized, however, that no matter how well AFL unions were able to maintain the no-strike pledge, labor's contribution would always be imperiled as long as the labor movement remained divided. Yet the war years did not alter his views on the requirements for an AFL-CIO reconciliation. Even though Lewis stepped down from the CIO presidency in 1940, Green continued to regard CIO leaders as selfish and immoral, and he would forgive them only after they had demonstrated genuine repentance. The war years did witness an outpouring of invitations from Green to the CIO to "return to the house of labor," but once again it was Lewis and not Green who stole the headlines by announcing a scheme for labor peace. As a member of the CIO's standing negotiating committee, Lewis proposed a peace formula that called for Green's retirement and the elevation of Meany to the presidency of a unified labor movement.[24]

The positive response of the Executive Council to Lewis's letter revealed that Green was fast becoming a nonentity in the Federation. Not one Council member argued that forcing Green's retirement was an unacceptable basis for negotiations. Green himself probably opposed the plan because it would have meant labor unity without a confession of responsibility for the split on the part of the CIO, and because it would have placed Lewis in the position of kingmaker at his expense. Nevertheless, Green dutifully followed the Executive Council's order to accept the peace overture and declared that he was "more than willing" to retire if it served the cause of peace. Unfortunately, CIO President Murray, who received no prior notice of Lewis's action, rejected the proposal. Acknowledging that Lewis's peace proposal was a test of his personal authority, Murray informed Lewis that all initiatives on behalf of labor unity had to originate in the office of the CIO president.[25]

Murray was thus placed in the uncomfortable position of appearing to block labor unity while Green faced forced retirement. Roosevelt came to their rescue, however, with an alternative plan. Roosevelt's plan did not call for a merger. Rather, he suggested that a committee of six members, three each from the AFL and CIO, meet together with the president to discuss war policies affecting labor. Green and Murray embraced the president's proposal, who thereupon established the Combined War Labor Board. An indication of the Executive Council's lukewarm acceptance of the new board was the selection of Green as chief AFL representative.[26] And although the board met frequently, it never became an important formulator of labor policy, and it encouraged neither Green nor Murray to pursue workable strategies for labor unity. Indeed, while both the AFL and CIO supported Roosevelt throughout the war, the Second World War did not lessen the tensions between the rival labor federations.

If the continued division in organized labor weakened Green's dream of a cooperative war effort, the dream all but collapsed under the strains of a wartime economy. One of the most serious economic problems on the domestic front was that of inflation, which Roosevelt sought to check to limiting wage increases. Prices rose considerably in the early months of the war, and the National War Labor Board granted numerous wage increases so that wages could keep pace with the cost of living. By July 1942, the board worked out a formula to determine the amount of future wage increases. In practice, this so-called "Little Steel Formula" meant that wages could not be increased more than fifteen percent above rates prevailing in January 1941.[27]

Green was horrified by the government's interference on the wage issue. For Green, as for most labor leaders, determination of wages was the exclusive domain of collective bargaining. Even during the war emergency, the government had no right to interfere in the adjustment of wages. Upon the announcement of the Little Steel Formula, Green wrote a scathing letter to the president condemning the "invasion of Labor's basic rights. It is not necessary to freeze wages and suspend collective bargaining in order to prevent inflation."[28]

In an effort to prove his point, Green devised his own program to curb inflation. Green's plan called for the creation of joint labor-management commissions, free from government control, that voluntarily would work out wage stabilization agreements. Labor and capital could work out arrangements whereby future wage increases would be paid in war bonds to be cashed in at the end of the war. In addition, he suggested a restructuring of the tax system to curtail war profiteering by industry and, finally, he demanded rent and price controls.[29] Thus Green was willing to accept wage limitation only if collective bargaining remained intact and only if prices were held in check by government decree.

Roosevelt completely ignored Green's plan. On October 2, 1942, the president signed legislation creating the Office of Economic Stabilization and outlawing all wage increases not approved by the National War Labor Board. Furthermore, the NWLB was prohibited from raising wages beyond those prevailing on September 15, 1942. This amounted to no less than an effort to freeze wages, and it angered Green and the Executive Council. Some members, including William Hutcheson, argued that the wage freeze justified a renunciation of the no-strike pledge. But Green spoke for the majority on the Council when he said that, despite their objections, the AFL "will cooperate fully" with the president's anti-inflation program.[30]

Although Green continued to express his dissatisfaction with wage controls, he did so with little effect. The president could effectively ignore Green and the Executive Council because he realized that the AFL hierarchs would never challenge the presidency and undermine the war effort. Indeed, Green's patriotism knew no bounds. He considered it his personal duty, as a citizen of the U.S., "to respond to every request that the President of the United States may make and to every order which he may issue as Commander in Chief."[31]

At the conclusion of the war, Green championed the AFL's desire to return to unrestricted collective bargaining. He called for the abolition of the National War Labor Board and railed against those who hoped to maintain wage controls in peacetime. In October 1946, he declared that "the way to establish and maintain industrial peace and stability is to remove government control of wages immediately." It was imperative, according to Green, to abolish governmental control, restore normal collective bargaining, and allow wages to rise to their "proper" level.[32]

Patriotism and loyalty to Roosevelt go a long way toward explaining why Green ultimately acquiesced in the establishment of wartime wage controls, but acceptance of the Little Steel Formula had been made much more palatable by a National War Labor Board decision of June 1942. Green understood that the Little Steel Formula could undermine union organization. Why would unorganized workers join unions if unions had little hope of securing wage increases? Indeed, Green's opposition to wage controls had as much to do with his concern over union membership as the standard of living. In an attempt to temper the opposition of Green and other labor leaders to the Little Steel Formula, the NWLB introduced the maintenance of membership clause.

Maintenance of membership applied to all unions that had signed contracts with employers. In practice, the formula stated that all newly-hired workers were permitted fifteen days to declare their unwillingness to join the union. If workers failed to exercise this option, they automatically became dues-paying union members and thus subject to dismissal for failure to abide by all union regulations. Since few workers made use of the escape clause, the AFL enjoyed substantial growth in the war years, climbing from a membership of 5.1 million in 1941 to almost 6.9 million in 1945.[33] While maintenance of membership softened Green's reaction to wage controls, he willingly gave it up after the war to return to unfettered collective bargaining. He did not believe maintenance of membership was a fair trade for government interference in the collective bargaining arena.

Wage regulation and the continued division in the labor movement were damaging blows to Green's vision of a cooperative war effort. The hostility of Congress provided the knockout punch. In the depression years, Green had hoped to curtail strike activity in an effort to prove to employers that workers were responsible members of society who deserved the right to form unions. In the war years, he hoped to maintain the no-strike pledge in order to convince employers and government officials that workers were patriotic and loyal, willing to sacrifice their self-interest to defeat the enemy. In return, employers and representatives would treat labor with respect, maintaining wages and protecting labor's political rights. Just as this approach failed as an organizing strategy in the 1930s, during the war years the approach failed to safeguard labor's political position.

Anti-labor sentiment in Congress during he war rose and fell with the level of strike activity. As long as workers refrained from strikes, which they did to a remarkable degree in 1942, even conservatives were appeased. But as the number of strikes increased in 1943, Congress reacted with a vengeance. Although the number of strikes was only slightly higher in 1943 than in 1942, the number of days lost more than tripled the figure of 1942. Yet it was not the combination of skyrocketing living costs and wage controls that disrupted the no-strike pledge. One man was largely responsible for the increased strike activity of 1943. Over two-thirds of the days lost in that year resulted from several United Mine Worker strikes.[34] John L. Lewis again would topple the cooperative dream of William Green. He had done so in the 1930s by manipulating worker militancy and undermining labor unity, and he would do so during the war by making a mockery of the no-strike pledge and bringing down on labor the wrath of Congress.

The 1943 UMW strikes brought to the surface, for the first time, the differences among labor leaders during the war. Aside from a handful of Trotskyists, active at the local level in both the AFL and CIO, who viewed the war as an opportunity to undermine the social order, three distinct leadership styles emerged. First, there was the militancy of John L. Lewis, the only major labor leader who challenged directly both government and industry during the war. Lewis believed that other labor leaders had made themselves slaves to the Roosevelt Administration. They had exchanged labor's only weapon, the strike, for a government promise to maintain union memberships. They had become, in essence, the henchmen of government and industry as they forced discipline on their own rank-and-file. Lewis vowed to continue the fight for economic advance without giving up that which had built his union in the first place—the economic muscle of the rank-and-file.[35]

Phil Murray and the craft union leaders of the AFL represented the most common leadership style during the war. They made a calculated decision to trade the strike weapon for tangible union gains. Their strategy paid off in terms of membership growth, increases in union treasuries, and increased prestige within the Democratic party. But the price was very high. reliance on government agencies led to an ever-increasing bureaucratization of union activities during and after the war. Further, their role as enforcers of the no-strike pledge often placed them in opposition to their own membership. The gap between union members and their leadership widened during the war.[36]

Green represented a third style. Unlike Lewis, Green had abandoned long ago the use of economic force. His goal, as always, was to secure union advances by proving labor was respectable and responsible. The war provided an excellent opportunity to realize that goal. Unlike Murray and the craft union leaders, there was for Green no question of a trade-off between the right to strike and maintenance of membership. Enforcing the no-strike pledge was his moral and patriotic duty, not a calculated strategy. While he chafed at the growing involvement of the state in labor affairs, he was willing to sacrifice temporarily the interests of the movement for the sake of victory in war.

Thus Green was livid when Lewis led the coal miners on strike in 1943. The public, the Roosevelt Administration, and Congress shared his hostility. Largely in response to the coal strikes, Congress passed the Smith-Connally War Labor Disputes Act over Roosevelt's veto in June 1943. The act was a direct assault on labor's right to strike, requiring unions to file strike notices, maintain a thirty-day cooling off period, and submit to a strike vote by the National Labor Relations Board. Green and Murray responded in a joint memorandum that attacked the act as a real threat to collective bargaining. It was a "wicked, vicious" measure "born of revenge and malice."[37]

Although the Smith-Connally Act was the only major piece of anti-labor legislation passed during the war, numerous other bills were introduced intended to curb union activity. State legislatures in the South and West also launched anti-union crusades.

George Meany, not William Green, led the AFL's battle against restrictive laws. Green's influence in the Federation was dying as surely as was his dream of a cooperative war effort. From the sidelines, then, Green complained that Congress sought to undermine labor's rights even though the Federation was giving its utmost to the war effort. The AFL had a marvelous strike record, AFL members had purchased millions of dollars worth of war bonds, and in every way, Green and the AFL had proven to be shining examples of patriotism and sacrifice.[38] Green had shown employers and shown employers and government representatives that the majority of AFL members were, in fact, responsible and respectable. He had kept his part of the bargain. But his efforts had not led to a spirit of cooperation. Only the close ties with the Roosevelt Administration and the need for labor's assistance in the war effort saved the labor movement from severely restrictive legislation. If Green hoped to avoid a conservative onslaught after the war, he would have to do more than dream of cooperation. He would have to reassess his political assumptions, in particular the effectiveness of nonpartisanship.

Organized labor emerged from the war a powerful economic and political force in the nation. "Measured in numbers, political influence, economic weight, or by any other yardstick," conceded the president of the U.S. Chamber of Commerce in 1944, "labor is a power in our land." At the end of the war, the combined membership of the AFL, CIO, and independent unions stood at 15 million, a five-fold increase since 1933. According to historian David Brody, "political action . . . held out seemingly boundless opportunity for the exertion of labor's power at the close of World War II. It did not appear beyond reason to anticipate a role comparable to that played by the labor movement in British political life."[39] Many CIO officials recognized the political possibilities and emerged from the war with schemes to radicalize the Democratic party or launch a third party.

The AFL lagged far behind the CIO in terms of political thinking, but even Green and the old guard moved to expand labor's political interests. Among the sources of the AFL's heightened political awareness were the Great Depression, which proved that labor's well-being could not be isolated from the health of society as a whole, the strong identification with the New Deal, and also the dramatic increase in size and resources that obligated the AFL to look beyond its narrow interests. By the late 1930s, and certainly by the end of the 1940s, the AFL, for the most part, had committed itself to the ideal of the welfare state—that government had a responsibility to provide a decent living standard for all its citizens. In the halls of Congress, Green battled for an adequate minimum wage for all workers, the extension of social security benefits, the establishment of a national system of health insurance, the improvement of public education, and government housing programs.[40] Yet although Green exhibited a growing concern for social welfare legislation, he did not recognize the need to alter the nature of the Federation's participation in politics. He doggedly adhered to the principle of nonpartisanship.

In the early years of the AFL, nonpartisanship was at times an effective policy. It had strengthened labor's bargaining power with both the Democrats and Republicans. But by the 1930s, nonpartisanship no longer suited the political environment. The original justification for the AFL's political policy—the rough equivalence of the two parties on labor issues—was no longer true after the election of Roosevelt. The vast majority of workers voted Democratic in the 1930s and 1940s, and most labor officials were ardent New Dealers. But the AFL's influence within the Democratic party was crippled by the unwillingness of Green and other AFL leaders to abandon nonpartisanship and establish institutional ties with the party.

If the policy of nonpartisanship was outmoded in the 1940s, why then did Green not pursue a different political course? One significant reason was the continued existence of a powerful anti-New Deal bloc within the Federation. In 1939, ten AFL officials publicly attacked the Roosevelt

Administration, much to the embarrassment of Green and the Executive Council majority. William Hutcheson resigned from the Council in 1936 to protest the Council's support for New Deal legislation. Hutcheson returned to the Council in 1940 and served as the leading Republican until John L. Lewis and the UMW reaffiliated in 1946.[41] Since the AFL was a voluntary institution, Green did not have the power to coerce these anti-New Dealers into any new political venture.

An even more important factor was the dead hand of tradition. By the end of the war, Green was simply too complacent, too set in his ways to take full advantage of labor's potential political strength. The aged Federation president found it much easier to mouth time-worn slogans about the merits of nonpartisanship than to look creatively at the future. Even after the disastrous elections of 1946, Green argued that "the best interests of the AFL's entire membership have been protected and conserved through a strict adherence to a nonpartisan political policy."[42]

A third reason for Green's failure to capitalize on the postwar situation was the coming of the Cold War. Green's dread of Communism—and like many others he tended to stigmatize all political and economic dissenters as Communists—did not become moderated with the passage of time. At almost every AFL convention, Green made sure to attack the "Red menace" and to link it, at least by implication, with CIO unions. Thus it was easy for him to dismiss the CIO officials' advocacy of national planning, and economic policy designed to insure full employment, or a third party as Communist-inspired. In 1946, he lashed out at the CIO's Political Action Committee, which had been created in 1944 to bring the CIO's political force to bear in national elections. Although the CIO PAC endorsed Roosevelt, Green declared that the ultimate purpose of the committee was the imposition "upon our nation a form of foreign-conceived ideology totally unsuited to our American way of life."[43] Green's penchant for linking political innovation to Communism intensified as relations between the Soviet Union and the U.S. deteriorated.

Green was a life-long Democrat. He was a vocal supporter of New Deal candidates and contributed money to their campaigns. But the force of tradition, the anti-New Deal bloc within the Federation, and the Cold War all locked him into a nonpartisan stance. In the Congressional elections of 1946, Green refused to recognize the need for a change in policy. In a letter to all affiliates, he wrote that voting a straight party ticket did not make for good government. He explained that the "nonpartisan political policy of the American Federation of Labor is based on the principle that the workers should elect the friends and defeat the enemies regardless of their political affiliation."[44] The election results demonstrated the fallacy of this approach. Republicans won control of both houses of Congress for the first time since 1930 and put through the infamous Taft-Hartley Act.

Among other restrictions, Taft-Hartley outlawed the closed shop, restored the use of injunctions, proscribed jurisdictional strikes and secondary boycotts, and prohibited unions from making any contributions in connection with national elections or primaries. When the bill passed over Truman's veto and became law of the land in 1947, Green felt tricked and troubled. In vain did he plead with conservative politicians and their industry supporters that their anti-union objectives could not be effected without endangering economic prosperity, if not the capitalist system itself. On the platform and in periodicals, Green preached the gospel of high wages and defended the rights of free institutions with passionate eloquence. He wailed that Taft-Hartley would drive workers, out of desperation, into the camp of radicals. Nevertheless, Green urged compliance with the provisions of the "slave law."[45] Thus Green became a truly thwarted and indignant man—the implacable enemy of radicals and the rejected defender of capitalism.

Passage of Taft-Hartley devastated Green. After more than twenty years trying to demonstrate that the interests of capital, organized labor, and the state were in harmony, he was faced with the fact that both the public and men of power still regarded labor with suspicion. He had failed to bring unions into the mainstream of American political and economic life. Yet even Taft-Hartley could not shake Green's conviction that his approach to union advance was a dead end. The old man once again refused to abandon caution, conservatism, and respectability. To the bitter end, he shunned economic force and pursued accommodation with industry and the succoring of public support. When AFL members flooded his office with demands that he call a twenty-four-hour general strike to protest passage of the act, Green responded that such action was unthinkable because it "would influence the public against labor."[46]

Taft-Hartley did jolt Green into the recognition that the AFL's political program had to be intensified. He sided with the majority at the 1947 convention in ordering the creation of a special political agency, Labor's League for Political Education. Financed by voluntary contributions, the LLPE was set up to acquaint workers with the economic and political views of the AFL and to prepare and disseminate information on the labor records of candidates.[47] Although Green was anxious to use the LLPE as a means to influence party platforms, he sought to avoid too close an alliance with either the Democrats or Republicans. When the Executive Council discussed the policy to be pursued in the 1948 presidential election, Green sided with the majority and argued for strict adherence to the traditional policy of no endorsement.[48]

Until his death, Green refused to accept the arguments of George Meany and his growing band of followers that LLPE could be more effective if it endorsed a presidential candidate. In Green's view, such an endorsement was tantamount to party endorsement, a clear violation of nonpartisanship. As his health declined and as he found it necessary to return to Coshocton for extended periods of rest, Green carried less and less weight in Federation circles. As his influence declined, Meany's increased. In 1952, Meany persuaded the Executive Council to hold the AFL convention after the Republican and Democratic nominating conventions, but before the national elections. This deft move allowed delegates to the AFL convention to hear first hand from both candidates, Dwight D. Eisenhower and Adlai Stevenson. Stevenson, the Democrat, came out in favor of the repeal of Taft-Hartley while Eisenhower waffled. Faced with such a clear-cut choice, the AFL, for the first time in its history, endorsed a candidate from a major party for the presidency.[49] This shift in political strategy was a result of Meany's maneuvering and symbolized the end of Green's influence.

That Green was a sick, failing man was painfully obvious to everyone at the September 1952 AFL convention. Weak though he was, he insisted on presiding and making several long speeches, attending committee meetings and conferences. "It was a sad thing," an AFL employee said. "Green was so near the end of the road, and he seemed to realize it. He didn't want to turn loose." After adjournment, Green spoke to Secretary-Treasurer Meany, telling him "I'm tired, and I think I'll go home for a few days and rest."[50]

Green returned to his hometown and spent two days at the Coshocton Memorial Hospital, where doctors discovered that he was suffering from exhaustion and a failing heart. Then he went home to bed. Always thinking of the AFL, he kept in touch with headquarters by telephone. He was saddened when voters on November 4 failed to elect Stevenson. Then a few days later came another hard blow—the sudden death of Phil Murray. Despite their union differences, the two old miners had respected and liked one another personally, and Green felt the death keenly. He did not try to go to Murray's funeral, and he telephoned Meany to say, "It doesn't look like I'm going to be back in the office for a while; you have the authority to do whatever needs to be done. Good luck."[51]

On Thursday, November 20, 1952, in his home at 409 South Fourth Street, William Green suffered a heart attack. He sank rapidly in the night and on Friday, at 1:22 in the afternoon, his heart stopped beating. On Monday, Green was laid to rest in South Lawn Cemetery, not far from where he was born, not far from where he had dug coal and become a trade unionist.[52]

Afterword

O RGANIZED LABOR in the 1980s faces a crisis as serious as any it has faced since the 1930s. By any measure— membership, political power, bargaining might—the movement is weaker now than it has been for decades. Anti-labor forces within government and industry reign supreme, and the public image of unions continues to decline. When the Executive Council of the AFL-CIO met in February 1985, it invited academics and industrial relations experts to help devise a strategy to combat the current crisis. The solution? The AFL-CIO should mount a public relations campaign to sell the idea of unionism to the public. It should down-play union militancy and confrontational tactics and stress instead the valuable role unions play in terms of productivity and efficiency.

The parallels between this strategy and Green's program for the 1920s, 1930s, and 1940s are obvious. And even though current leaders of labor are guided by more practical concerns than Christian idealism, a study of Green's presidency still seems a natural first step for those who would understand the conservatism of today's labor leaders. Green's career links the infancy of organized labor in the late nineteenth century and its maturity in the 1980s. A study of his life not only fills a void in the historical record, it reveals the often surprising continuity of thought among labor leaders across several generations.

Labor historians invariably depict William green as a bumbling incompetent, vain and ignorant, the cheerful servant of selfish and reactionary craft unionists, and the person most directly responsible for the split in organized labor in the 1930s. As one historian put it, Green was "depressingly cautious and almost completely without imagination. Whatever forward motion the labor movement made from Green's accession to the AFL presidency in 1924 to his death in the 1950s was made despite Green

173

rather than because of him."[1] Other historians describe his "weakness of character," his "naivete," and his "ineptitude."[2] These harsh judgments contain elements of truth, but they also serve as a myth that obscures an understanding of the man and his values. In large measure, Green is a victim of the strong CIO bias held by labor historians who follow the lead of early CIO bigwigs, especially John L. Lewis, and use Green as a whipping boy to personify the backwardness of the AFL.

This is not to deny that Green was a weak labor leader. His deficiencies contributed to the failure of the AFL in the 1920s and 1930s to meet the needs of millions of unskilled workers in mass-production industries. His dogged commitment to time-worn labor traditions such as exclusive jurisdiction, political nonpartisanship, and union autonomy prevented the AFL from exercising real political and economic power during his tenure. Under his leadership, the Federation remained a weak and conservative organization of mostly skilled workers. But Green himself was not a narrow-minded craft unionist, and to place him in the same camp with Arthur Wharton of the Machinists, William Hutcheson of the Carpenters, and John P. Frey of the Metal Trades Department is to misunderstand him. Green was above all a decent, honorable, and even courageous man who recoiled at economic injustice and labored unsparingly to bring all workers into the trade union fold.

Green's commitment to the organization of all workers was revealed in his consistent support for the principle of industrial unionism. In public speeches and in the private meetings of the AFL Executive Council, Green steadfastly maintained that if mass-production workers were to be organized, the Federation would have to abandon its craft union structure. Yet just as Gompers had realized the limits of the AFL presidency in the nineteenth century when he failed in his efforts to establish a central strike fund and remove racist clauses from affiliates' constitutions, so, too, did Green realize that the friendly persuasion of the AFL president could not sway the outmoded way of thinking on the part of craft union chieftains. Green's inability to alter the structure of the Federation was not proof that Green was the happy servant of craft unionists. Throughout his career, he was an outspoken champion of the need for industrial unionism.

Green's impotency as a labor leader stemmed not from personal weakness, selfishness, or lack of effort but from an inflexible adherence to an unworkable strategy. His inability to abandon the notion that the union cause could be advanced only to the extent that employers and workers embraced the spirit of cooperation proved his undoing. He never accepted the fact that militancy, or at least militant posturing, could be an effective strategy. At best, he believed, militancy might yield short term material gains. But in the long run, militancy damaged the supposedly moral relationship that existed between labor and capital. For Green, the "development of moral standards in relations between those whose incomes depend on employment and those who operate the industries that provide jobs" was the "most important contribution" the labor movement could make.[3]

Even by his own standards, Green was a failure. As he himself understood, true cooperation began after employers recognized unions and collective bargaining was initiated. His pursuit of labor-management cooperation as an organizing strategy was an absurdity in the 1920s and 1930s. It played into the hands of those who hoped to stymie the organization of mass-production workers—craft union leaders and employers. His strategy failed to influence a single employer and it alienated millions of workers willing to join the AFL. CIO leaders pursued cooperation with industry in the sense that they, too, believed that once collective bargaining was established, unions and employers could work toward industrial peace. However, CIO leaders understood that rank-and-file combativeness could be used as a weapon to compel union recognition. The CIO's reluctance to sanction militancy once collective bargaining was established has been cited by historians as an indication of the movement's essentially conservative character. Green must then be condemned forever as a labor leader unwilling to take at least this forward step. Indeed, his moral opposition to militancy led him to attack the CIO with a fervor he never exhibited when dealing with even the most reactionary employer.

Green also suffered from what John L. Lewis described as an "innate craving for orthodox respectability."[4] His appearance, his personal habits, and his professional activities all exuded respectability. Even as a youth, Green never flirted with radical ideas, never questioned established beliefs and conventions, never showed an interest in anything not completely acceptable to middle-class society. As a labor official, he sought public approval for all his actions and was morbidly concerned lest he offend anyone by his comments. Indeed, he was so cautious and conventional in his opinions and actions that he failed to inspire those whom he supposedly led. To American workers the AFL president seemed distant and singularly unremarkable. The craving of respectability is shared to some extent by all entrenched labor bureaucrats. By the end of their careers both Gompers and Lewis had grown fat and complacent, unwilling to take risks. But both continued to command the allegiance of working people because of their finely-honed leadership talents, talents that Green never possessed.

Another downfall of Green's presidency was his lack of a sophisticated understanding of the depth and breadth of economic injustice. He remained convinced that all problems between capital and labor were ultimately moral and not economic. Even in the midst of depression, Green never once considered the possibility that the interests of capital and labor were divergent. As unemployment mounted in 1931 and 1932, Green could not understand why employers shirked their "moral obligation" to maintain employment. All friction between those who toil and those who own industry, from the shop floor to the halls of Congress, would disappear once both sides began to live according to the Golden Rule and the dictates of the Bible. Green's understanding of economics never extended far beyond biblical platitudes.

Above all, Green's career reminds us that moral idealism in itself is a weak tool for the advancement of the working class. Labor leadership then and now must possess confidence in the ability of working people themselves to improve the conditions of their existence. Leaders must also possess a critical appreciation of the nature of economic injustice. While one might applaud Green's vision of society perfected through Christianity, one must also recognize that this vision ultimately led to his failure as a labor leader.

Notes

Preface

1. The best analyses of labor unrest in southern Appalachia and the AFL's campaign in the South are Irving Bernstein, *The Lean Years: A History of the American Worker, 1920–1933* (Boston, 1960), pp. 1–43; and Jean Trepp McKelvey, *AFL Attitudes Toward Production, 1900–1932* (Ithaca, 1952), pp. 99–113.

2. Bernstein, *The Lean Years*, p. 34.

3. American Federation of Labor, *Report of the Proceedings of the Forty-Ninth Annual Convention* (1929), pp. 60, 265–283. (Convention proceedings will be cited hereafter as AFL, *Proceedings*, with the year following.)

4. McKelvey, p. 102.

5. AFL, *Proceedings*, 1930, p. 86.

6. Address to Atlanta Central Labor Union, February 14, 1930, Reel 7, William Green Collection, Ohio Historical Society (hereafter cited as WGC OHS).

7. Lewis Lorwin, *The American Federation of Labor: History, Policies, and Prospects* (Washington, D.C., 1933), p. 258.

8. McKelvey, p. 106.

9. On the Danville strike, see Bernstein, *The Lean Years*, pp. 36–40; McKelvey, pp. 108–111; Lorwin, pp. 254–256.

10. Lorwin, pp. 256–258.

Chapter I

1. "Biographical Note," William Green Collection, Biographical File, AFL-CIO Archives.

2. Katherine Harvey, *The Best-Dressed Miners* (Ithaca, 1969), p. 20.

3. Wills and Marriages, Coshocton County, 1925.

4. Norman N. Hill, *History of Coshocton County* (Newark, Ohio, 1881), p. 605.

5. *United Mine Workers Journal* (hereafter cited as *UMWJ*), April 17, 1902; Andrew Roy, *A History of the Coal Miners of the United States* (Columbus, 1907), pp. 56–58; Raymond Boryczka and Lorin Lee Cary, *No Strength Without Union: An Illustrated History of Ohio Workers, 1803–1980* (Columbus, 1982), pp. 4, 65.

6. Hill, pp. 604–606.

7. Ninth Census of the United States, 1870.

8. Boryczka and Cary, p. 66; McAlister Coleman, *Men and Coal* (New York, 1943), pp. 34–35.

9. Tenth Census of the United States, 1880; "Biographical Note," William Green Collection, Biographical File, AFL-CIO Archives.

10. Address to Kenyon College, October 22, 1949, Reel 17, WGC OHS.

11. Ibid.

12. "Miscellaneous," William Green Collection, Biographical File, AFL-CIO Archives.

13. Benjamin Stolberg, "Sitting Bill," *Saturday Evening Post*, October 18, 1941, p. 90.

14. Hill, p. 606; Max Danish, *William Green: A Pictorial Biography* (New York, 1952), p. 7.

15. Quoted in Thomas R. Brooks, *Clint: A Biography of a Labor Intellectual, Clinton S. Golden* (New York, 1978), p. 7.

16. Stolberg, p. 90.

17. Green to Macon Reed, Jr., September 5, 1936, William Green Collection, Biographical File, AFL-CIO Archives.

18. See Boryczka and Cary, pp. 66–67.

19. William Green, *Labor and Democracy* (Princeton, 1939), p. 22.

20. "Speech," April 21, 1936, Reel 17, WGC OHS.

21. Green to Thomas Van Lear, January 9, 1925, Reel 4, WGC OHS.

22. John Brophy, *A Miner's Life* (Madison, 1964), p. 34.

23. William Atherton, "The Making of William Green," unpublished essay, Reel 6, WGC OHS.

24. Green's frequent trips to Coshocton are recorded in his "Expense Accounts," Reel 14, WGC OHS.

25. "Biographical Sketch," Reel 1, WGC OHS.

26. Ibid.

27. Address to Kenyon College, October 22, 1949, Reel 17, WGC OHS.

28. See Herbert Gutman, "Protestantism and the American Labor Movement: The Christian Spirit in the Guilded Age," *American Historical Review*, 72 (October 1966), pp. 74–101; David Alan Corbin, *Life, Work, and Rebellion in the Coal Fields: The Southern West Virginia Miners* (Urbana, 1985), pp. 146–175.

29. *UMWJ*, April 30, 1891; *UMWJ*, May 7, 1891.

30. See *UMWJ*, March 23, 1893.

31. Ibid., February 15, 1894.

32. Ibid., June 28, June 14, May 3, April 19, April 5, 1894; Brophy, pp. 22–23.

33. *UMWJ*, June 6, 1895; *UMWJ*, March 21, 1895.

34. Coleman, p. 57.

35. Circular Letter, October 3, 1893, Reel 3, WGC OHS.

36. *UMWJ*, July 15, 1897.

37. Ibid., August 12, July 15, 1897.

38. Ibid., August 3, August 28, 1898; Coleman, p. 58.

39. K. Austin Kerr, "Labor-Management Cooperation: An 1897 Case," *Pennsylvania Magazine of History and Biography*, 49 (January 1975), 45–71; James P. Johnson, *The Politics of Soft Coal* (Urbana, 1979), p. 26; Coleman, pp. 49–50.

40. Kerr, p. 71.

41. Address to the Harvard Union, March 30, 1925, Reel 14, WGC OHS.

42. *UMWJ*, January 3, 1901.

43. Ibid., December 26, 1901.

44. Ibid., October 3, September 5, May 30, 1901.

45. Ibid., December 26, 1901.

46. Warren Van Tine, *The Making of the Labor Bureaucrat* (Amherst, 1973), pp. 80–81.

47. *UMWJ*, December 26, 1901, December 11, 1902.

48. *Coshocton Daily Age*, January 12, January 4, January 1, 1906.

49. Ibid., January 12, 1906.

50. Coleman, pp. 77–78.

51. *UMWJ*, February 3, 1906; Coleman, p. 76.

52. *Coshocton Daily Age*, February 5, 1906.

53. *UMWJ*, April 5, 1906.

54. Ibid., June 21, 1906.

55. Coleman, pp. 79–80; *UMWJ*, March 30, January 23, 1908.

56. John Mitchell to William B. Wilson, July 20, 1909, John Mitchell Papers, Catholic University of America (Hereafter cited as JMP CUA).

57. Mitchell to Green, July 17, 1909, JMP CUA.

58. Mitchell to John Walker, July 27, 1909; William B. Wilson to Mitchell, July 28, 1909; Green to Mitchell, July 20, 1909; Mitchell to Green, July 16 and July 17, 1909, JMP CUA.

59. William Green, "To the Officers and Members of Local Unions of the United Mine Workers of America," November 25, 1909, JMP CUA.

60. Edwin Perry to Mitchell, October 13, 1909; Mitchell to Green, September 29, 1909; John Walker to Mitchell, September 25, 1909; Mitchell to John Walker, September 22, 1909, JMP CUA.

61. *UMWJ*, October 21, 1909.

62. Green to Mitchell, December 13, 1909, JMP CUA.

63. *UMWJ*, December 30, December 23, 1909.

64. Mitchell to John P. White, December 23, 1910, Mitchell to Green, March 2, 1910, JMP CUA; Edwin Perry to Green, November 17, 1909, Reel 1, WGC OHS.

65. Green to Mitchell, February 2, 1911, Reel 1, WGC OHS; Coleman, p. 82.

66. Green to Mitchell, March 7, 1911, JMP CUA.

67. E. E. Vorhies to Green, November 16, 1911, Reel 1, WGC OHS; Danish, p. 18.

68. Hoyt Warner, *Progressivism in Ohio, 1897–1917* (Columbus, 1964), pp. 265–266.

69. Patrick Reagan, "The Ideology of Social Harmony and Efficiency: Workmen's Compensation in Ohio, 1904–1919," *Ohio History*, 90 (Autumn 1981), 317–331.

70. Green to W. K. Field, January 6, 1925, Reel 4; John Moore to Green, January 2, 1925, January 7, 1925, January 15, 1925, and no date, Reel 1, WGC OHS.

71. Phillip Foner, *History of the Labor Movement in the United States, Volume IV: The Industrial Workers of the World, 1905–1917* (New York, 1965), pp. 381–383.

72. Green to Mitchell, March 7, 1912, JMP CUA; *UMWJ*, June 27, 1912; James Mercer, *Ohio Legislative History, 1909–1913* (Columbus, n.d.), pp. 499–500.

73. Green to W. K. Field, January 6, 1925, Reel 4, WGC OHS.

74. John P. White to Mitchell, December 26, 1910, JMP CUA; "Biographical Sketch," Reel 1, WGC OHS.

75. Frank Farrington to Green, September 8, 1934, Reel 8, WGC OHS.

76. Green to Macon Reed, Jr., September 5, 1936, William Green Collection, Biographical File, AFL-CIO Archives.

77. On the social gospel, see Henry F. May, *Protestant Churches and Industrial America* (New York, 1949); and Robert T. Handy, ed., *The Social Gospel in America* (New York, 1966).

78. Quoted in Gutman, p. 100.

79. Jacob Henry Dorn, *Washington Gladden: Prophet of the Social Gospel* (Columbus, 1967), pp. 205–208.

80. Ibid., p. 221.

81. *UMWJ*, December 21, 1911, November 28, 1912.

82. Quote and information on Labor Forward are from Elizabeth and Kenneth Fones-Wolf, "Trade-Union Evangelism; Religion and the AFL in the Labor Forward Movement," in *Working-Class America: Essays on Labor, Community, and American Society*, eds. Michael H. Frisch and Daniel J. Walkowitz (Urbana, 1983), pp. 153–184.

83. Charles A. Madison, *American Labor Leaders: Personalities and Forces in the Labor Movement* (New York, 1962), pp. 110–111.

84. *UMWJ*, November 21, 1912.

85. Ibid., November 28, 1912.

86. AFL, *Proceedings,* 1915, pp. 498–499; Philip Taft, *The A. F. of L. in the Time of Gompers* (New York, 1960), pp. 364– 365.

87. Melvyn Dubofsky and Warrren Van Tine, *John L. Lewis: A Biography* (New York, 1977), pp. 37–40.

88. Ibid., pp. 100–101.

89. "Extracts from UMWA Executive Board Meeting," January 25, 1925, Reel 4, WGC OHS; AFL, *Proceedings,* 1921, pp. 451–454.

90. Quoted in Philip Taft, *The A. F. of L. from the Death of Gompers to the Merger* (New York, 1970), p. 1.

91. On Green's election, see Madison, p. 108; Stolberg, p. 27; Dubofsky and Van Tine, p. 110; and Taft, *The A. F. of L. in the Time of Gompers,* pp. 486–487.

92. *Coshocton Age,* January 10, 1907.

93. Quoted in James R. Green, *The World of the Worker: Labor in Twentieth-Century America* (New York, 1980), p. 123.

94. *American Federationist,* January 1925, p. 29.

95. Quoted in Irving Bernstein, *The Lean Years: A History of the American Worker, 1920–1933* (Boston, 1960), p. 92.

Chapter II

1. On the internal and external problems facing organized labor in the 1920s, see Irving Bernstein, *The Lean Years: A History of the American Worker, 1920–1933* (Boston, 1960), pp. 85–90.

2. On the shift in AFL policy in the 1920s, see Jean Trepp McKelvey, *AFL Attitudes Toward Production, 1900–1932* (Ithaca, 1952), pp. 79–98.

3. Address at Reading, Pennsylvania, May 14, 1927, Reel 16, WGC OHS.

4. Labor Sunday Address, New York City, September 5, 1926, Reel 16, WGC OHS.

5. McKelvey, pp. 90–91.

6. See, for example, Green's editorial in the *American Federationist,* October 1925, pp. 873–874.

7. On the AFL's new wage theory, see McKelvey, pp. 80, 91–97, 117.

8. Address at State Normal School, Duluth, Minnesota, May 18, 1926, Reel 16, WGC OHS.

9. *New York Times,* October 5, 1926, p. 28:2.

10. AFL, *Proceedings,* 1927, p. 198.

11. Ibid., p. 217.

12. *New York Times,* July 31, 1927, p. 25:1; Charles A. Madison, *American Labor Leaders: Personalities and Forces in the Labor Movement* (New York: 1962), p. 112.

13. Labor Day Address, Philadelphia, September 6, 1926, Reel 14, WGC OHS; *New York Times,* January 11, 1926, p. 20:2.

14. AFL, *Proceedings,* 1926, pp. 103, 104, 197–207.

15. Green, "The Five-Day Week," January 1927, Reel 16, WGC OHS.

16. *American Federationist,* July 1927, p. 786; Green, "The Five-Day Week," January 1927, Reel 16, WGC OHS; *Literary Digest,* March 31, 1928, pp. 12–13; *American Federationist,* January 1927, p. 23.

17. Address to Rotary International Convention, October 17, 1928, Reel 15, WGC OHS.

18. Green, "American Trade Unionism," Radio Speech, delivered at Kansas City, Missouri, May 2, 1925, Reel 14, WGC OHS.

19. On the AFL's relations with the military, see James O. Morris, *Conflict Within the AFL: A Study of Craft Versus Industrial Unionism, 1901–1938* (Ithaca, 1958), pp. 71–81.

20. Quoted in Morris, pp. 71–72.

21. *New York Times,* May 25, 1929, p. 10:8; Green to General R. L. Bullard (president of the National Security League), November 12, 1928, Reel 12, WGC OHS; Green to James L. Moss (president of the U.S. Flag Association), April 15, 1929, Reel 13, WGC OHS.

22. Green, "American Trade Unionism," Radio Speech, delivered at Kansas City, Missouri, May 2, 1925, Reel 14, WGC OHS.

23. Bernstein, *The Lean Years,* p. 103.

24. *New York Times,* October 3, 1927, p. 3:1.

25. Bernstein, *The Lean Years,* p. 103.

26. Ibid., pp. 103–104; Phillip Taft, *The A. F. of L. from the Death of Gompers to the Merger,* (New York, 1970), p. 7; Green to Matthew Woll, February 17, 1927, Reel 6, WGC OHS.

27. Bruce Minton and John Stuart, *Men Who Lead Labor* (New York, 1937), p. 4.

28. *New York Times,* August 10, 1925, p. 14:3.

29. AFL, *Proceedings,* 1925, pp. 139–143, 152–153.

30. Bernstein, *The Lean Years,* pp. 139–141.

31. *New York Times,* January 13, 1927, p. 41:3.

32. Bernstein, *The Lean Years,* p. 139; Green to Frank X. Sullivan, June 15, 1927, Reel 16, WGC OHS; *New York Times,* March 12, 1927, p. 17:4; Green to International Unions, February 14, 1928, Reel 6, WGC OHS.

33. Bernstein, *The Lean Years,* pp. 140–141.

34. "Interview," March 3, 1929, Reel 16, WGC OHS.

35. *New York Times,* February 14, 1925, p. 28:5.

36. Morris, pp. 87–88.

37. Ibid., pp. 89–90.

38. Ibid., pp. 90–93.

39. Ibid., pp. 94–95.

40. Green to Robert Fechner, January 11, 1927, Reel 6, WGC OHS.

41. *American Federationist,* April 1927, p. 402.

42. Green to Martin F. Ryan, June 3, 1927, Reel 6, WGC OHS.

43. Morris, pp. 113–116; *American Federationist,* April 1927, p. 402.

44. AFL *Proceedings,* 1928, pp. 315–323.

45. *New York Times,* April 6, 1929, p. 13:1.

46. Labor Sunday Address, New York City, September 5, 1926, Reel 16, WGC OHS.

47. Address at Vassar College, March 18, 1929, Reel 15, WGC OHS.

48. Ibid.

49. *New York Times,* October 18, 1928, p. 31:8.

50. Bernstein, *The Lean Years,* pp. 97–102.

51. Lorwin, pp. 243–244.

52. Morris, p. 57.

53. Green to Max S. Hayes, September 10, 1926, Reel 6, WGC OHS.

54. *American Federationist,* November 1926, pp. 1305–1307.

55. "Extract from AFL Executive Council Minutes, January 11–19, 1927," Convention File 11, AFL-CIO Archives.

56. Green to Paul Smith, June 24, 1927, Convention File 11, AFL-CIO Archives.

57. Paul Smith to Green, July 27, 1927; Green to Paul Smith, July 29, 1927, Convention File 11, AFL-CIO Archives.

58. Morris, pp. 61–63; Lorwin, pp. 247–248.

59. Green to Joseph Shepler, January 7, 1927, Reel 6, WGC OHS.

60. AFL, *Proceedings*, 1927, pp. 8–10.

61. Ibid., 1928, pp. 50–51.

62. *New York Times*, October 5, 1929, p. 9:1.

63. Labor Day Address, Philadelphia, September 6, 1926, Reel 14, WGC OHS.

64. *New York Times*, September 5, 1927, p. 3:7.

65. See, for example, *New York Times*, September 3, 1928, p. 6:2.

66. Morris, p. 83.

67. Address to the Harvard Union, March 30, 1925, Reel 14, WGC OHS.

68. M. B. Hammon to Green, December 26, 1924, Reel 3, WGC OHS.

69. Bernstein, *The Lean Years*, p. 237.

70. *American Federationist*, February 1925, p. 110; *New York Times*, October 10, 1925, p. 17:1.

71. Address to the Ohio State Federation of Labor, Steubenville, Ohio, August 10, 1925, Reel 16, WGC OHS.

72. Ibid.

73. Bernstein, *The Lean Years*, p. 237.

74. Ibid., pp. 195–206.

75. Address to Fellowship Council Meeting, New York City, April 12, 1926, Reel 14, WGC OHS.

76. Ibid., frame 737.

77. Bernstein, *The Lean Years*, p. 395.

78. Ibid., p. 396; *New York Times*, February 11, 1928, p. 9:1; *New York Times*, February 12, 1928, p. 9:1.

79. Taft, *The A. F. of L. from the Death of Gompers to the Merger*, p. 23.

80. AFL, *Proceedings*, 1929, pp. 194–198, 317–325, 325– 333, 340–352.

81. Bernstein, *The Lean Years*, p. 200.

82. *New York Times*, April 6, 1930, p. 1:1.

83. Quoted in Taft, *The A. F. of L. from the Death of Gompers to the Merger*, p. 22.

84. *New York Times*, May 8, 1930, p. 2:3.

85. Bernstein, *The Lean Years*, pp. 409–410.

86. *New York Times*, September 12, 1930, p. 5:4.

87. Bernstein, *The Lean Years*, pp. 413–414.

88. *American Federationist*, April 1932, pp. 426–428.

Chapter III

1. Quoted in Art Preis, *Labor's Giant Step: Twenty Years of the CIO* (New York, 1964), p. 5.

2. Irving Bernstein, *The Lean Years: A History of the American Worker, 1920–1933* (Boston 1960), p. 252.

3. *New York Times*, November 23, 1929, p. 1:6.

4. David Brody, "The Rise and Decline of Welfare Capitalism," in *Change and Continuity in Twentieth Century America: The 1920s*, ed. John Braeman et al. (Columbus: 1968), pp. 172–173.

5. Bernstein, *The Lean Years*, p. 335.

6. Ibid., p. 337.

7. On Hoover's labor views, see Robert H. Zieger, *Republicans and Labor, 1919–1929* (Lexington, Ky., 1969), pp. 60–68.

8. *American Federationist*, July 1930, p. 787.

9. Ibid., March 1931, p. 273.

10. *New York Times*, July 19, 1930, p. 18:2.

11. *American Federationist*, July 1930, p. 788.

12. Ibid., March, 1931, p. 273.

13. *New York Times*, July 19, 1930, p. 18:2.

14. Ibid., July 15, 1931, p. 3:1.

15. *American Federationist*, July 1931, p. 923.

16. Quoted in *New York Times*, January 26, 1932, p. 5:1.

17. AFL, *Proceedings*, 1932, pp. 4–7.

18. *New York Times*, November 30, 1932, p. 18:1.

19. AFL, *Proceedings*, 1932, pp. 422–424.

20. Roosevelt Distinguished Service Medal Presentation, New York City, October 27, 1930, Reel 7, frame 414, WGC OHS.

21. Roosevelt Distinguished Service Medal Acceptance Speech, New York City, October 27, 1930, Reel 15, WGC OHS.

22. *American Federationist*, January 1929, p. 21.

23. Ibid., April 1928, p. 403.

24. *New York Times*, March 15, 1929, p. 34:2.

25. *American Federationist*, April 1928, p. 403.

26. Ibid.

27. *AFL Weekly News Service*, December 6, 1930.

28. Frank Duffy to Green, May 26, 1930, Reel 7, frame 340, WGC OHS; Green to Frank Duffy, June 19, 1930, Reel 7, frame 364 WGC OHS.

29. Bernstein, *The Lean Years*, p. 334.

30. Green to Hoover, November 24, 1930, Reel 7, frame 382, WGC OHS.

31. *New York Times*, November 29, 1930, p. 1:5.

32. J. Joseph Huthmacher, *Senator Robert F. Wagner and the Rise of Urban Liberalism* (New York: 1968), pp. 61–63; Lorwin, pp. 288–289.

33. *American Federationist*, August 1930, p. 913.

34. Huthmacher, p. 82.

35. Ibid., pp. 71–85.

36. *New York Times*, March 11, 1931, p. 5:1.

37. Ibid.

38. AFL, *Proceedings*, 1931, pp. 397–398.

39. Address to ILGWU Convention, May 1932, Reel 12, frame 457, WGC OHS.

40. *American Federationist*, July 1930, p. 786.

41. *New York Times,* June 10, 1931, p. 4:2; Labor Day Address, September 3, 1931, Reel 15, frame 358, WGC OHS.

42. Lorwin, pp. 292–294; Bernstein, *The Lean Years,* pp. 349–350; *New York Times,* October 16, 1931, p. 22:4.

43. AFL, *Proceedings,* 1931, p. 79.

44. Bernstein, *The Lean Years,* p. 351.

45. AFL, *Proceedings,* 1932, p. 9.

46. John Frey to Clarence Ross, December 12, 1932, Container 13, Frey Papers, Library of Congress.

47. AFL, *Proceedings,* 1930, p. 3.

48. Bernstein, *The Lean Years,* pp. 477, 481.

49. AFL, *Proceedings,* 1932, pp. 284–296.

50. Ibid., 1932, p. 296.

51. Ibid., 1932, p. 317.

52. Quoted in Elizabeth Brandeis, "Organized Labor and Protective Labor Legislation," in *Labor and the New Deal,* ed. Milton Derber and Edwin Young (Madison, Wisc., 1957), p. 203.

53. Ibid., pp. 202–204.

54. Ibid., p. 204.

55. Quoted in Irving Bernstein, *Turbulent Years: A History of the American Worker, 1933–1941* (Boston, 1970), p. 26.

56. Ibid., p. 27.

57. Ibid., pp. 24–26; Bernard Bellush, *The Failure of the NRA* (New York, 1975), pp. 7–8; Brandeis, pp. 199–204.

58. Arthur M. Schlesinger, Jr., *The crisis of the Old Order, 1919–1933* (Boston, 1957), p. 393.

59. *New York Times,* October 8, 1930, p. 14:2.

60. See, for example, Sidney Lens, *Radicalism in America* (New York, 1969), p. 305.

61. *New York Times,* October 11, 1930, p. 8:2; *New York Times,* October 22, 1930, p. 11:8; Maxwell C. Raddock, *Portrait of an American Labor Leader: William L. Hutcheson* (New York, 1955), pp. 177–178.

62. *New York Times,* September 9, 1932, p. 4:4.

63. Bernstein, *The Lean Years*, p. 512.

64. *New York Times*, December 16, 1932, p. 14:2.

65. Ibid., December 20, 1932, p. 9:4.

66. Green to Tobin, December 21, 1932, Reel 14, frame 332, WGC OHS.

67. *New York Times*, March 3, 1933, p. 2:6.

68. Green to Tobin, March 10, 1933, Reel 14, frame 524, WGC OHS.

69. Bernstein, *Turbulent Years*, p. 30.

70. Morris, p. 141.

71. *American Federationist*, April 1933, p. 372.

72. Irving Bernstein, *The New Deal Collective Bargaining Policy* (Berkeley, 1950), pp. 25, 30–31.

73. Bernstein, *Turbulent Years*, pp. 31–32; Brandeis, p. 205.

74. Bradeis, p. 205.

75. Ibid.

76. Bernstein, *Turbulent Years*, p. 32.

77. Ibid.

78. *New York Times*, June 4, 1933, p. 2:3.

79. Bernstein, *Turbulent Years*, pp. 33–34.

80. Green to Presidents of International Unions, May 27, 1933, Reel 8, WGC OHS.

81. *American Federationist*, July 1933, p. 678.

82. Bellush, p. 37.

83. *American Federationist*, July 1933, p. 678.

84. Ibid., February 1933, p. 117.

85. Bellush, pp. 12–14, 36–38, 45.

86. Ibid., pp. 41–43; *New York Times*, June 28, 1933, p. 1:6; *New York Times*, June 29, p. 1:5.

87. Sidney Fine, *The Automobile Under the Blue Eagle* (Ann Arbor, 1963), p. 48.

88. Ibid., pp. 53–55.

89. Ibid., p. 55.

90. Ibid., p. 58.

91. Ibid., p. 63.

92. Ibid., p. 64.

93. Ibid., p. 65.

94. Green to William Collins, September 18, 1933, Reel 9, WGC OHS.

95. Fine, *Automobile*, p. 73.

96. *New York Times*, September 1, 1933, p. 12:2.

97. Green to William Collins, August 28, 1933, Reel 9, WGC OHS.

98. *American Federationist*, December 1933, p. 1332.

99. James A. Gross, *The Making of the National Labor Relations Board, 1933–1937* (Albany, 1974), p. 21.

100. Ibid., p. 21.

101. Ibid., pp. 37–38, 54–55.

102. Ibid., pp. 37–39, 73.

103. Ibid., p. 39.

104. Ibid., p. 50.

105. *American Federationist*, July 1933, p. 678.

106. Ibid., April 1934, p. 356.

107. Bernstein, *Turbulent Years*, p. 193.

108. Gross, p. 73.

109. Bernstein, *Turbulent Years*, p. 193.

110. Bellush, pp. 170–171.

111. Bernstein, *Turbulent Years*, p. 349; *New York Times,* June 20, 1935, p. 1:5.

112. *New York Times*, September 5, 1933, p. 1:5.

113. Ibid;, September 5, 1933, pp. 1:5.

114. AFL, *Proceedings*, 1933, pp. 6–11.

115. *American Federationist*, July 1933, pp. 473–480.

116. Green, "Speech," June 7, 1935, Reel 15, WGC OHS.

117. *American Federationist*, July 1935, p. 693.

Chapter IV

1. AFL, *Proceedings*, 1933, pp. 8–9.

2. Green to Presidents of International Unions, May 27, 1933, Reel 8, WGC OHS.

3. James O. Morris, *Conflict Within the AFL: A Study of Craft Versus Industrial Unionism, 1901–1938* (Ithaca, 1958), p. 151.

4. AFL, *Proceedings*, 1931, pp. 45, 63.

5. *American Federationist*, July 1933, pp. 790–791.

6. Ibid., May 1934, p. 465.

7. Philip Taft, *The A. F. of L. from the Death of Gompers to the Merger* (New York, 1970), p. 99; Sidney Fine, *The Automobile Under the Blue Eagle* (Ann Arbor, 1963), p. 39.

8. Fine, *Automobile*, p. 39.

9. Collins to Green, August 5, 1933, Reel 18, WGC OHS.

10. Wharton to Green, July 29, 1933, National Union File 6 (Machinists), AFL-CIO Archives.

11. Green to Hayes, July 28, 1933, Reel 17, WGC OHS.

12. Fine, *Automobile*, pp. 142–143.

13. Green to Wharton, August 2, 1933, National Union File 6 (Machinists), AFL-CIO Archives.

14. William Green, "A Great American Institution," *American Teacher*, 20 (November-December 1935), 4.

15. Wharton to Green, August 8, 1933, National Union File 6 (Machinists), AFL-CIO Archives.

16. AFL Executive Council Minutes, September 7, 1933, AFL-CIO Archives.

17. Ibid., September 7, 1933.

18. Irving Bernstein, *Turbulent Years: A History of the American Worker, 1933–1941* (Boston, 1970), p. 95.

19. Green to United Automobile Workers, December 1, 1933, Reel 19, WGC OHS.

20. *New York Times*, February 2, 1934, p. 1:4; *New York Times*, February 3, 1934, p. 8:2.

21. Green to United Automobile Workers, December 23, 1933, Reel 19, WGC OHS.

22. Green to United Automobile Workers, January 8, 1934, Reel 19, WGC OHS.

23. Fine, *Automobile,* pp. 213–218.

24. Bernstein, *Turbulent Years,* pp. 183–184.

25. *New York Times,* March 18, 1934, p. 29:1.

26. Bernstein, *Turbulent Years,* pp. 184–185.

27. Taft, *The A. F. of L. from the Death of Gompers to the Merger,* p. 101.

28. Fine, *Automobile,* p. 291.

29. Ibid., pp. 291–292.

30. Ibid., p. 291.

31. Ibid.

32. *New York Times,* October 1, 1933, p. 28:1.

33. Ibid.

34. *American Federationist,* November 1933, p. 1178.

35. Bernstein, *Turbulent Years,* p. 220; Fine, *Automobile,* pp. 274–275.

36. Green to Branch, May 17, 1934, AFL Strike File, Local 18384, AFL-CIO Archives.

37. Ibid.

38. Green to Coleman Claherty, May 25, 1934, AFL Strike File, Local 18384, AFL-CIO Archives; Fine, *Automobile,* p. 279; Bernstein, *Turbulent Years,* p. 224.

39. Fine, *Automobile,* p. 283.

40. Green to Collins, May 26, 1934, Reel 19, WGC OHS.

41. Fine, *Automobile,* p. 296.

42. Ibid.

43. *New York Times,* June 24, 1934, p. 19:1; Fine, *Automobile,* p. 297.

44. *New York Times,* June 25, 1934, p. 6:2.

45. Wyndham Mortimer, *Organize!: My Life as a Union Man* (Boston, 1971), p. 77.

46. Fine, *Automobile,* pp. 299–300, 304.

47. Mortimer, p. 77.

48. Ibid.

49. Green to Shipley, November 26, 1934, Reel 20, WGC OHS.

50. Fine, *Automobile,* p. 306.

51. Ibid., pp. 381–2.

52. Dillon to Green, November 13, 1934, Reel 20, WGC OHS.

53. *New York Times,* January 30, 1935, p. 2:3.

54. Ibid., February 16, 1935, p. 7:7.

55. Fine, *Automobile,* p. 383.

56. *New York Times,* February 24, 1935, p. 6:1.

57. Fine, *Automobile,* p. 383.

58. Ibid.

59. Green to Reeves, March 18, 1935, Reel 21, WGC OHS.

60. *New York Times,* April 10, 1935, p. 13:5.

61. Fine, *Automobile,* pp. 384–385.

62. Green to Shipley, February 7, 1935, Reel 21, WGC OHS.

63. Address to Toledo Central Labor Union, February 17, 1935, Reel 17, WGC OHS.

64. *New York Times,* February 24, 1935, p. 6:1.

65. Fine, *Automobile,* p. 385.

66. Ibid., p. 366.

67. *New York Times,* April 24, 1935, p. 5:5.

68. Sidney Fine, "The Toledo Chevrolet Strike of 1935," *Ohio Historical Quarterly* 67 (October 1958), pp. 326–332.

69. Ibid., p. 337.

70. Ibid., p. 345; Green to Dillon, May 9, 1935, AFL Strike File, Local 18384, AFL-CIO Archives.

71. Fine, "Chevrolet Strike," p. 346.

72. Ibid., pp. 347–348.

73. *American Federationist,* June 1935, p. 588.

74. Fine, "Chevrolet Strike," p. 352.

75. Green to William K. Siefke, June 19, 1935, AFL Strike File, Local 18384, AFL-CIO Archives.

76. Fine, "Chevrolet Strike, p. 355.

77. Fine, *Automobile,* p. 401.

78. Bernstein, *Turbulent Years,* pp. 374–377; Walter Galenson, the CIO *Challenge to the AFL: A History of the American Labor Movement 1935–1941* (Cambridge, Mass., 1960), pp. 124–125; Taft, *The A. F. of L. from the Death of Gompers to the Merger,* pp. 104–107.

79. Taft, *The A. F. of L. from the Death of Gompers to the Merger,* p. 106.

80. Galenson, pp. 124–125.

81. Ibid., p. 125.

82. Ibid.

83. Ibid.

84. Fine, *Automobile,* pp. 406–407.

85. Green to Wharton, August 25, 1935, Reel 22, WGC OHS.

86. Bernstein, *Turbulent Years,* p. 377.

87. Ibid., p. 378.

88. Fine, *Automobile,* p. 417.

89. Ibid.

90. Ibid., p. 418.

91. Bernstein, *Turbulent Years,* p. 378; Fine, *Automobile,* p. 418.

92. Bernstein, *Turbulent Years,* p. 378.

93. Ibid., p. 379.

94. Ibid.

95. Fine, *Automobile,* pp. 406–409.

96. Louis Adamic, "Will Rubber Snap," *The Nation,* March 20, 1935, pp. 334–336.

97. Ruth McKenney, *Industrial Valley* (New York, 1939), pp. 109–110.

98. Matthew Josephson, *Sidney Hillman: Statesman of American Labor* (New York, 1952), p. 385.

99. Bernstein, *Turbulent Years*, pp. 381–382.

100. Ibid.

101. Galeson, p. 267.

102. Ibid., pp. 267–268.

103. Ibid., p. 268.

104. Staughton Lynd, "The Possibility of Radicalism in the Early 1030s: The Case of Steel," *Radical America* 6 (November-December 1972), pp. 36–65.

105. Ibid., pp. 198–203.

106. Galenson, p. 76.

107. Ibid.

108. Ibid., p. 76–77.

109. Green to *Amalgamated Journal*, August 15, 1935, Reel 9, WGC OHS.

110. Morris, pp. 158–159.

111. Green, "Speech," June 7, 1935, Reel 15, WGC OHS.

112. Ibid.

113. Bernstein, *Turbulent Years*, pp. 38–40.

114. Jerold S. Auerbach, *Labor and Liberty: The LaFollette Committee and the New Deal* (Indianapolis, 1966), p. 97.

115. Ibid., p. 99.

116. Ibid., p. 101.

117. *New York Times*, October 9, 1933, p. 17:1.

118. Bernstein, *Turbulent Years*, p. 370.

Chapter V

1. For description of Green, see Bruce Minton and John Stuart, *Men Who Lead Labor* (New York, 1937), pp. 3–29; Charles A. Madison, *American Labor Leaders: Personalities and Forces in the Labor movement* (New York, 1962), pp. 108–135; Irving Bernstein, *The Lean Years: A History of the American Worker, 1920–1933* (Boston, 1960), pp. 94–97; Max Danish, *William Green: A Pictorial Biography* (New York, 1952), pp. 13–15.

2. Raymond Clapper, "Labor's Chief: William Green," *Review of Reviews*, 88 (November 1933), 21.

3. Bernstein, *The Lean Years,* p. 95; Len DeCaux, *Labor Radical: From the Wobblies to the CIO* (Boston, 1970), p. 191.

4. DeCaux, pp. 191–192.

5. Melvyn Dubofsky and Warren Van Tine, *John L. Lewis: A Biography* (New York, 1977), p. 282.

6. Ibid.

7. Bernstein, *The Lean Years,* p. 121.

8. Dubofsky and Van Tine, p. 206.

9. *American Federationist,* January 1932, p. 17.

10. Bernstein, *The Lean Years,* p. 123.

11. "Extracts from UMWA Executive Board Meeting," January 1925, Reel 4, WGC OHS.

12. *UMWJ,* January 1, 1925.

13. Dubofsky and Van Tine, pp. 145–146; Philip Taft, *The A. F. of L. from the Death of Gompers to the Merger* (New York, 1970), p. 17.

14. Taft, *The A. F. of L. from the Death of Gompers to the Merger,* pp. 17–18.

15. Green to President Hoover, November 24, 1930, Reel 7, WGC OHS.

16. Dubofsky and Van Tine, pp. 163–167; Bernstein, *The Lean Years,* pp. 366–377.

17. Taft, *The A. F. of L. from the Death of Gompers to the Merger,* p. 20.

18. Green to John Walker, March 6, 1930; John Walker to Green, March 8, 1930; Green to John Walker, March 20, 1930, Reel 9, WGC OHS.

19. John L. Lewis, "The United Mine Workers of America," *American Federationist,* October 1931, pp. 1211–1218.

20. See AFL, *Proceedings,* 1933, p. 284.

21. Dubofsky and Van Tine, p. 214.

22. Ibid., p. 192.

23. Ibid., pp. 289–290, 181–202.

24. Ibid., pp. 205–206.

25. Address to Toledo Central Labor Union, September 17, 1934, Reel 15, WGC OHS.

26. Gerald N. Grob, *Workers and Utopia: A Study of Ideological Conflict in the American Labor Movement, 1865–1900* (Chicago, 1961), p. 141.

27. Irving Bernstein, *Turbulent Years: A History of the American Worker, 1933–1941* (Boston, 1970), p. 355.

28. *Dictionary of American Biography,* 6, pp. 218–219.

29. Ibid., 6, pp. 706–707.

30. Ibid., 5, pp. 339–340.

31. Ibid., 5, pp. 690–691.

32. Walter Galenson, *The CIO Challenge to the AFL: A History of the American Labor Movement, 1935–1941* (Cambridge, Mass., 1960), p. 8.

33. AFL, *Proceedings*, 1935, p. 570.

34. *Machinists' Monthly Journal,* August 1936, p. 481.

35. Frey to Thomas J. Donnelly, November 16, 1935, Container 8, Frey Papers, Library of Congress.

36. AFL, *Proceedings*, 1934, p. 453.

37. Bernstein, *Turbulent Years*, pp. 354, 360.

38. Taft, *The A. F. of L. from the Death of Gompers to the Merger*, pp. 52–53.

39. Quoted in Bernstein, *Turbulent Years*, p. 352.

40. Bernard Mandel, *Samuel Gompers: A Biography* (Yellow Springs, Ohio, 1963), pp. 96–99.

41. AFL, *Proceedings*, 1887, p. 3.

42. See, for example, David Brody, "The Emergence of Mass-Production Unionism," in *Change and Continuity in Twentieth Century America*, ed., John Braeman et al (Columbus, 1964) p. 223; Galenson, p. 8.

43. AFL, *Proceedings*, 1933, pp. 501–504.

44. The federal labor unionists made their complaint in *Labor Action,* February 1, 1934.

45. "Proceedings of the Conference of Presidents of National and International Unions Held in Washington, D.C., January 24–25, 1934," National Union File 1, AFL-CIO Archives.

46. Ibid.

47. Bernstein, *Turbulent Years*, p. 360.

48. AFL, *Proceedings*, 1934, pp. 581–586.

49. Ibid., 1934, pp. 586–587, 598.

50. *New York Times*, October 21, 1934, p. 2:1.

51. Charles Beard, "Confusion Rules in Washington," *Current History*, 41 (December 1934), 337.

52. AFL, *Proceedings*, 1934, p. 683.

53. Ibid., 1934, pp. 589, 594–595.

54. Frey to Lawrence O'Keefe, July 15, 1936, Container 5, Frey Papers, Library of Congress.

55. AFL, *Proceedings*, 1934, pp. 681–682.

56. *New York Times*, May 4, 1935, p. 2:4.

57. Ibid., June 30, 1935, p. 2:5.

58. Frey to Victor Olander, July 19, 1935, Container 5, Frey Papers, Library of Congress.

59. Dubofsky and Van Tine, p. 214.

60. *New York Times*, September 4, 1935, p. 11:1.

61. Quoted in Dubofsky and Van Tine, p. 214.

62. AFL, *Proceedings*, 1935, p. 7.

63. Ibid., 1935, pp. 521–524.

64. James O. Morris, *Conflict Within the AFL: A Study of Craft Versus Industrial Unions, 1901–1938* (Ithaca, 1958), p. 209.

65. AFL, *Proceedings*, 1935, pp. 725–727.

66. *New York Times*, October 20, 1935, p. 1:7.

67. Quoted in Joseph Goulden, *Meany* (New York, 1972), p. 88n.

68. AFL, *Proceedings*, 1935, pp. 698–699.

Chapter VI

1. Walter Galenson, *The CIO Challenge to the AFL: A History of the American Labor Movement, 1935–1941* (Cambridge, Mass., 1960). p. 5.

2. Philip Taft, *The A. F. of L. from the Death of Gompers to the Merger* (New York, 1970), pp. 149–150.

3. Melvyn Dubofsky and Warren Van Tine, *John L. Lewis: A Biography* (New York, 1977), p. 223.

4. Ibid., p. 226.

5. Christopher Tomlins, "AFL Unions in the 1930s: Their Performance in Historical Perspective," *Journal of American History* 65 (March, 1979), 1023.

6. *American Federationist,* December 1935, pp. 1281–2.

7. Dubodsky and Van Tine, p. 224.

8. William Green to John L. Lewis et al., November 23, 1935, AFL Papers, Office of the President, File C, Box 1, State Historical Society of Wisconsin (hereafter cited as SHSW).

9. Lewis to Green, November 23, 1935, AFL Papers, Office of the President, File C, Box 1, SHSW.

10. Galenson, p. 6.

11. Charles P. Howard to Green, December 2, 1935, AFL Papers, Office of the President, File C, Box 1, SHSW.

12. Lewis to Green, December 7, 1935, AFL Papers, Office of the President, File C, Box 1, SHSW.

13. Green to Lewis, December 9, 1935, Adolph Germer Papers, Box 2, SHSW.

14. Irving Bernstein, *Turbulent Years: A History of the American Worker, 1933–1941* (Boston, 1970), pp. 405–407.

15. Galenson, p. 648 n. 25.

16. Ibid., p. 11.

17. *Proceedings 1936 Convention,* United Mine Workers of America, pp. 11, 164, 173–179.

18. Ibid., pp. 303–309.

19. Ibid., p. 309.

20. Dubofsky and Van Tine, p. 231.

21. Green to W. E. Ingersoll, February 8, 1936, AFL Papers, Office of the President, File C, Box 1, SHSW.

22. Green to James Maloney, February 11, 1936, AFL Papers, Office of the President, File C, Box 1, SHSW.

23. Bernstein, *Turbulent Years,* p. 436.

24. Tobin to Green, February 26, 1936, AFL Papers, Office of the President, File C, Box 2, SHSW.

25. Arthur Wharton to Green, February 28, 1936; Matthew Woll to Green, February 29, 1936; Felix Knight to Green, March 6, 1936; Joseph Weber to Green, February 27, 1936; and Harry Bates to Green, February 25, 1936, AFL Papers, Office of the President, File C, Box 2, SHSW.

26. Green to the Presidents of International Unions, March 2, 1936; "Replies to Letters of March 2, 1936," AFL Papers, Office of the President, File C, Box 2, SHSW.

27. Bernstein, *Turbulent Years*, p. 439.

28. Dubofsky and Van Tine, p. 237.

29. AFL, Information and Publicity Service, June 5, 1936, CIO Folder 1, AFL-CIO Archives.

30. Lewis to Green, June 30, 1936, AFL Papers, Office of the President, File C, Box 1, SHSW.

31. Green to All Affiliate Organizations, April 23, 1936, AFL Papers, Office of the President, File C, Box 3, SHSW.

32. Green to George Berry, April 27, 1936, AFL Papers, Office of the President, File C, Box 3, SHSW.

33. Bernstein, *Turbulent Years,* p. 414.

34. Taft, *The A. F. of L. from the Death of Gompers to the Merger,* p. 156.

35. Cited in Seymour Martin Lipset, Martin Trow, and James Coleman, *Union Democracy: The International Politics of the International Typographical Union* (Garden CIty, N.Y., 1956), p. 272.

36. *American Federationist,* September 1936, p. 923.

37. On Lewis's suppression of insurgency, see Dubofsky and Van Tine, pp. 112–131.

38. *American Federationist,* September 1936, p. 922.

39. Bernstein, *Turbulent Years,* pp. 413–414.

40. Green to Lewis et al., June 2, 1936, AFL Papers, Office of the President, File C, Box 2, SHSW.

41. Ogburn to Green, July 8, 9, and 13, 1936, AFL Papers, Office of the President, File C, Box 2, SHSW.

42. Taft, *The A. F. of L. from the Death of Gompers to the Merger,* pp. 162–163.

43. Ibid.; Green to Lewis et al., July 16, 1936, AFL Papers, Office of the President, File C, Box 2, SHSW.

44. The United Automobile Workers and the United Rubber Workers joined the CIO on July 2, 1936. The Typographical Union and the Hatters were not prosecuted because neither were affiliated with the CIO.

45. Taft, *The A. F. of L. from the Death of Gompers to the Merger*, pp. 164–165; Bernstein, *Turbulent Years*, p. 419.

46. John L. Lewis et al. to Green, July 21, 1936, AFL Papers, Office of the President, File C, Box 1, SHSW.

47. Ogburn to Green, July 22, 1936, AFL Papers, Office of the President, File C, Box 2, SHSW.

48. Taft, *The A. F. of L. from the Death of Gompers to the Merger*, pp. 172–180; Bernstein, *Turbulent Years*, pp. 421– 422.

49. Bernstein, *Turbulent Years*, p. 422.

50. Ibid.

51. Taft, *The A. F. of L. from the Death of Gompers to the Merger*, p. 166.

52. Bernstein, *Turbulent Years*, pp. 423–424.

53. Green to ALL Affiliate Organizations, September 5, 1937, AFL Papers, Office of the President, File C, Box 3, SHSW.

54. David Brody, "The Emergence of Mass-Production Unionism," in *Change and Continuity in Twentieth Century America*, ed., John Baeman et al. (Columbus, 1964), p. 234.

55. Brody, pp. 238–51.

56. Sidney Fine, *Sit-Down: The General Motors Strike of 1936–1937* (Ann Arbor, 1969), pp. 304–310.

57. *New York Times*, February 5, 1937, p. 1:7.

58. Fine, *Sit-Down*, p. 289–290.

59. Ibid.

60. Ibid.

61. *New York Times*, February 12, 1937, p. 19:1.

62. Fine, *Sit-Down*, p. 330.

63. *New York Times*, February 13, 1937, p. 9:2.

64. Ibid., February 16, 1937, p. 1:8.

65. Galenson, pp. 90–96.

66. *New York Times,* March 4, 1937, p. 2:2.

67. Green, "Why I Am Unalterably Opposed to the Sit-Down Strike," *Liberty Magazine,* October 16, 1937, pp. 4–6.

68. Ibid.

69. Labor Day Address, Dallas, September 6, 1937, Reel 15, frames 723–724, WGC OHS.

70. Tomlins, p. 1023.

71. Bernstein, *Turbulent Years,* pp. 682–685.

72. Taft, *The A. F. of L. from the Death of Gompers to the Merger,* p. 197; James O. Morris, *Conflict Within the AFL: A Study of Craft Versus Industrial Unionism, 1901–1938* (Ithaca, 1958), p. 248.

73. Taft, *The A. F. of L. from the Death of Gompers to the Merger,* p. 188.

74. Ibid.

75. AFL, *Proceedings,* 1937, pp. 105–106.

76. Taft, *The A. F. of L. from the Death of Gompers to the Merger,* p. 191.

77. Green to Salaried and Special Organizers, June 14, 1937, AFL Papers, Office of the President, File C, Box 3, SHSW.

78. Bernstein, *Turbulent Years,* p. 500.

79. Tomlins, p. 1023.

80. Dubofsky and Van Tine, pp. 300–334.

81. AFL, *Proceedings,* 1937, pp. 5–15.

82. Ibid., 1937, pp. 377–417.

83. Philip Murray to Frank Morrison, October 16, 1937, AFL Papers, Office of the President, File C, Box 24, SHSW.

84. AFL, *Proceedings,* 1937, pp. 8, 11.

85. See, for example, Green to National and International Unions, State Federations of Labor, City Central Bodies, and Directly Affiliated Unions, December 19, 1937; and Green to AFL Organizers, January 24, 1938, AFL Papers, Office of the President, File C, Box 21, SHSW.

86. Green to State Federations of Labor and City Central Bodies, February 24, 1937, AFL Papers, Office of the President, File C, Box 21, SHSW.

87. Taft, *The A. F. of L. from the Death of Gompers to the Merger,* pp. 201–202.

88. Ibid.

89. *New York Times,* February 16, 1937, p. 1:5; *New York Times,* May 18, 1937, p. 1:2.

90. Ibid., January 23, 1938, p. 22:3.

91. Green's letter is reprinted in *American Federationist,* March 1938, pp. 249–257.

92. AFL, Information and Publicity Service, February 11, 1938, CIO Folder 2, AFL-CIO Archives.

93. *New York Times,* February 16, 1937, p. 9:3.

94. Cited in McAlister Coleman, *Men and Coal* (New York, 1943), p. 183.

95. Ibid., p. 177; Bernstein, *Turbulent Years,* p. 696.

96. Bernstein, *Turbulent Years,* pp. 697–699.

97. *American Federationist,* December 1938, p. 1281.

98. *New York Times,* October 7, 1938, p. 3:5.

99. Taft, *The A. F. of L. from the Death of Gompers to the Merger,* p. 131; Bernstein, *Turbulent Years,* pp. 660–661.

100. Bernstein, *Turbulent Years,* pp. 665–667.

101. AFL, *Proceedings,* 1941, p. 115.

102. Jerome Auerbach, *Labor and Liberty: The LaFollette Committee and the New Deal* (Indianapolis, 1966), p. 164.

103. *New York Times,* October 12, 1934, p. 6:2; AFL, *Proceedings,* 1934, pp. 330–333; Phillip S. Foner, *Organized Labor and the Black Worker, 1619–1981* (New York, 1981), pp. 205, 211.

104. AFL, *Proceedings,* 1934, pp. 331–334.

105. William Green, "Our Negro Worker," *Messenger,* 7 (September 1925), 332; William H. Harris, *The Harder We Run: Black Workers Since the Civil War* (New York, 1982), pp. 73–74.

106. Brailsford Brazeal, *The Brotherhood of Sleeping Car Porters* (New York, 1946), pp. 129–149.

107. Harris, p. 90; Foner, *Black Worker,* p. 208.

108. Harris, p. 91; Foner, *Black Worker,* p. 209–211.

109. AFL, *Proceedings*, 1935, pp. 818–819.

110. Cited in Foner, *Black Worker*, pp. 213–214.

111. See Horace Cayton and George Mitchell, *Black Workers and the Unions* (Chapel Hill, 1939); and James R. Green, *The World of the Worker: Labor in Twentieth-Century America* (New York, 1980), pp. 161, 166.

112. Galenson, pp. 627–628.

113. Foner, *Black Worker*, p. 235.

114. Ibid.

115. Dubofsky and Van Tine, pp. 323–364.

116. AFL, *Proceedings*, 1939, pp. 582–585.

117. Joseph Goulden, *Meany* (New York, 1972), p. 79.

118. Ibid., pp. 78–81, 92, 114, 116–117.

Chapter VII

1. See, for example, Green to Meany, May 14, 1947; October 12, 1950, Reel 19, WGC OHS.

2. Green to meany, June 14, AFL Papers, Office of the President, File A, Box 13, SHSW; "Green Articles," AFL Papers, Office of the President, File A, Box 15, SHSW; Joseph Goulden, *Meany* (New York, 1972), pp. 72, 81.

3. *New York Times*, January 26, 1946, p. 2:1; *New York Times*, October 7, 1946, p. 8:2.

4. AFL, *Proceedings*, 1933, p. 142; AFL, *Proceedings*, 1934, pp. 385–390, 570–571.

5. *AFL Weekly News Service*, September 26, 1936.

6. Green to Walter Citrine, January 25, 1938, AFL Papers, Office of the President, File C, Box 23, SHSW.

7. *American Federationist*, October 1939, p. 1051.

8. AFL, *Proceedings*, 1939, pp. 11–13.

9. See, for example, Address delivered at Dinner for the Benefit of the Leon Blum Colony in Palestine, New York City, June 26, 1940, Reel 15, WGC OHS.

10. Labor Day Address, Denver, Colorado, September 2, 1940, Reel 15, WGC OHS.

11. Walter Galenson, *The CIO Challenges to the AFL: A History of the American Labor movement, 1935–1941* (Cambridge, Mass., 1960), pp. 618–619.

12. Joel Seidman, *American Labor from Defense to Reconversion* (Chicago, 1953), pp. 28–29.

13. Labor Day Address, Denver, Colorado, September 2, 1940, Reel 15, WGC OHS.

14. AFL, *Proceedings*, 1940, pp. 10–11.

15. See, for example, Speech to Passaic County American Legion, May 11, 1941, Reel 17, WGC OHS.

16. *New York Times*, August 13, 1941, p. 37:7.

17. Address to the Rotary Club of Philadelphia, April 2, 1941, Reel 15, WGC OHS.

18. See, for example, New York Times, March 30, 1941, p. 31:1.

19. Address to the Rotary Club of Philadelphia, April 2, 1941, Reel 15, WGC OHS.

20. *New York Times*, June 13, 1941, p. 12:3.

21. Ibid., December 17, 1941, p. 1:1.

22. *AFL Weekly News Service*, December 17, 1941.

23. Seidman, pp. 80–81; Philip Taft, *The A. F. of L. from the Death of Gompers to the Merger* (New York, 1970), p. 222; *New York Times*, December 21, 1941, p. 11:1.

24. *New York Times*, January 18, 1942, p. 1:2.

25. Melvyn Dubofsky and Warren Van Tine, *John L. Lewis: A Biography* (New York, 1977), pp. 405–407; *New York Times*, January 20, 1942, p. 1:1.

26. *New York Times*, January 25, 1942, p. 1:1.

27. On Little Steel, see Nelson Lichtenstein, *Labor's War at Home: The CIO in World War II* (New York, 1982), p. 70.

28. Green to Roosevelt, July 20, 1942, Reel 20, WGC OHS.

29. *AFL Weekly News Service*, February 9, 1943.

30. *New York Times*, October 5, 1942, p. 12:1; Taft, *The A. F. of L. from the Death of Gompers to the Merger*, p. 223.

31. *New York Times*, October 7, 1942, p. 52:1.

32. AFL, *Proceedings*, 1946, p. 485; *New York Times*, October 15, 1945, p. 2:2.

33. Christopher Tomlins, "AFL Unions in the 1930s: Their Presence in Historical Perspective," *Journal of American History,* 65 (Mach 1979), p. 1023; on maintenance of membership, see Seidman, pp. 91–108.

34. Seidman, p. 133.

35. See Dubofsky and Van Tine, p. 417.

36. This argument is presented throughout Lichtenstein.

37. *New York Times,* June 18, 1943, p. 1:1.

38. See, for example, AFL, *Proceedings,* 1943, p. 99.

39. David Brody, *Workers in Industrial America: Essays on the Twentieth Century Struggle* (New York, 1980), pp. 173–174, 215.

40. Taft, *The A. F. of L. from the Death of Gompers to the Merger,* pp. 277–302.

41. Ibid., p. 455; Galenson, p. 608; Dubofsky and Van Tine, pp. 457–458.

42. *AFL Weekly News Service,* November 27, 1946.

43. Ibid., October 29, 1946.

44. Ibid.

45. AFL, *Proceedings,* 1947, p. 14; *New York Times,* May 28, 1947, p. 2:7.

46. *New York Times,* June 27, 1947, p. 3:3.

47. Arthur F. McClure, *The Truman Administration and the Problems of Postwar Labor, 1945–1948* (Cranbury, N.J., 1969), p. 217.

48. Taft, *The A. F. of L. from the Death of Gompers to the Merger,* pp. 311–312.

49. Ibid., pp. 320–323.

50. Quoted in Goulden, pp. 177–179.

51. Ibid.; *New York Times,* November 22, 1952, p. 1:2; *New York Times,* November 25, 1952, p. 22:3.

52. *New York Times,* November 25, 1952, p. 22:3; *American Federationist,* December 1952, pp. 2–23.

Afterword

1. David A. Shannon, *Between the Wars: America, 1919–1941* (Boston, 1965), p. 90.

2. Melvyn Dubofsky and Warren Van Tine, *John L. Lewis: A Biography* (New York, 1977), p. 225; Philip Taft, *The A. F. of L. from the Death of Gompers to the Merger* (New York, 1970), p. 98; Bruce Minton and John Stuart, *Men Who Lead Labor* (New York, 1937), p. 27.

3. *American Federationist,* June 1951, p. 19.

4. *New York Times,* August 30, 1950, p. 1:2.

Bibliography

Primary Sources

Manuscript Materials

Adolph Germer Papers. State Historical Society of Wisconsin, Madison.

American Federation of Labor Papers. State Historical Society of Wisconsin, Madison.

American Federation of Labor: Letter Press Copybooks of Samuel Gompers and William Green, 1883–1924, Manuscript Division, Library of Congress, Washington, D.C.

American Federation of Labor Executive Council Minutes of Meetings. George Meany Memorial Archives, Silver Springs, Maryland. Used by permission of AFL-CIO Secretary-Treasurer Thomas Donahue.

John P. Frey Papers. Manuscript Division, Library of Congress, Washington, D.C.

Mary (Mother) Jones Papers. Department of Archives and Manuscripts, The Catholic University of America, Washington, D.C.

Lewis G. Hines Papers. Manuscript Division, Library of Congress, Washington, D.C.

William Green Papers, 1915–1952. American Federation of Labor-Congress of Industrial Organizations Archives, Washington, D.C.

William Green Papers. Ohio Historical Society, Columbus, Ohio.

Convention Proceedings and Union Journals

American Federation of Labor. *Report of the Proceedings of the Annual Conventions, 1913–1952.*

209

American Federationist.

American Federation of Labor Weekly News Service.

International Teamster.

Labor Action.

Machinists Monthly Journal.

United Mine Workers of America. *Proceedings of the Conventions, 1891–1938.*

United Mine Workers Journal.

Reminiscences and Autobiographies

Brophy, John. *A Miner's Life.* Edited and supplemented by John O. P. Hall. Madison: University of Wisconsin Press, 1964.

DeCaux, Len. *Labor Radical: From the Wobblies to the CIO.* Boston: Beacon Press, 1970.

Gompers, Samuel. *Seventy Years of Life and Labor.* 2 vols. New York: Dutton, 1925.

Green, William. *Labor and Democracy.* Princeton: Princeton University Press, 1939.

Jones, Mary H. *Autobiography of Mother Jones.* Edited by Mary Field Parton. Chicago: Kerr, 1925.

Mortimer, Wyndham. *Organize!: My Life as a Union Man.* Edited by Leo Fenster. Boston: Beacon Press, 1971.

Perkins, Frances. *The Roosevelt I Knew.* New York: Viking, 1946.

Secondary Sources

Books

Alinsky, Saul D. *John L. Lewis: An Unauthorized Biography.* New York: Putnam, 1949.

Anderson, Jervis. *A Phillip Randolph: A Biographical Portrait.* New York: Harcourt Brace Javonovich, 1973.

Auerbach, Jerold S. *Labor and Liberty: The LaFollette Committee and the New Deal.* Indianapolis: Bobbs-Merrill, 1966.

Bellush, Bernard. *The Failure of the NRA.* New York: Norton, 1975.

Bernstein, Irving, *The Lean Years: A History of the American Worker, 1920–1933*. Boston: Houghton Mifflin, 1960.

———. *The New Deal Collective Bargaining Policy*. Berkeley: University of California Press, 1950.

———. *Turbulent Years: A History of the American Worker, 1933–1941*. Boston: Houghton Mifflin, 1970.

Bornet, Vaughn Davis. *Labor Politics in a Democratic Republic: Moderation, Division, and Disruption in the Presidential Election of 1928*. Washington, D.C.: Spartan Books, 1964.

Boryczka, Raymond, and Cary, Lorin Lee. *No Strength Without Union: An Illustrated History of Ohio Workers, 1803–1980*. Columbus: Ohio Historical Society, 1982.

Brazeal, Brailsford. *The Brotherhood of Sleeping Car Porters*. New York: Harper, 1946.

Brody, David. *Workers in Industrial America: Essays on the Twentieth Century Struggle*. New York: Oxford University Press, 1980.

Brooks, Robert R. R. *Unions of Their Own Choosing: An Account of the National Labor Relations Board and Its Work*. New Haven: Yale University Press, 1939.

Brooks, Thomas R. *Clint: A Biography of a Labor Intellectual, Clinton S. Golden*. New York: Atheneum, 1978.

Cayton, Horace, and Mitchell, George. *Black Workers and the Unions*. Chapel Hill: University of North Carolina Press, 1939.

Cochran, Bert. *Labor and Communism: The Conflict that Shaped American Unions*. Princeton: Princeton University Press, 1977.

Coleman, McAlister. *Men and Coal*. New York: Farrar and Rinehart, 1943.

Corbin, David Alan. *Life, Work, and Rebellion in the Coal Fields: The Southern West Virginia Miners*. Urbana: University of Illinois Press, 1985.

Danish, Max D. *William Green: A Pictorial Biography*. New York: Inter-Allied Publications, 1952.

Derber, Milton, and Young, Edwin. *Labor and the New Deal*. Madison: University of Wisconsin Press, 1957.

Dorn, Jacob Henry. *Washington Gladden: Prophet of the Social Gospel*. Columbus: Ohio State University Press, 1967.

Dubofsky, Melvyn, and Van Tine, Warren R. *John L. Lewis: A Biography*. New York: Quadrangle, 1977.

Fast, Howard. *Power* (a novel about John L. Lewis). Garden City, N.Y.: Doubleday, 1962.

Fine, Sidney. *The Automobile Under the Blue Eagle.* Ann Arbor: University of Michigan Press, 1963.

———. *Sit-Down: The General Motors Strike of 1936–1937.* Ann Arbor: University of Michigan Press, 1969.

Fink, Gary M., ed. *Biographical Dictionary of American Labor Leaders.* Westport, Ct.: Greenwood Press, 1974.

Foner, Phillip S. *History of the Labor Movement in the United States.* 5 vols. New York: International Publishers, 1947–1975.

———. *Organized Labor and the Black Worker, 1916–1981.* New York: Praeger, 1982.

Foster, William Z. *Misleaders of Labor.* Chicago: Trade Union Educational League, 1927.

Frisch, Michael H., and Walkowitz, Daniel J., eds. *Working-Class America: Essays on Labor, Community, and American Society.* Urbana: University of Illinois Press, 1983.

Galbraith, John K. *The Great Crash, 1929.* New York: Avon, 1980.

Galenson, Walter. *The CIO Challenge to the AFL: A History of the American Labor Movement, 1935–1941.* Cambridge, Mass.: Harvard University Press, 1960.

Gluck, Elsie. *John Mitchell, Miner: Labor's Bargain with the Gilded Age.* New York: John Day, 1929.

Goldberg, Arthur J. *AFL-CIO: Labor United.* New York: McGraw Hill, 1956.

Goulden, Joseph C. *Meany.* New York: Atheneum, 1972.

Green, James R. *The World of the Worker: Labor in Twentieth-Century America.* New York: Hill and Wang, 1980.

Greenstone, J. David. *Labor in American Politics.* Chicago: University of Chicago Press, 1977.

Grob, Gerald N. *Workers and Utopia: A Study of Ideological Conflict in the American Labor Movement, 1865–1890.* Evanston: Northwestern University Press, 1961.

Gross, James A. *The Making of the National Labor Relations Board, 1933–1937.* Albany: State University of New York Press, 1974.

Gutman, Herbert G. *Work, Culture and Society in Industrializing America: Essays in American Working-Class and Social History.* New York: Vintage Books, 1977.

Handy, Robert T., ed. *The Social Gospel in America*. New York: Oxford University Press, 1966.

Harris, Herbert. *Labor's Civil War*. New York: Knopf, 1940.

Harris, William H. *The Harder We Run: Black Workers Since the Civil War*. New York: Oxford University Press, 1982.

Harvey, Katherine. *The Best-Dressed Miners: Life and Labor in the Maryland Coal Region, 1835–1910*. Ithaca: Cornell University Press, 1969.

Held, Adolph. *A Tribute to William Green*. New York: Jewish Labor Committee, 1952.

Higgins, George G. *Voluntarism in Organized Labor in the United States, 1930–1940*. Washington, D.C.: Catholic University of America, 1944.

Hill, Norman N. *History of Coshocton County*. Newark, Ohio: A.A. Graham and Company, 1881.

Horowitz, Ruth l. *Political Ideologies of Organized Labor: The New Deal Era*. Nw Brunswick, N.J.: Transaction Books, 1978.

Huthmacher, J. Joseph. *Senator Robert F. Wagner and the Rise of Urban Liberalism*. New York: Atheneum, 1968.

Johnson, James P. *The Politics of Soft Coal*. Urbana: University of Illinois Press, 1979.

Josephson, Matthew. *Sidney Hillman: Statesman of American Labor*. Garden City, N.Y.: Doubleday, 1952.

Karson, Marc. *American Labor Unions and Politics, 1900–1918*. Carbondale: Southern Illinois University Press, 1958.

Laslett, John H. M. *Labor and the Left: A Study of Socialist and Radical Influences in the American Labor Movement*. New York: Basic Books, 1970.

Lens, Sidney. *Radicalism in America*. New York: Crowell, 1969.

Levinson, Edward. *Labor on the March*. New York: Harper, 1938.

Lichtenstein, Nelson. *Labor's War at Home: The CIO in World War II*. New York: Cambridge University Press, 1982.

Lipset, Seymour Martin, Trow, Martin, and Coleman, James. *Union Democracy: The Internal Politics of the International Typographical Union*. New York: Free Press, 1956.

Lorwin, Lewis. *The American Federation of Labor: History, Policies, and Prospects*. Washington, D.C.: The Brooklings Institution, 1933.

McClure, Arthur F. *The Truman Administration and the Problems of Postwar Labor, 1945–1948*. Cranbury, N.J.: Associated University Presses, 1969.

McKelvey, Jean Trepp. *AFL Attitudes Toward Production, 1900– 1932*. Ithaca: New York State School of Industrial and Labor Relations, Cornell University, 1952.

McKenney, Ruth. *Industrial Valley* (a novel). New york: Harcourt Brace, 1939.

Madison, Charles A. *AMerican Labor Leaders: Personalities and Forces in the Labor Movement*. New York: Harper, 1952.

Mandel, Bernard. *Samuel Gompers: A Biography*. Yellow Springs, Ohio: Antioch Press, 1963.

May, Henry F. *Protestant Churches and Industrial America*. New York: Harper, 1949.

Mercer, James. *Ohio Legislative History, 1909–1913*. Columbus; E. T. Miller, n.d.

Millis, Harry A., and Brown, Emily Clark. *From the Wagner Act to Taft-Hartley: A Study of National Labor Policy and Labor Relations*. Chicago: University of Chicago Press, 1950.

Milton, David. *The Politics of U.S. Labor: From the Great Depression to the New Deal*. New York: Monthly Review Press, 1982.

Minton, Bruce, and Stuart, John. *Men Who Lead Labor*. New York: Modern Age, 1937.

Morris, James O. *Conflict Within the AFL: A Study of Craft Versus Industrial Unions, 1901–1938*. Cornell Studies in Industrial and Labor Relations, vol. 10. Ithaca: New York State School of Industrial and Labor Relations, Cornell University, 1958.

Nadworny, Milton. *Scientific Management and the Unions, 1900– 1932*. Cambridge, Mass.: Harvard University Press, 1955.

Preis, Art. *Labor's Giant Step: Twenty Years of the CIO*. New York: Pioneer, 1964.

Raddock, Maxwell C. *Portrait of an American Labor Leader: William L. Hutcheson*. New York: American Institute of Social Science, 1955.

Roberts, Harold S. *The Rubber Workers*. New York: Harper, 1944.

Robinson, Archie. *George Meany and His Times*. New York: Simon and Schuster, 1981.

Roy, Andrew. *A History of the Coal Miners of the United States*. Columbus: J. L. Trauger, 1907.

Schlesinger, Arthur M., Jr. *The Age of Roosevelt*. 3 vols. Boston: Houghton Mifflin, 1957–1960.

Seidman, Joel. *American Labor from Defense to Reconversion*. Chicago: University of Chicago Press, 1953.

Shannon, David A. *Between the Wars: America, 1919–1941*. Boston: Houghton Mifflin, 1965.

Stolberg, Benjamin. *The Story of the CIO*. New York: Viking Press, 1938.

Taft, Philip. *The A. F. of L. from the Death of Gompers to the Merger*. New York: Octagon Books, 1970.

———. *The A. F. of L. in the Time of Gompers*. New York: Harper, 1957.

———. *Organized Labor in American History*. New York: Harper, 1964.

Thorne, Florence C. *Samuel Gompers: American Statesman*. New York: Philosophical Library, 1957.

Van Tine, Warren R. *The Making of the Labor Bureaucrat: Union Leadership in the United States, 1870–1920*. Amherst: University of Massachusetts Press, 1973.

Walsh, J. R. *C.I.O.—Industrial Unionism in Action*. New York: Norton, 1937.

Warner, Hoyt. *Progressivism in Ohio, 1897–1917*. Columbus: Ohio State University Press, 1964.

Zieger, Robert H. *Republicans and Labor, 1919–1929*. Lexington, Ky.: University of Kentucky Press, 1969.

Articles

Adamic, Louis, "Will Rubber Snap," *The Nation*, March 20, 1935, pp. 334–336.

Beard, Charles. "Confusion Rules in Washington," *Current History*, 41 (December 1934), 336–338.

Broun, Heywood. "Mr. Lewis and Mr. Green," *The Nation*, November 28, 1936, pp. 634–636.

Cotkin, George B. "The Spencerian and Comtian Nexus in Gompers' Labor Philosophy: The Impact of Non-Marxian Evolutionary Thought," *Labor History*, 20 (Fall 1979), 510–523.

Derber, Milton. "Labor-Management in World War II," *Current History*, 48 (December 1965), 340–345.

Fine, Sidney. "The Toledo Chevrolet Strike of 1935," *Ohio Historical Quarterly*, 67 (1958), 325–356.

Green, James R. "Working Class Militancy in the Depression," *Radical America*, 6 (November-December 1972), 1–35.

Gutman, Herbert G. "Protestantism and the Labor Movement: The Christian Spirit in the Gilded Age," *American Historical Review,* 62 (October 1966), 74–101.

Keeran, Roger R. "Communist Influence in the Automobile Industry, 1920–1933: Paving the Way for an Industrial Union," *Labor History,* 20 (Spring 1979), 189–225.

Kerr, K. Austin. "Labor-management Cooperation: An 1897 Case," *Pennsylvania Magazine of History and Biography,* 99 (January 1975), 45–71.

Koistinen, Paul A. C. "Mobilizing the World War II Economy: Labor and the Industrial-Military Alliance," *Pacific Historical Review,* 42 (1973), 443–478.

Lichtenstein, Nelson. "Ambiguous Legacy: The Union Security Problem During World War II," *Labor History,* 18 (Spring 1977), 214–238.

Lynd, Staughton. "The Possibility of Radicalism in the Early 1930s: The Case of Steel," *Radical America,* 6 (November-December 1972), 36–65.

Nash, George H. "Charles Stelzle: Apostle to Labor," *Labor History,* 11 (Spring 1970), 151–174.

Nelson, Daniel. "Origins of the Sit-Down Era: Worker Militancy and Innovation in the Rubber Industry, 1934–1938," *Labor History,* 22 (Spring 1982), 198–225.

Pomper, Gerald. "Labor and Congress: The Repeal of Taft-Hartley," *Labor History,* 2 (Summer 1961), 323–343.

Reagan, Patrick D. "The Ideology of Social Harmony and Efficiency: Workmen's Compensation in Ohio, 1904–1919," *Ohio History,* 90 (Autumn 1981), 317–331.

Rogin, Michael. "Voluntarism: The Political Functions of an Antipolitical Doctrine," *Industrial and Labor Relations Review,* 14 (1962), 521–535.

Stolberg, Benjamin. "Sitting Bill," *Saturday Evening Post,* October 18, 1941, pp. 27, 90, 92–93, 95, 97, 99.

Tomlins, Christopher. "AFL Unions in the 1930s: Their Presence in Historical Perspective," *Journal of American History,* 65 (March 1979), 1021–1042.

Widick, B. J. "Two Defeats for William Green." *The Nation,* October 9, 1935, pp. 412–413.

Unpublished Material

Farber, Milton L., Jr. "Changing Attitudes of the American Federation of Labor toward Business and Government, 1929–1933." Ph.D. Thesis, The Ohio State University, 1959.

Gowaskie, Joseph Michael. "John Mitchell: A Study in Leadership." Ph.D. Thesis, The Catholic University of America, 1968.

Reagan, Patrick D. "Early Social Insurance Reform in Ohio: 1910–1919." M.A. Thesis, The Ohio State University, 1976.

Rose, Patricia Therpack. "Design and Expediency: The Ohio State Federation of Labor as a Legislative Lobby, 1883–1935." Ph.D. Thesis, The Ohio State University, 1975.

Tate, Juanita Diffay. "Phillip Murray as a Labor Leader." Ph.D. Thesis, New York University, 1962.

Index